Omraam Mikhaël Aïvanhov

A Biography

Omraam Mikhaël Aïvanhov

A Biography

By

LOUISE-MARIE FRENETTE

Translated from the French by
Violet Nevile

SUR🌱OMA
The Full Spectrum of Life
United Kingdom - Australia

Published by Suryoma

Copyright© Suryoma, Ltd. 1999

Suryoma Ltd.
P.O. Box 307
Liverpool L69 4QF
U.K.
and
P.O.Box 798
Brookvale, NSW2100
Australia

Original title:
Omraam Mikhaël Aïvanhov et le chemin de Lumière
Published by Éditions A.L.T.E.S.S. Paris

British Library Cataloguing in Publication Data

A catalogue record for this book is available
from the British Library

ISBN 0 9536889 0 9

Printed in the United Kingdom by Biddles Ltd.,
Guildford and King's Lynn

Table of Contents

Part Three:
Brother Mikhaël 145

Part Four:
The Master 231

children; his philosophy of education of children; cosmic moral laws; importance of music & singing; a brotherhood centre in Switzerland; oriental Masters; union of East & West; three paths of evolution; degrees of silence; occasional visits to the Pyrenees.

Introduction

All human beings seek happiness. All aspire to great things. In fact, we all have a desire for perfection, this ideal to which we often give different names. 'Those who are seeking tenderness, wealth, beauty, or power,' said Omraam Mikhaël Aïvanhov, 'are they not really seeking God?'

The teaching that this great Bulgarian-born spiritual Master, Omraam Mikhaël Aïvanhov, dispensed so generously between 1938 and 1985 has already helped thousands of human beings to transform their lives. His methods are simple and within the reach of all, but they are also extraordinarily powerful and effective.

The major themes of this teaching have always existed, for their source is in the highest spheres of the invisible worlds, and they have been taught by all of mankind's most enlightened spiritual guides. In our times it has been given to Omraam Mikhaël Aïvanhov to bring them before us in his own unique way. Every element in his teaching has its practical application. In words so clear and simple that a child could understand, he speaks of the inborn potential possessed by all human beings to become perfect 'as the heavenly Father is perfect,' and to transform the world in which they live. He speaks of the quest for sanctity and perfection as the most enthralling work possible. And if he constantly uses the word 'work', it is because in his eyes every aspect of our existence is meant to be made use of: spiritual work is essential, but equally important is work on the physical plane. He insists that it is by means of the events of our daily lives that we can arrive at perfection, that initiation no longer takes place in temples but in everyday life, and that all our faculties –

our senses, emotions, and activities – can serve as springboards in this quest for perfection.

Central to Omraam Mikhaël Aïvanhov's teaching is light, which he defines as the most perfect expression of divine reality. He explains how we can use it to transform ourselves and become radiant as the sun. Another theme to which he refers constantly is the 'yoga of nutrition', a way to physical and psychic health through assimilation of the subtlest and most potent elements concealed in food. In addition, he astonishes and vivifies us with his unique perspectives on the meaning of love and sexuality; on the great laws of 'cosmic morality'; on true purity which is to have a heart as transparent as crystal; on the way in which mothers can work to perfect the child in their womb. He explains how to purify oneself, how to bring good out of evil, and how to bring oneself into harmony with the four elements and learn to use their power creatively.

He himself is an example. In the course of his eighty-six years he endured a great many of the trials known to humanity and used them consciously as tools of transformation. He was still very young when he began the work of self-perfection to which every human being is called. At the age of six, a booklet on the life of a great saint triggered a first spiritual experience which marked him profoundly. In adolescence, his inner life was borne along on a powerful current that led him to illumination and ecstasy at the age of fifteen. The twenty years he spent under the guidance of the Bulgarian Master Peter Deunov were years of intense spiritual work during which he strove to develop the qualities and virtues of a true son of God. Finally, his life in France, initially as the representative of Peter Deunov and later as a spiritual Master in his own right, bears witness to the immensity of the love that animated him and his exceptional wisdom and greatness of soul.

The spiritual work and discoveries of his early years gave a special flavour to the way he taught. In the course of more than five thousand talks, principally in France, over a period of forty-seven years, he often used the experiences of his youth to illustrate a point or spur his audience on to greater spiritual efforts. His reminiscences evoked a colourful picture of the child and youth he had been, as well as of the country in which he lived until the age of thirty-seven.

Far from portraying himself as the hero of events, however, he often referred to his own role with self-depreciatory humour, knowing that those who were capable of doing so would decipher the underlying lesson and grasp the essential. He never claimed to have been a model child or adolescent. On the contrary, he emphasized his mistakes and failings, asserting that from whatever level one started it was always possible to rise to greater heights. On the other hand, when he revealed an exceptional mystical or psychic experience, he often added in tones of great seriousness: 'As heaven is my witness, what I am telling you is true. I cannot lie to you.'

No one who approached him could fail to sense that his one burning desire was to be useful to humanity, to all those he encountered, and in particular to his 'brothers and sisters', as he called his disciples. His sole concern was to enlighten them, to accompany them in their personal evolution, as a guide leads and accompanies mountain climbers on their way to the summit.

Omraam Mikhaël Aïvanhov takes his place in the ranks of the great spiritual Masters of humanity. His spiritual kinship with those exalted beings is manifest in every aspect of his life. An incarnation such as his is like a great river bearing powerful currents from the higher planes of existence. It transforms all that lies in its path and rejuvenates countless individuals, galvanizing them into leaving the backwaters and joining the mainstream of the servants of light.

*
* *

I discovered Omraam Mikhaël Aïvanhov's teaching in 1976, in Canada. The following year I visited the Bonfin, in France, where he had been giving daily talks to his disciples every summer since 1953. Subsequently, until the year of his death, I had the joy of meeting him several times.

Five years after he left this world, I began to formulate the project of a book, in association with Violet Nevile who had already translated into English many of the published volumes of his teaching, and who collaborated in various phases of the work. With a fully documented biography in mind, we conducted months of extensive research into everything Omraam Mikhaël Aïvanhov had said about himself in the course of several thousand talks, and methodically sorted and indexed the relevant documents. Once this first step was taken, I began to draft the biography, which went through many stages and underwent innumerable corrections and transformations. In the course of seven years of work, I was constantly discovering new texts and receiving new information, advice, and explanations from some of those who had been close to Omraam Mikhaël Aïvanhov in his lifetime. My long quest twice led me to Bulgaria, and several times to France and Switzerland. More than one hundred interviews also provided a rich harvest of reflection, anecdotes, and reminiscences which all contributed something to the creation of this book.

The events I have mentioned were thus gleaned from many different sources: Omraam Mikhaël Aïvanhov's own talks; his mother's reminiscences, reported by her granddaughters, as well as those of other members of his family and many friends and disciples. I have scrupulously respected what he said about himself: in describing what he thought or understood, his state of mind or his feelings at different moments, I have used only his own reflections. With a single exception (a conversation in a park, in Pau, mentioned in Chapter 18), even the dialogues are drawn from his own account of events.

It was often difficult, however, to pinpoint the exact moment of some of the mystical experiences of his childhood and youth. When he mentioned them it was with a pedagogical purpose in mind, and he was not too concerned about details; the age he gave for a given event was not always the same. It seems that in his eyes the time was unimportant. From the point of view of the soul, events occur in a present unbounded by space and time; what counts is their reality, the repercussions they have in the heart and soul, and the links they forge with the subtler worlds. After considerable comparison and deduction I settled on the chronology which was most frequently given and which seemed the most logical.

This work has been a life-experience that was both elating and difficult, all the more difficult because it is impossible to portray or circumscribe the full dimensions of such a being. The years in which I have studied the events of Omraam Mikhaël Aïvanhov's life, observed his reactions in the face of difficulty and adversity, and explored his teaching in ever greater depth have been a pilgrimage in his company which has filled me with a deep sense of admiration and gratitude.

This book is both a biography and a spiritual itinerary. It is intended for all those who find inspiration in the lives of great human beings. Nobody knows better than I that he alone could have told the story of his life as it deserves to be told, but in telling it I have followed the advice he gave his disciples in reference to extrasensory phenomena. On March 28th, 1946, he said: 'There are things that only God can explain; we ourselves know so little. I have given you a few bits and pieces, and it is up to you to stitch them together.' This is what I have done. I have gathered all the bits and pieces I could find and threaded them on my loom in an attempt to reconstitute the great tapestry of his life.

Louise-Marie Frenette
Sherbrooke, Québec
September 1997

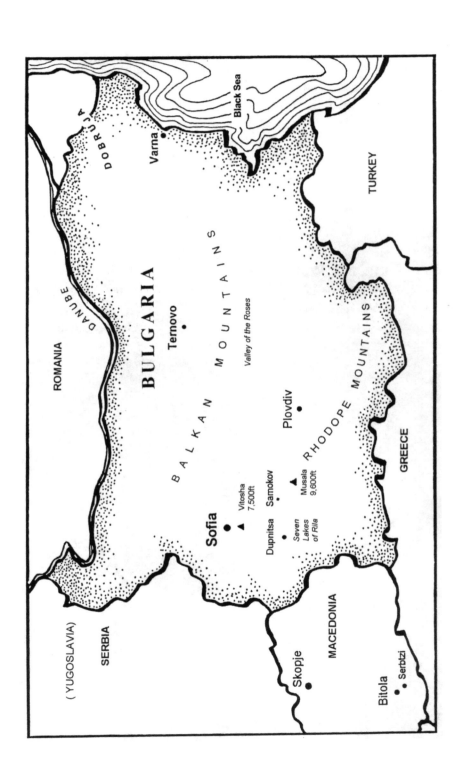

Acknowledgements

I would like to express my sincere gratitude to all those, too numerous to name, who have contributed in so many different ways to the completion of this work: by submitting to long and frequent interviews, by assisting with secretarial or research work, by contributing financially, by reading and making suggestions as the manuscript gradually took shape, and by accompanying me on my research trips to France, Switzerland, and Bulgaria.

Part One:
Youth

When we look at the lives of great human beings, our attention is drawn in a special way to their background and the path they followed in life. Our interest in them depends to a great extent on whether we can follow the same path and benefit from their experiences, and for this it is important to find out what first triggered their decision to work on themselves and become great.

Peter Deunov

1

Everything is Foreshadowed in Childhood

Omraam Mikhaël Aïvanhov was born in the little village of Serbtzi in Macedonia at the dawn of the 20th century. In the early morning hours of January 31st, 1900, as the villagers slept under the watchful eye of the Grandmother Mountain, the first cockcrow announced the beginning of a new day. It was bitterly cold out of doors, but in the house in which a baby boy had just opened his eyes a great fire blazed in the hearth.

Mikhaël was born early at eight months, and before the day was out, his mother asked the village priest to come and baptize him, for in those mountain villages at that time, the chances of survival were slim for a premature baby. But if the adults were afraid to lose him, the new baby seemed happy to find himself in this world and determined to hold on to life.

Dolia, Mikhaël's mother, had dedicated her child to God from the moment of his conception. She could not know then that he would one day become a great spiritual Master with thousands of disciples, but she hoped above all things for a child who would be a true servant of God, who would devote his life to a divine mission. While she was carrying him, she had constantly wished for him all that was most beautiful and perfect.

The world into which this child was born was one of extreme hardship. At the beginning of the 20th century, Macedonia – like Bulgaria and most of the Balkans – was still subject to Ottoman rule. The region, whose population included some two million Bulgarians, was in a state of social and economic chaos. Coveted by its neighbours, it was the arena of ongoing skirmishes between

Turks, Serbs, Greeks, and Bulgarians, all of whom laid claim to it. For decades, the people had known nothing but armed incursions, abortive popular uprisings, and cruel reprisals in which crops and villages were burned and the population decimated. Again and again, at the first warning of the approach of armed men, the women and children fled in terror to hide in the forests.

Mikhaël's grandmother, Astra, was one of the countless victims of those troubled times. In 1875 or thereabouts, she had been widowed and her life thrown into disarray when, during an armed raid on the village, her husband was killed and their house destroyed. Pregnant at the time with Dolia – Mikhaël's mother – she found herself alone and forced to work as never before to provide for the needs of her family.

Astra was a remarkable woman. She was widely known for her skill as a midwife and reputed to be one of the region's finest healers. As has always been the case in countries in which medical services were unavailable, those who lived in rural areas were accustomed to call on a local healer for help in sickness. For the most part these were women with a keen intuition and an exceptional knowledge of nature – gifts often passed on from mother to daughter – which enabled them to relieve suffering and sometimes to cure even serious illnesses. In the region of Mount Pelister, toward the end of the 19th century, people came from far and near to consult Astra. Thanks to her knowledge of the healing properties of plants, she successfully treated people suffering from a variety of illnesses. Many of her remedies included secrets handed down from ancient times, particularly those involving the beneficial properties of aromatic plants, the magnetic currents found in certain spots on earth, or the influence of sunlight and stars on the human body.

Astra's work as a midwife meant that she was often called out at night. Without hesitation and seemingly tireless, she often trudged miles through deep snow to a distant cottage or farmstead. Payment for the services of a midwife traditionally consisted of a towel and a piece of soap. Rarely did she receive more. And as the financial rewards for her work as a healer were hardly more lavish, she earned barely enough to support her small family. From her patients she received a great deal of love and gratitude – veneration even – but times were hard for all, and money was scarce.

Her daughter, Dolia, grew into a lively and spirited young girl. In striking contrast to her short, slight frame, she manifested a remarkable degree of inner strength. Spontaneous and outgoing by nature, she was full of affection for her family and friends. At the age of fourteen she was married to a young man called Ivan Dimitrov,[1] one of a large family of farmers from the village of Serbtzi.

All the members of her new family, men and women alike, shared in the work of the farm, taking turns labouring in the fields or tending to domestic chores. In keeping with local tradition, the family pooled their efforts with their neighbours, sowing and harvesting together in one plot of land after another. It was Dolia's mother-in-law who initiated the young bride into her new duties, and she did so with unfailing kindness. Since the age of four – like all children in these mountain villages – Dolia had learned to share the work in her mother's house and garden, and now, when her turn came, she began to toil in the fields, carrying heavy buckets of water to the field-workers, or looking after their children. It was not long before she became an indispensable element of harmony in her new family, who learned to rely on her kind heart and ready sense of humour.

When Mikhaël was born, Dolia was twenty-four. Her first-born, a boy, had died as an infant and her second child, a girl, was at this time about five.

Matured by the traumas and hardships of life in an unforgiving environment, Dolia had already experienced the loneliness suffered by many women at the time. Conditions in the mountain villages of Macedonia and Bulgaria were so difficult that the men often left to seek their fortune in the towns or with the charcoal-burners in the forests. With hope and physical strength as their only resource, they left their wives and children, convinced that they would soon find the work that would make them rich. Those who were successful

---

1. In Bulgaria, as in Russia, children are called by the family name to which is added the first name of their father. Thus Mikhaël would be called Mikhaël Ivanov Dimitrov, meaning Mikhaël, son of Ivan Dimitrov. For most of his life he would be known as Mikhaël Ivanov. Note that the final 'v' in Bulgarian is pronounced as 'f'. This is why, when Mikhaël first went to France, he would spell his name as 'Ivanoff' so that it would match the pronunciation. It was only later (see Chapter 20), that the surname Ivanov was changed to Aïvanhov.

visited their families briefly every two or three years, returning home for good only when they could no longer work. Like most of the married women she knew, Dolia had endured her husband's absence for long periods at a time. Some years before Mikhaël was born, Ivan had established his own charcoal business in Bulgaria, in a forest on the outskirts of the Black Sea port of Varna. It was a long way from Serbtzi, the work was demanding, and his visits home were rare.

Mikhaël's childhood was thus marked by the absence of his father, but also by insecurity and terror, by the constant political and social upheaval that reigned in Macedonia. Dolia, like many others, was more than once obliged to save herself and her two children by hiding in the forest. In addition to trials of this kind, she experienced other more personal sorrows: two or three years after Mikhaël's birth, her little girl, aged six or seven, died suddenly. It was not in Dolia's nature, however, to pine or withdraw into herself. She went about her work, taking her full share of responsibility in her husband's family, and in that most precious duty of all, the education of her son.

Mikhaël was probably four or five when he first took part in one of his country's most beautiful customs. On New Year's day, small boys became the messengers of good fortune, invested with the power to call down blessings on their neighbours and friends. Warmly wrapped up against the cold and carrying a twig of dogwood decorated with coloured ribbons, they went from house to house, tapping each person present with the twig while reciting wishes for good health and abundant harvests in the new year. The adults thanked them by putting an apple, some sweets, or a sugar bun into the bag carried by each child.

Some of Dolia's neighbours, eager to receive the first blessing of the year from Mikhaël, begged his mother to send him to them very early, before the other children. Dolia awakened him before dawn, dressed him, and before they set out together, made sure that he remembered the greeting he was to recite. It must have been hard for the small child to brave the darkness and battle against the snow and the cold wind, but he knew the meaning of what they were doing, for Dolia had explained it to him, and he did his best.

*
* *

The things to which Mikhaël was attracted as a child were significant: he loved threads and every kind of string; the water gushing from a spring; fire, and tall trees. These four 'childhood passions', as he called them, played an important part in his development, pointing him very early in life toward the reality that each one represented. Threads came to symbolize the complexity of relationships that bind human beings and the different elements of creation to each other. The clear, transparent water which flowed from the ground spoke to him of purity. The fire which gives light, warmth and life led him gradually to a 'solar' philosophy. Tall trees awoke in him the love of heights. As he would say later: 'Everything in our lives is foreshadowed in the events of childhood, but we pay no attention.'

Speaking of his love of threads, he said that he had been born with the idea of cutting the constraints that hold human beings prisoner, of freeing them from their bonds. At the age of four, with infinite patience, he picked up and treasured every scrap of string, every thread of wool or cotton he could find. One room in the family home had a particular fascination for him, for in it was a loom and around the walls hung skeins of brightly coloured thread. From the doorway, he watched his cousin weaving, spellbound by the movement of her hands as they danced over the warp, gradually transforming the separate threads into a piece of cloth. It was then that he began to have his first dim perception of the true meaning of threads, which speak not only of binding and unbinding, but which can be woven into something useful, beautiful, and durable.

One day when the weaver was out, Mikhaël ventured into the room and stood by the loom, gazing with fascination at all those bright threads stretched over the frame. Suddenly, moved by an irresistible impulse that seemed to well up from the depths of his being, he seized a pair of scissors, and barely conscious of what he was doing, cut them all off the loom. He was still there, clutching his precious harvest of coloured threads, when his cousin found him. And what a to-do followed: the poor woman crying out in horror at the devastation, others rushing in and scolding, while Mikhaël, although he realized that what he had done was wrong, barely heard the angry tumult around him. He was too full of his new-found sense of the hidden meaning of those threads.

It goes without saying that he was punished by his mother, who had to spend the best part of the night repairing the damage. Only years later did he really understand the hidden symbolism of this strange childhood passion. In previous incarnations,[2] he explained, he must have been aware of the significance of threads, and learned to tie and untie them: 'Obviously, at that age, it was unconscious, but there was certainly a hidden intelligence urging me on.' Later, he would often speak of the threads that make up the fabric of life. His constant desire was to help his fellow human beings, disciples, and friends to link themselves to divine energies and free themselves from the bonds that held them prisoner. His work was a continual weaving of ties between the spiritual and the physical worlds.

His second great passion, the love of water, was born in him when he was not yet five. On a voyage of exploration around the family home, he found water bubbling from a tiny spring and flowing away under the foliage. Intrigued, he lay face-down in the grass for a long time, watching this marvel of nature. In the days and months that followed, the spring drew him like a magnet. Fascinated by the transparency of the water, he spent hours gazing at it and was astonished to see that it never stopped flowing. If someone asked where Mikhaël was, the answer was always:

'Mikhaël? He must be by the spring.'

And that is where they found him.

The image of the spring took root deep within his mind. As a child of Aquarius, he was always drawn to water: rivers, waterfalls and the sea were a constant source of wonder and delight to him.

Of his four childhood passions, however, it was his love of fire that was foremost. The fires set by the peasants to burn off weeds or stubble; the oil lamp that lit the evening meal; the tiny votive light that burned before the holy icon; the flames blazing in the fireplace; all these manifestations of fire enchanted him. At the age

---

2. Maeterlinck, referring to the Hindu doctrine of reincarnation, wrote: 'Never has there been a more beautiful, just, moral, fruitful, consoling, or – up to a point – more credible belief. With its doctrine of successive expiations and purifications, it alone accounts for all social inequality, all the abominable injustices of destiny.' Quoted by E. Bertholet in *La Réincarnation*, P. Genillard, Lausanne, 1978, p. 8.

of five he began to light his own little fires of straw or twigs, just for the pleasure of watching them burn. For a time, no one caught him in the act, but eventually this dangerous pastime ended in near-disaster. One day, while exploring his parents' hay-loft, he found some rotten straw, so black and ugly that he decided to put a match to it.

'It's too old. It must be burned,' he thought to himself.

Without hesitation, raking it into a heap, he set it alight and watched the leaping flames, thinking he had never seen anything so beautiful. Before long, however, his delight changed to concern as the fire became more than he could handle and he realized his helplessness. Suddenly, alerted by the smoke, some adults came rushing in with buckets of water to throw on the blazing straw, while Mikhaël, still half engrossed in his delight, began to realize that this new escapade was serious and would certainly cost him his supper. Taking to his heels, he ran to take refuge with his grandmother Astra.

This had become a habit with him whenever one of his pranks ended badly and he knew that his mother would have to scold him. Convinced that no one would know where he was, he was always astonished when they found him there. But it was his grandmother's 'clairvoyance' that really astonished him, for she always seemed to know when he had committed some crime. How could she tell? On this occasion, seeing the anxiety in his eyes as he arrived, she immediately said:

'Aha, I see you have been up to mischief again!'

'How do you know?' asked Mikhaël uneasily.

'I can see it in your face!' she replied, and to give him time to summon up the courage to face his mother, who ruled him with great firmness, she added:

'Never mind! Come and hide with me.'

Mikhaël had a special relationship with this grandmother who was always so loving and understanding. For the little boy, Astra was the good fairy who always protected him, who cared for him when he was ill. In his eyes she was a truly exceptional being whose hands were skilled in bringing little children into the world, whose immense knowledge enabled her to restore sick people to health.

Speaking of her, in later life, he would say that it was because she was so full of love that she had been given the power of healing.

In spite of the remorse he experienced after the fire in the hayloft, his love of fire did not diminish any more than his love of water. In his words:

> Ever since I was born I have had a special leaning toward fire, and although, when I was young, I used to set fire to barns, later I understood that I would do better to leave physical fire alone and set fire to my own heart and the hearts of others.[3]

Instinctively, he sensed the role of water and fire in nature, and his passion for them presaged the importance they would have in his life and his future teaching. The beauty, the purity, and the symbolism of these two elements would always be a source of nourishment and inspiration to him, as well as key instruments in his spiritual work.

But fire and water were not the only natural phenomena for which he had a passion; there were also trees. He had a special affection for the tall poplars in the village, whose leaves whispered in response to every breath of wind and whose soaring trunks made him dream of great heights. As soon as he was strong enough to climb from branch to branch all the way to the top, he would perch there for hours, looking out over the surrounding countryside. Delighting in the beauty of nature that revealed itself to him in all its splendour, he felt like a bird, ready to spread his wings and fly. Dolia knew that when Mikhaël was not near the spring, he was sure to be found in the highest branches of a tree. When she called him, he would grasp the trunk in his arms and slide to the ground.

This passion for heights revealed a marked tendency in his character which became constantly more imperative, an innate impulse to look at everything from the highest possible point of view. Later, he would recall the experiences of his childhood and use the example of a child perched at the top of a tree, who can see things that his father, in spite of his great learning, is incapable of seeing from ground level. He would speak of the importance of

---

3. April 10th, 1968 (*The Splendour of Tiphareth*, p. 252).

placing oneself above circumstances and events, so as to see farther and understand more clearly the meaning of life.

*
* *

The natural environment in which Mikhaël spent his early childhood was harsh. Serbtzi was in a rugged, mountainous part of Macedonia, dominated by the great mass of Mount Pelister. At the beginning of the 20th century, physical conditions in these parts were still very primitive. The houses were without comfort, and people slept on beds of straw covered with mats. In winter, the snow and icy winds made all outdoor work painfully laborious, and the villages were cut off from each other.

Most of the schools were one-room huts, built of a wooden frame filled in with mud and straw. They were heated by wood-burning stoves, and if anybody had the misfortune to break a window it was replaced with paper to keep out the cold, for there was no money to buy a new pane of glass. In winter it was the duty of each of the thirty or forty pupils to find a log in the forest and carry it to school with them. If some of them forgot their contribution, the cold gradually crept back into the classroom toward the end of the day, making it impossible for the children to pay attention to their lessons.

During his first year of school, Mikhaël was enthralled when the teacher read the Bible account of creation. It was a revelation of such beauty that he was eager to share it with his family. As quickly as possible, he learned the story by heart, and when he was ready to recite it to them, he did so with such detail and contagious enthusiasm that the adults listened in silence, taken aback both by his knowledge and his talent as a storyteller. For the rest of his life, Mikhaël had a special fondness for the Book of Genesis. The picture of God, whose word creates such wondrous things, remained alive in his mind for many years.

On his sixth birthday Mikhaël received a booklet about St Athanasius, whose feast fell on that day. Captivated and deeply moved by the beauty of a life of great purity and loving dedication, he decided then and there that he too would become 'impeccable.' This little book was to be an important milestone in his life. Like all true mystics, his great sensitivity urged him not only to seek beauty in the world around him but also to withdraw into himself in search of the divine source within. At the age of four he had already made up his mind to serve God and not to marry. Even though he was too young to understand why he renounced marriage, he was deeply convinced that he should do so.

As a small child he was capable of concentrating for hours at a time, observing some phenomenon of nature. He often went off alone to reflect on some words of his mother or grandmother that he had taken to heart or to puzzle over something that intrigued him. The conclusions he drew from these observations and reflections were to remain with him for life, and the experiences of these early years became a constant source of lessons both for himself and others. But as he was to say later, he was a high-spirited child, and the effects of this first 'conversion' at the age of six were soon eroded by the reality of life at school and by the difficulties caused by his fiery temperament: 'I was a bit of a rascal,' he confessed with a smile.

Indeed, the little boy's turbulence was often a problem for his neighbours and a source of concern to his mother. There is no doubt that the energy and exceptional inner strength with which he was endowed would prove indispensable for his future work, but his curiosity about everything often led him into trouble. Although his family were ready to recognize that he meant well, they could not help but be angry and administer punishment when his good intentions ended in disaster. When the neighbours, exasperated by his experiments with fire and the explosions of his firecrackers, complained to his mother, she always stood up for him and asked them to be patient.

'You don't know what he's really like. He is troublesome now, but just wait: you will see how he turns out.'

Mikhaël used to say that his mother had been his first model. The education she gave him left an indelible mark. With unerring intuition she found the words and images that helped him to control his turbulent energies. She was always calm and never beat him for his pranks, neither did she try to force him to change. Instead, she appealed to his intelligence by painting a vivid picture of what he would become if he behaved badly or, on the other hand, if he learned to control his impulses.

'Now you know what is in store for you. The choice is up to you,' she used to say, repeating the Bulgarian axiom:

Krivdina do pladnina; pravdina do veknina.

'What is twisted will last until noon tomorrow; what is straight will last eternally.'

Her methods had a powerful effect on the child. Each time she spoke to him in this way he longed to throw himself into her arms and beg to be forgiven. Only his childish pride held him back. As soon as he was alone, he shed tears of remorse, for Dolia had appealed to the best in him, to his most noble ideal. He could never forget her words. He knew that what she said was true: all that is just and noble lasts for eternity. His love for his mother went very deep, and the example of her patience, her devoted selflessness, and her love played a crucial role in his life: 'It was she who taught me to love and respect all women.'

His grandmother Astra was also an important influence in his life. He spent long moments at her knee listening to fantastic stories, mystical legends and fairy-tales, vivid accounts of the epic battles between black and white magicians in which good triumphed over evil. Naturally, Mikhaël was always on the side of the white magicians, and although he knew in advance that every tale would end in the victory of good, like all children he thrilled to a gamut of emotions as he listened to the dangerous adventures of his heroes.

In the absence of Mikhaël's father, the essential task of forming and guiding the growing boy fell to his mother and grandmother. These two exceptional women had certainly been put by his side to sustain him with their love and wisdom, to help him to discover his innate possibilities and teach him to channel all his forces in the service of light. They did not know what the future held for this child – the extreme poverty, and the derision, calumnies, and betrayals that he would have to endure before his mission would be fulfilled – but they prepared him to the best of their ability for his future work.

Some of the family elders also had considerable influence on him. Most of them had no book-learning and had never been to school, but their attitude manifested so much kindness and dignity that

Mikhaël considered them living examples. He had a special admiration for one old man who was also called Mikhaël. When he talked, weighing every word and every gesture, he seemed to the child the personification of wisdom. Like Astra, he was a wonderful story-teller, and whenever he came to spend the evening with the family, he regaled Mikhaël with tales of the triumph of love over hatred, of light over darkness. These old folk tales, full of esoteric symbolism, nourished the child's mind and stimulated his ideal to become a true champion of the light.

2

Varna

A few months after Mikhaël's seventh birthday a tragic event changed the course of his life. One day, as he was walking by himself outside the village, he saw a troop of armed men on the road. They were still some distance away but approaching rapidly. In alarm, Mikhaël ran as fast as he could toward the village, shouting a warning to a group of peasants at work in the fields and gesturing to them to flee. With great presence of mind he led them to the river where they would be concealed by the tall reeds that lined the river bank. With his mother and other members of the family and all the villagers who had been warned in time, Mikhaël spent the rest of the day and well into the night plunged to the neck in the icy water, while the soldiers looted and set fire to the houses, shooting all those who had been unable to flee.

That night Dolia made up her mind to leave with Mikhaël and join her husband in Varna, in the north-east of Bulgaria. Sadly, this meant leaving Astra, who decided to remain in the village with those who planned to rebuild their houses. For Mikhaël, who had such a close relationship with his grandmother, the departure from Serbtzi must have been deeply distressing. In haste, with a small group of villagers who had also decided to leave, Dolia and Mikhaël set out for the north, travelling mainly on foot or in mule-drawn carts, avoiding towns and villages for fear of meeting other bands of marauders. After a while they were able to board a train that took them to the Black Sea coast.

In 1907, Varna, the ancient Black Sea port of Odessos founded by the Greeks in the 6th century, was a city of some 40,000 inhabitants.

On their arrival, Dolia and Mikhaël found temporary shelter with a Macedonian friend, while Ivan looked for something more permanent in the vicinity of his own office in the Turkish quarter.

The accommodation he found for them was a single room in the home of another Macedonian friend. It was a spacious house in Pleven Street – now renamed Kan Petko Voï Voda Street – which had once belonged to the *bey*, the Turkish governor of the district, and the present owner had taken in several families of Macedonian refugees, each of which occupied one room.

For the little boy, the difference between this new home and his former environment was extreme. At the time, the Turkish quarter was virtually a slum, a labyrinth of narrow, dusty alleys and miserable shacks in the south-east of the town, close to the sea. Many of the houses had a secret door concealed within the walls leading into the next house – a useful precaution in these troubled times, when the Ottoman police were still very active.

Relations between the families of the neighbourhood – Turkish, Macedonian, and Bulgarian – seem to have been amicable enough, and the children spoke both Bulgarian and Turkish. But all that Mikhaël saw and heard was unfamiliar, not least the Turkish priest – the Mullah – who occasionally visited the owner of the house and his numerous tenants. There were no more fields of wheat, no fresh vegetables or milk. All their food had to be bought from the market stalls or shops. And most of the children he met in the streets were wild and unruly. The urban population of those times was deeply marked by interminable years of civil war and a brutal political regime, and the children, left to their own devices, often formed gangs and fell into bad ways. In such a neighbourhood, Mikhaël's choice of playmates was limited, and on several occasions they tried to lead him astray and persuade him to steal or join in their vandalism. They soon learned that although his dynamic temperament and his openness and eagerness to explore and learn about everything made him as adventurous as any of them, he could never be persuaded to wrong another human being.

Although Mikhaël's parents were quite well off at this period they always lived simply like those around them. Because of his work, Ivan chose to live in the poorest quarter of the town, but his business had been established for about ten years and was now a prosperous concern with twenty or more employees working in a large tract of forest outside Varna. He was in a position to make plans for his son's education.

*
*   *

Mikhaël's first spring in a town must have been very different from that he had known in his native village. Here in Varna, peach and almond trees were coming into flower and the occasional walnut tree was breaking into leaf in the backyards and spare plots of land. Even the Turkish quarter took on a festive air when its few meagre trees began to blossom, but it could not compare with Serbtzi, where with the coming of the first warm days, the whole of nature seemed to burst out in an explosion of joy.

Every year on March 1st, it was the custom for young and old alike to celebrate the approach of spring by wearing a red and white pompon or bow, while the girls plaited ribbons in their hair. The significance of this age-old tradition had long been forgotten, but it was still honoured both in town and country. Naturally, Mikhaël knew nothing of the symbolism at the time, but many years later he explained that red and white represent the masculine and feminine principles at work in nature.

The decorations were worn until the appearance of the first storks, omens of good fortune, when it was the custom for everyone to make a wish. Dolia, like all the other mothers, gave Mikhaël two little balls of red and white wool to wear, and soon the coming of the storks gave him the opportunity to make one of those wishes that are born only in the hearts of children. For weeks after those first days of spring, every bush, railing, or lamppost was decorated with discarded red and white pompons and ribbons.

For Mikhaël, the highlight of this period was the feast of Easter. His family, like most Bulgarians, belonged to the Orthodox Church. Each evening Ivan lit the small votive lamp in front of the icon in their home while the family prayed together for protection during the night, and before each meal they asked God to be present at their table.

The people of Bulgaria had been Christian since AD 865, during the reign of King Boris I, and throughout the five centuries of

Ottoman rule the majority had held staunchly to their Christian faith. But the dioceses in Bulgaria were subject to the Greek Orthodox patriarchate of Constantinople, and little by little, Greek had replaced Bulgarian as the language in the churches and even the schools. At the beginning of the 20th century, however, the vernacular was beginning to come into its own again. Not many years before, Konstantin Deunovski, the priest in charge of the local parish, had restored the liturgy in Bulgarian. Ten years later, it was Peter Deunov, the son of this priest, who was to become Mikhaël's spiritual guide.

During the week before Easter a great bustle of preparations went on in all the families. On Holy Thursday, quantities of sweet rolls had to be baked and hard-boiled eggs painted. The first egg was always painted red, the colour that symbolizes life, and placed before the family icon. Other eggs were then painted all the colours of the rainbow. Toward eight or nine o'clock on Saturday evening, the faithful gathered in the church for the liturgy that would last until the early hours of Sunday morning. For Mikhaël, this was the high point, a ceremony that was a magical manifestation of light. The shimmering vestments of the celebrants, the golden crown encrusted with precious stones, the voices of men and women rising in great waves of sacred music that filled the church, the shadows that gradually receded and disappeared as the congregation lit their candles – all this impressed itself indelibly on his memory. Looking at the multitude of flames that lit the people's faces, dissolved the darkness and illuminated the gold of the icons, he had the impression that cohorts of fire were on the march.

But the ceremony lasted for several hours, and he was relieved when at last he could go out into the fresh air and join other children in the game of striking their eggs together, each attempting to break others while keeping their own intact. The broken eggs were eaten on the spot while those that remained unbroken, seen as symbols of life, were placed before the family icon until the following year.

*
* *

At the age of eight Mikhaël was already very attentive to all that went on around him. Each experience in these years of childhood was necessary to his future understanding of the inner workings of the material world. The long moments he spent reflecting on each new discovery were vital to his intelligence, which sought instinctively to draw the right conclusions from the phenomena stored in his memory. Paradoxically, he often seemed to be absent, as though his soul floated on a higher plane, as though his spirit had not fully taken possession of his body.

As he explained later, the first years of life are a special period during which a child often lives outside itself, as if in a cloud, while subconsciously preparing to receive the spirit. The length of this period may vary considerably; in his case it lasted until he was nearly nine. Instead of mixing with other children and taking part in their games, he often stood aside and reflected about things. Also, he was subject to occasional feelings of sadness that swept over him for no apparent reason, feelings which he later attributed to a deeply distressing experience his mother had suffered shortly before he was born.

Eventually, when he did begin to associate with other children, he was so guileless and so ignorant of their sly ways of avoiding punishment that he often became their scapegoat. When they took to their heels after some misdeed, he remained glued to the spot with nothing to say in his own defence. And as he never named the true culprits, he was often beaten in their place. Even his mother punished him sometimes, when he had been with a group of children that had done some serious damage. But Mikhaël was not completely naïve: after igniting a fire-cracker he was quick to run away, even though he knew he would have to face the music when he returned home, for the neighbours would have already complained to his mother.

One day, however, having been falsely accused yet again, he was so upset by his parents' lack of understanding that he decided to leave home. Not knowing where to go, he wandered down Dounavska Street to the railway station, where he spent some time watching the passengers coming and going, and thinking about his situation.

Suddenly, the busy scene lost all interest for him. Anxiety gripped him when he realized that, for the first time in his life, he was faced with a serious problem that he was quite unable to resolve by himself. Night was coming on; it was growing rapidly colder, and in spite of his unhappiness, he was beginning to be hungry. Above all, he had no idea where he could sleep that night. Unable to bring himself to return home, he decided that his most urgent problem was to find a bed for the night. Leaving the station, he set out briskly in the direction of the sea. To his relief the solution soon presented itself in the shape of a large bale of straw. 'That will do perfectly,' thought Mikhaël to himself, and it was with a sense of real freedom that he slipped under a layer of straw and, forgetful of his empty stomach, was soon fast asleep.

Meanwhile, Dolia was scouring the streets in search of him. As the evening wore on she became more and more worried, unable to prevent herself from imagining all the terrible things that might have happened to him.

Early next morning Mikhaël was awoken by a railway worker, who asked him what he was doing there.

'I've left my family…'

'What, left your family? Go home right away or I'll hand you over to the police!'

Mikhaël plucked up courage and made his way home, where his parents greeted him with exclamations of joy. His mother, who understood him so well, hugged him close, without a word of reproach.

Reassured and comforted by such a welcome, Mikhaël realized that nowhere in the world could he be better off than with his own family. He had to admit in all honesty that in leaving home he had wanted to make his parents feel that they misunderstood him. Speaking of this in later years, he said that, afterwards, his 'inner counsellors' had talked to him at length about his behaviour, and he had taken what they said to heart. But most human beings, he added, behave in this way toward their heavenly parents: they want to be free and independent, so they 'leave home' and look for happiness elsewhere. 'We want to punish God for reprimanding us and trying to get us to mend our ways.'

*

* *

The happiness that Mikhaël appreciated so much in his family lasted barely a year and a half. In the autumn of that year his father fell seriously ill and within a few days was at death's door. Realizing the gravity of his illness, Ivan worried about leaving his wife alone to fend for herself, Mikhaël, and the new baby of three months, and advised Dolia to marry a good friend of his. On October 3rd, 1908 he died.

Dolia knew nothing about her husband's business and was at a loss to know what to do to save it. A number of people took advantage of her ignorance to cheat her out of her due, and by the time they had had their way, she found herself at the age of thirty-three with two children, in mourning for her husband, and almost destitute. Her anguish was so great that she fell seriously ill.

In this time of distress Mikhaël did his best to take care of his mother. He prepared the meals, looked after his baby brother, and tried to keep their room clean and tidy. He had been doing his share of domestic chores for some time by then, so it was not this aspect of the situation that he found hardest: it was his mother's extreme desolation that alarmed him. Not quite nine years old, he felt terribly young and helpless. One day, at last, help was forthcoming: the Macedonian friend who had sheltered them on their arrival in Varna appeared at the door laden with a big bag of food. She had come to take care of his mother and the baby.

As soon as Dolia was up and about again she took steps to save her little family from utter ruin. After discussion with the shareholders of her husband's business she finally succeeded in obtaining some compensation for all she had lost: she was given the use of a house in Dounavska Street, not far from where she had lived for such a short time with Ivan.

Their new home was a small, rustic house built of wood and cob in the Turkish style, divided into tiny rooms. A separate kitchen in which they could have their meals was built at right angles to the main building. Part of the ground floor was set off from the house to serve as a stable, and to Mikhaël's great delight, a buckthorn had taken root in the floor of the stable and grown out through the window, shading the front of the house with its luxuriant foliage.

The security afforded by this little house was relative, for Dolia had no income, and it was almost impossible for a woman alone to provide for herself and two children. Once the period of mourning was past, seeing no alternative, she agreed to marry the friend Ivan had spoken about, a widower with one small boy.

Now, at least, Dolia was not alone, but the extreme poverty in which they lived only seemed to get worse as time went on, for her husband was not always able to earn enough for their needs. In spite of her efforts to save every penny, Dolia often found herself unable to provide the three children with the food they needed. Like all housewives of her country, she spent long hours spinning, weaving, or sewing their clothes, but she had no money to buy shoes for them, and for years they went barefoot.

In later years Mikhaël would say that it was the difficulties of this life of poverty that had allowed him to cultivate the most essential moral qualities and acquire strength of character and will-power. The obligation to rise above material privations had helped him to develop his innate mysticism. Like so many other young children in those troubled times, he was deprived of a father, but Dolia, his unassuming but tireless guide and mentor, was a little lamp that illuminated his path.

In the spring following his father's death, an apparently insignificant incident threw a tiny ray of light on one of the aspects of his future. Several comrades arrived one day in great excitement to tell him that the gypsies had pitched their tents in the town. Nomadic gypsies or tziganes were a familiar part of the Bulgarian landscape. They claimed to have come originally from India – their language contained a number of words of Indian origin – and every spring they moved from village to village, camping with their tents and caravans wherever there was work to be had in the fields. On the outskirts of the towns they set up as showmen, fortune-tellers or tinkers.

One of the gypsies that had just arrived in Varna was a well-known clairvoyant, and Mikhaël decided to go with his friends to see her. He had long been familiar with the existence of clairvoyants and healers, and his mother had often told him amazing tales about the famous clairvoyant Cortez. What would this gypsy woman have to say about his future? As soon as he approached, without looking at his hand as was customary, she said:

'You have many enemies.'

'How can I have many enemies?' asked Mikhaël in astonishment.

At nine years old… How could he have many enemies? Flustered and obviously ill at ease, the old crone added:

'Don't worry. You have many friends as well.'

But Mikhaël protested:

'Why do you keep saying something different?'

Her only reply was a surly mutter:

'I can't tell you more than that. Everything is mixed up in my head.'

Without looking at him, she held out her hand as though to ask for money, but almost immediately withdrew it and hurried off to her wagon. Mikhaël went home, disappointed that the old gypsy woman had not lived up to her reputation. It was only many years later, faced with the destructive forces that would try to crush him and destroy his work, that he was to remember the old woman's words and the veiled portent they contained.

*
*   *

During the school holidays, Mikhaël had his first experience of work as apprentice to the local blacksmith. For months prior to this, he had taken every opportunity to watch the smith in his forge, and had become ever more eager to try his hand at the work. Each time he saw a piece of dull, opaque metal gradually becoming red and incandescent, he experienced a thrill of astonishment that kept drawing him back to the forge. The thing that impressed him most was to see iron, when plunged into the red-hot coals, beginning to resemble fire and becoming malleable and luminous.

One day he made up his mind: abandoning his observation post by the door, he walked boldly into the smithy and asked to be taken on as an apprentice. He was hired on the spot, and the first thing he learned was to pump the bellows that kept the fire hot. Not long after this, his dream came true: the smith, seeing his perseverance, agreed to teach him to hammer a piece of incandescent iron and give it a new shape.

Mikhaël watched closely and each time the big burly man in his leather apron brought his hammer down on the anvil, he did the same, trying to keep to the same rhythm. To his delight, every blow produced sheaves of sparks which fell all around them. Many of the sparks burned his bare feet, but he continued undeterred. In the evening he returned home exhausted, his feet covered with blisters, and proudly handed his mother the twenty stotinki (cents) he had earned that day.

Mikhaël's apprenticeship at the forge lasted several weeks. It was an opportunity for him to observe and reflect on the phenomenon of fire, on the behaviour of the smith, and on the effect the work had on himself. This, his first job, seems to have been an event of importance in his youth. In later years, he was fond of talking about how a flame communicates its heat and light to metal. He compared a human being to a piece of iron, saying that each of us, in contact with divine fire, is capable of becoming radiant, luminous, and full of warmth.

His love of fire led to other discoveries as well. One day he noticed that this element that had such a vital role in nature could be extremely beneficial for his health. Intuitively, he understood that a wood fire contained subtle, curative elements. Sometimes, having failed to take precautions against the cold and finding himself chilled and feverish, he lit a fire in the stove, and settling down by it, held his hands to the flames and gazed into them for a long time. Later, he explained that his fingertips, like antennae, picked up the solar energy stored in the tree that had been turned into charcoal. After a while he would fall asleep, his whole body pervaded by a feeling of gratitude and well-being, and when he awoke he was cured.

It was about this time that Mikhaël first discovered music, and it came about through his encounter with a strange man known to the inhabitants of Varna as 'the madman.' Once a well-known conductor, he had lost his reason owing to a great personal tragedy. Since then, asking permission from no one, he had taken up residence in the clock tower near the cathedral and spent his days wandering the streets, a beatific smile on his face. When children laughed at or tormented him, he simply smiled and patted them on the head. Sometimes, to the delight of passers-by, he broke into loud and soulful song.

It was this eccentric being who first introduced Mikhaël to music. He became fond of the little boy who listened with such respect to his singing and who never tried to bait him. When Mikhaël climbed to the top of the clock tower in search of him, the old man welcomed him warmly and sang for him. Little by little, the child became familiar with the music he heard in this way, and soon he was proud to be able to say:

'Sing me something from Trovatore. Sing me an aria from Aida.'

At this, the old man would close his eyes, letting inspiration come to him. Then, his expression radiant, he would jump on the pendulum of the great clock and swing from it, singing all the songs his young friend asked for. There was something about those arias that had great appeal for Mikhaël's sense of the romantic. Poetic scenes filled his imagination and mystical sensations seemed to flow through his whole being. He listened to his strange teacher for hours, often joining his voice to his, and was soon able to sing a great many classical arias. These new horizons transformed his life and from then on he developed a passionate love of music.

Once a child discovers music, other doors are open to him, for there is a subtle link between the arts, each one stimulating and nurturing the others. Thus Mikhaël also learned to love the theatre and the cinema – to which he was probably introduced at school – but as he had no pocket-money, he could never buy a ticket for the performances. One day he decided to try to slip into the cinema by mingling with the crowd of spectators, and to his delight, no one noticed or stopped him. Emboldened by his success, he returned again and again, often seeing the same film or play several times in succession. Before long, this became much easier when some of the actors befriended him and gave him free tickets.

Stimulated by the theatre, his powers of observation developed rapidly. In the years that followed, Mikhaël studied with passionate attention the subtleties of the actors' technique. Some seemed to him colourless and without personal magnetism. Listening to them he was astonished to realize that their tears, laughter, and anger were all equally unconvincing. There was a hollowness behind their words. While others could so easily make their audience laugh or cry, or transport them to a world of dreams. An Armenian called Chaxtoun was particularly remarkable: as soon as he came on stage a thrill of anticipation ran through the audience. Even when his back was turned, his whole being vibrated with such an emotional charge that the audience held their breath.

In spite of his youth, Mikhaël sensed the invisible reality underlying the things he observed and was deeply struck by the realization that the spiritual essence emanating from a human being is capable of moving great numbers of people, even the most apathetic. Also, when he saw two actors having a drink together one day, after quarrelling violently moments before on stage, he realized that the theatre reflected life. Those actors were like enemies, who, meeting in the next world after death, understood how stupid they had been to fight over things of no importance. Realizing that the purpose of all the obstacles, criticism, and opposition they had encountered was to teach them something and stimulate their development, they were able to embrace and forgive each other.

3

'Hear, my Child'

That year, Mikhaël's life entered a new phase. He was now nine, and his childhood was slipping away. The death of his father, his mother's illness, his new responsibility toward his young brother, the self-discipline that his work in the smithy had required of him – all these things had matured him and prepared him for the powerful spiritual shock that came to him at this time.

Once again, it was a book that occasioned the event. Without fully realizing what it was, he borrowed the Book of Proverbs from the school library, and although still a little young for reading matter of this kind, was bowled over by certain passages about wisdom. He had the feeling that one in particular was directly addressed to him:

Hear, my child, your father's instruction,
and do not reject your mother's teaching;
for they are a fair garland for your head,
and pendants for your neck.
My child, if sinners entice you, do not consent.

He did not understand all that Proverbs said about wisdom, but he took the book home to reread the passages he liked best, those that filled him with ardour and nourished his ideal of becoming a great sage. Touched to the depths of his heart, his gaze turned inward:

There was a great upheaval within me: tears and sighs, and the longing to become a saint, a prophet. What a transformation! I cried for three days and nights, asking God to forgive my 'crimes'. Not that I had committed any crimes, but in my conscience I felt that I had![4]

---

4. Unpublished talk in 1960. Exact date unknown.

This new impetus to his heart and mind was the beginning of a spiritual ascent that continued without flagging amid all the difficulties normal to a growing boy. From this time on, he was committed to a personal quest for wisdom, and the orientation of his life began to take shape. Having been 'absent' until the age of nine, he had suddenly taken possession of the three rooms of his house – heart, mind and will. Everything was changed, and he did his best to live according to the precepts of the Book of Proverbs. With lightness of heart he determined to avoid any experiments that might endanger his own peace of mind and that of his neighbours.

At that age, however, as he admitted, the shock of his encounter with Solomon's wisdom could not transform him completely. The flame that had been lit within him gradually burned lower as the year went on, and his dynamic temperament led him to revert to his favourite pastimes. He gave up his experiments with fire, but he still occasionally produced explosions with black powder, wanting 'to let the neighbours hear some thunder.' The strategic battles waged by the children of the neighbourhood also provided a good outlet for his surplus energies. Before he completely discarded the ways of childhood, two more reminders would be necessary, one when he was ten, the other two years later.

One day, out for a stroll with a comrade, he came to a peddler's stall and began browsing through a booklet about a saint who had mastered his passions and become a great sage. Reluctantly, he put the book down, thinking, 'Ah, if only I could buy it!'

'It's only one lev,' said the peddler.

For Mikhaël that was a lot of money, and regretfully he turned away and walked on.

'If heaven lets me find the money,' he said to his friend, 'I'll buy the book and give whatever is left to a beggar.'

Suddenly he stopped; there at his feet was a lev. The book was his! Back in his room, he lost himself in the story, and once again an overwhelming enthusiasm for beauty, purity, and wisdom swept over him. At the same time, he reproached himself bitterly for his failure to live up to his ideal of perfection. Concentrating with all his might, he repeated over and over again: 'I will be a saint, a prophet.'

It was in the summer following his twelfth birthday that another book sounded a final alert. Mikhaël was spending the summer holidays in the forest outside the town with his stepfather and his fellow charcoal burners. While making himself useful in small ways, he spent much of his time watching the men at work as they cut two-foot lengths of wood, stacked them in a tall pyramids, and then covered them with soil, taking care to arrange small vents to ensure the minimum ventilation required. Two weeks were spent on these preparations, and another two weeks passed before the wood was completely charred and ready for use. The sacks of charcoal were then loaded on a donkey cart and taken to the town for sale.

The charcoal burners, who were fond of the young boy and treated him as their own son, built a tiny cabin for him in a tree, which he could reach by a ladder. One day, to give the boy something to do to while away his time, one of them took a small book from his pocket and handed it to him. When Mikhaël saw that it was a book of the Gospels, he climbed up into his tree to read it in peace.

The Gospels were not unknown to him, of course, for he heard passages read aloud every Sunday in church, but his encounter with them that day in the quiet of the forest was an experience of a totally different kind. As he read, his fascination grew, and the compassion and loving kindness of Jesus moved him deeply. It was when he reached the description of Jesus delivering a man of the demons that possessed him that something happened in his soul: he had a vivid sensation of being actually in Palestine with Jesus. He saw the poor wretch whom no one could control; he saw Jesus drive the demons from him and send them into a herd of swine; he saw the swine hurtling down the cliff and drowning. Unable to detach his gaze from the man who had once been possessed and who now sat at Jesus' feet, whole and perfectly calm, he found himself admiring his intelligent, sensitive face, his eyes illuminated by a new light of hope. And he sensed the crowd standing all about, dumbfounded by the metamorphosis they had witnessed.

Mikhaël found himself immersed anew in the atmosphere of Solomon's wisdom. He could think of nothing but that poor, crazed man who had been restored to his senses:

Again I wept. Again I determined to become a saint and a prophet. Again I saw myself as a worthless creature who spent his time pestering others. My mother had always taught me to behave wisely and rationally, but my good resolutions had never lasted very long. But this time was different. This time everything within me was in tumult because of that passage that had so impressed me and particularly because of those few, simple words describing the man sitting there 'in his right mind'.[5]

That long holiday in the midst of nature, far from the noise of city life and the distracting presence of his boisterous comrades, gave Mikhaël the setting he needed to assimilate this new spiritual experience in which Jesus had become his model. He felt happier and more at home in the forest than anywhere else. In the presence of all those trees he had a deep sense of contentment that seemed to rise from some mysterious memory hidden in the very cells of his body.

It must have been shortly after this encounter with the Gospels that he resolved to purify himself by fasting. As his mother recounted, at the age of twelve, he decided to fast for as long as possible with two comrades:

They hid in a cabin on the shore of a nearby lake. His friends soon abandoned their fast, but as they kept Mikhaël's hiding place secret, I spent several days searching everywhere for him, until one of the boys made up his mind to tell me where he was. When I finally found him I gave him the most severe scolding he had ever had from me, after which I burst into tears. Then I took him home and gave him a cup of light broth.

Although in this case the two other boys had been unable to stay the course, there were many occasions on which Mikhaël's friends followed his example. His influence with them was already considerable, and without realizing it himself, he was often their leader.

*
* *

The social context in which these children were growing up was extremely harsh. Periodical outbreaks of war and insurrection

---

5. Unpublished talk, July 17th, 1966.

ravaged the country, and the political situation was as unstable as that of Macedonia. The Ottoman yoke had been thrown off in 1908, but the country was still not at peace. Four years later, in October of 1912, church bells rang in Varna and throughout Bulgaria, announcing the mobilization of all the men fit to fight. The First Balkan War had begun. It did not last long: on December 3rd, an armistice was signed, and when the people of Varna learned that Turkey had lost almost all its territories in Europe, they poured into the streets to celebrate.

Like all the children of his time, Mikhaël had often heard of the atrocities perpetrated under Ottoman rule, and on the day of the armistice he joined in the general enthusiasm. Accompanied by a few friends, he ran to the Turkish legation with the intention of pulling down the Ottoman flag, the symbol of tyranny and injustice. Just as he had managed to remove it from its staff, however, the police appeared, and his comrades vanished into thin air. Mikhaël was left, still clutching the flag, to face the music alone.

Flanked by mounted police, he was marched through the town to the police station and told to wait. At first, standing in a corner of the room watching the policemen, he thought they looked very severe and felt sure he would be punished. Perhaps he would even be put in prison. But it was not long before he realized that the men could barely conceal their smiles as they whispered among themselves. In the end, with a half-hearted reprimand that deceived no one, they sent him home. Amused by the boldness of this young boy who had done something they were not at liberty to do, they could not find it in their hearts to punish him. They knew that for him and his comrades that flag represented oppression and tyranny. All children dream of heroic deeds and Mikhaël was no exception.

*
*   *

For the next few years, Mikhaël spent his summer holidays doing temporary work in various factories and workshops. The experience satisfied his eagerness to learn about life, to understand his fellow workers and the complexities of human relations. Also, he was delighted to be able to contribute what little he earned to the family's finances.

The different settings in which he worked provided ample matter for observation and reflection. His first experience was in a tailor's shop and lasted no more than a day, for he soon found the work too alien to his nature. To have to sit down all day long was torture to him, and after only a few hours he was so overcome with boredom that he fell fast asleep.

A little later he applied to a local sweet factory which was hiring workers. The foreman explained the task to him, but Mikhaël did not begin immediately. Only after watching the other employees to see how they carried out the different tasks did he start to work with concentration and precision. On that first day in the factory he was surprised to learn that the workers were free to eat as many sweets as they wanted. Enthusiastically availing himself of this permission, he was puzzled to see that each time he helped himself, his fellow workers exchanged amused glances, but it was not long before he understood, as his appetite for sweets vanished. He was never to forget the lesson: his employer obviously knew that a surfeit kills the appetite.

At another time he worked in a factory that produced pastels. By then he was beginning to be at ease in the working world, and once he had mastered the techniques he had been shown he ventured to invent a new method by which he achieved the same result as his fellow workers in less time and with less effort. His initiative won him a bonus from his employer, who had been watching this enterprising young worker.

Thanks to these summer jobs, Mikhaël learned the rudiments of several different trades, including that of mason and carpenter. All that he saw and experienced during these years became matter for reflection: the way people worked, the way their work affected them, relations between employers and employees, their discussions and disputes. He gained valuable insight into the problems, joys, and pains of their daily lives.

4

The Power of Thought

At the time of Mikhaël's youth, a child who wanted to read had no problem finding books, for most towns and villages in Bulgaria boasted a reading room. In fact, the public reading room was considered, together with church and school, to be one of the pillars of society. Mikhaël was already a regular visitor to the school library, and several of his teachers, aware of his thirst for learning and the extreme poverty of his family, were always ready to lend him books.

At home, however, he did not have the peace and quiet he needed for study and reflection. His brother and stepbrother were both much younger than he, and he now had two baby sisters. Dolia, seeing how much he suffered from his lack of privacy, managed to give him his own little room with a window that looked out on the roof of the kitchen. This room soon became a cherished haven in which Mikhaël passed long hours reading and learning to meditate.

His reading had already introduced him to the major themes of initiatic science of ancient Egypt, Greece, India, and Tibet, and at the age of thirteen he encountered the Buddha, who was to become for him a model second only to Jesus. Influenced also by his study of Hindu philosophers, he began to practise yoga in order, as he said later, to develop his will-power and his 'secret faculties'. A book by the American yogi Ramacharaka, author of several books about Hatha-yoga, made a powerful impression on him. On learning that the aim of Hatha-yoga – based principally on a technique of rhythmic breathing – was to lead adepts to the mastery of their thought processes through breath-control, Mikhaël began to practise these exercises every day with unrelenting resolve. Between the ages of twelve and fifteen his psychic and spiritual development seems to have been extremely rapid.

But books on spirituality were not the only kind that interested him; he also devoured adventure stories, and the novels of Jules Verne in particular opened fascinating new horizons. He sensed that authors like Verne, who were capable of describing unknown physical phenomena, must possess a highly developed intuition which gave them direct access to the invisible resources of nature. It was also in this sense that the study of chemistry held his attention for quite some time. With his mother's permission, he transformed the horse's stable into a laboratory, and by some prodigy of economy known only to herself, Dolia bought him a glass retort. His predilection for fire and eruptions being well known, no one was surprised when the first thing he did was to make some explosive.

Mikhaël was passionately interested in everything around him. His temperament continually drove him to get to the bottom of things, to investigate and extract the last drop of life-giving sap from every new discovery. The more he learned, the more convinced he became that every physical phenomenon was matched by a corresponding spiritual phenomenon. Thus the drop of mercury, like a bright, mobile jewel rolling in the hollow of his hand, showed that impurity tarnishes and divides, whereas purity ensures integrity and unity, for once broken into smaller drops and sprinkled with dust, the mercury could never become one again.

Gradually, however, Mikhaël was no longer content to confine his experiments to the physical plane. The object of his quest was on another level, and he turned his attention to the study of psychic phenomena. His first introduction to the books of Louis Jacolliot opened marvellous new perspectives on the powers of thought and the existence of mysterious, invisible forces that could be used by human beings in the visible world. Jacolliot claimed that, while in India, he had witnessed public demonstrations of the fantastic powers of fakirs: he had seen them plant a seed and within a few hours, by the power of thought alone, cause it to grow and produce flowers and fruit.

Mikhaël's reaction to this was to reflect that the tremendous power behind such exploits should be used for a nobler purpose than to impress the idle onlooker. He was determined to work on a higher plane than such fakirs. But first he needed to find out whether he was actually capable of getting results through mental concentration alone.

One of his first experiments took place in the *Morskata Gradina* (the Garden of the Sea) a park that runs along the shore of the Black Sea from north to south of Varna. Seeing that all the seats in the park were fully occupied, he focused on a man sitting on a distant bench, repeating in his mind: 'Get up. Go on, get up!' Within a few seconds the man stood up and walked away, and Mikhaël sat down in his place. He repeated the experiment several times to be sure that the result was not a question of chance. In the same way, he practised sending mental suggestions to his friends, directing them from a distance to make some harmless gesture: he persuaded one of them to take off his beret, another to pick up something from the ground. On one occasion, seeing a comrade coming toward him, he concentrated on his right foot to make him stop walking. But when he saw the boy pause and lean against a tree with a worried expression on his face, he hurried over to reassure him and everything was soon back to normal.

By the time he was fourteen, Mikhaël had begun to be aware of the immense powers of his own subconscious, and with this came a glimpse of the breathtaking possibilities before him. Judging by the experiments that absorbed his attention at that time, he was already familiar with concepts recognized by many different philosophies. He was aware, for example, of the existence of man's subtle bodies – astral, mental, causal, buddhic, and atmic – and of the system of the chakras, those subtle force-centres lying along the spinal column.

Exactly when Mikhaël discovered that human beings have the power, consciously or unconsciously, to leave their physical bodies and move about on the invisible planes is not known. He may not yet have been familiar with the spontaneous disassociation that is often triggered by the trauma of an accident or a surgical intervention, but we do know that several years later he was able to enlighten an ex-serviceman who told him that, when in a coma, he had found himself outside his physical body and had watched the surgeons at work on him as he lay unconscious on the operating table. But certainly, by the time he was fourteen, Mikhaël knew that the great mystics experienced phenomena of this sort, and it is evident that he had already discovered them for himself, for he began to introduce his friends to the idea that they, too, had this power.

From his extensive reading, he knew that if you can induce a 'higher state' in people, they will be capable of supernatural perceptions. He wanted so much to give his friends a chance to perceive these new horizons, in particular the splendours of the invisible world that were beginning to be revealed to him. When he proposed experiments of this kind to his friends, several of them agreed to let him hypnotize them. To be on the safe side, he invited their parents to be present. On his very first attempt, he succeeded in putting his subject into a disassociation trance, and the parents saw for themselves that their son could feel nothing in his physical body, for it was detached from his etheric body. One day, however, Mikhaël had great difficulty in bringing a subject out of his trance, and recognizing the dangers of this science which could so easily be used to dominate others, he abandoned it once and for all.

The experiments of those early years were no more than a preparation for things of far greater importance that lay in the future. It is impossible to say how many techniques he attempted to master before abandoning them when he realized that they could be used to exploit others. Later, he always advised his disciples not to use such practices without a very serious reason.

*
*   *

If the power of thought was one of Mikhaël's most important discoveries during his adolescence, the yoga of nutrition was another. At the age of fourteen he had an experience which caused him to reflect on the hidden properties of food. One morning, his mother found that she had nothing to give him for breakfast before he left home for the day. She did, however, have some flour, and with this she made a small bread roll for him. For Dolia, bread was the one great staple that could always be relied on when one had no money to buy anything else. While kneading the dough and thinking of her eldest son, who so often had to make do with an inadequate diet, she infused it with all her energy, every ounce of her strength. When Mikhaël came home that evening, he asked:

'Mother, what did you put into that bread?'

He was both intrigued and impressed, for having eaten it he had not felt hungry for the rest of the day. Dolia told him:

'While I was making it, I prayed that it would sustain you and give you strength for the day.'

Mikhaël found that his mother was far wiser than most of his teachers. He could not count the number of times she had given him good advice. But as usual, he needed to understand for himself the question of the energy contained in food. One day, when he had nothing to eat but a small piece of bread and a morsel of cheese, it occurred to him that he should chew each mouthful for a long time so as to draw from it all its hidden qualities. The result of the experiment was astonishing: a powerful sensation of well-being, joy, and peace flooded him, and he became aware of a host of subtle energies flowing from the food into his whole being.

His intuition thus confirmed, he reflected that the food we eat possesses a secret life of its own, far beyond its physical properties, and that it is important to eat slowly. Gradually, he understood that the mouth is especially designed to absorb the subtler energies contained in food, while the stomach assimilates principally the physical elements. On the other hand, he also began to see that his digestion was greatly influenced by physical conditions, as well as by his feelings, at the time of eating. He noticed, for instance, that his muscles were sometimes tense during meals, and realizing that this tension drained energy from his body, he began to do a few simple exercises of relaxation before eating.

For him, nutrition was already a form of yoga, a beneficial exercise, a discipline for life. He ate only when he was hungry, partly because he felt much better when he did so, but above all because he wanted to 'subordinate the ordinary way of life to the spiritual life.' From this time on, in taking what he needed to sustain the life of mind and body, he always tried to choose elements that were pure: water from unpolluted springs, natural food, books that inspired and elevated the mind.

These choices should have contributed to his fitness, but in spite of them his health at this period was not good; the poverty of his family and constant privations left him an easy prey to infection. During the greater part of the year he went barefoot, wearing his one pair of sandals only when it snowed in winter to make them last longer. In the mornings when there was no food in the house, he went to school without breakfast and sat through his classes, drowsy from hunger. Fortunately, when he fell ill, his mother always managed to pull him through, and Mikhaël conceived a lasting gratitude for the devotion and patience with which she nursed him.

Dolia, learning from her mother's example, had developed her own gift for healing. Sustained and guided by the principles that had guided Astra, she had also followed her intuition and made discoveries of her own. In particular, she had found that by passing her hand lightly over a patient's solar plexus she could sense the nature of the ailment and the treatment that was called for. Mikhaël often saw her helping people in this way, and wanted to know how she did it.

'Mother, how do you heal? What do you do to a patient?'

Dolia reflected for a moment before answering.

'I have no strength of my own, but when I am with someone who is ill, I forget everything else and put my whole soul into healing him. I start by calling on God, on his power and love, and think of nothing else. My love for the sick person is so great that my soul becomes a conductor of universal love, and when I pour that love into him he is healed.'

For Mikhaël, always so keenly aware of the importance of links, Dolia's words were truly a source of inspiration. 'She says she is weak, but her love is powerful,' he thought to himself. Thanks to her great faith, she was a humble intermediary, holding in her hands, as it were, the wire through which a powerful current flowed from the divine world and restored the sick to health.

This was the current that Mikhaël was constantly seeking in his own life, this link with the spiritual worlds which can be forged into an indestructible bond through prayer and meditation. At this stage of his life he was striving for it with so much ardour that he had difficulty in paying attention to life at school, which seemed to him unutterably boring.

*
* *

At the King Boris Lycée, the secondary school he attended until the age of fifteen, Mikhaël was considered a mediocre pupil. 'I was the class dunce,' he often said laughingly. At an age when his fellow pupils were thinking of glory, of their future profession, of marriage and children, Mikhaël was thinking of something quite different. His only concern was the spiritual life. The teachers, not knowing quite how to judge a boy who failed to conform to the established norms of behaviour and whose mind was so free of conventional stereotypes, gave him only average marks. The truth is that Mikhaël took an interest in anything that could contribute to his spiritual growth and attached little importance to everything else. For his intellectual formation he relied more on the public libraries and reading rooms than on school:

> Because of this great longing to become perfect and full of love, I devoured books, meditated, and did all kinds of experiments. My studies suffered as a result. I was simply not interested in anything at school – neither the teachers nor the books.[6]

In fact, it was only thanks to his exceptional memory that he managed to assimilate what was taught in the classroom, for, as his parents could not afford to buy even the basic school texts, he was obliged to borrow them from his classmates and skim through them during recreation periods. In class he always sat at the back, where he was rarely questioned by the teachers and was free to pursue his own reflections and concentrate on essentials. Accustomed to examining all that he heard and read, and filtering out anything that seemed superfluous or trivial, his mind was developing freely, unconstrained by academic norms.

The most important aspect of his school experiences was the understanding he gained of his fellow human beings. Observing the teachers, he recognized that some were dreary and governed by routine while others had the presence and personal magnetism he had seen in certain actors. With the same clear-sightedness, he observed his fellow-students and determined not to become like so many who recited the lessons by heart without understanding what they were

---

6. Unpublished talk, January 19th, 1946.

saying. Mikhaël never tried to be top of the class: such an ambition simply made no sense to him. The undeniable influence he had over his comrades was not that of a brilliant student, it was far subtler.

On the rare occasions that the teacher called on Mikhaël to answer a question, a murmur of pleasurable anticipation ran through the classroom. Then, knowing that he needed a moment in which to collect his thoughts and find something interesting to say, pupils and teacher alike waited in silence. And each time, drawing on his extensive reading, he recounted an adventure or an excerpt from a play that had struck him as important, and his vivid imagination and sense of fun led him to integrate into his tales amusing details that lightened the austere atmosphere of the class. In spite of themselves, even the most severe teachers had to smile, and most of them, slightly perplexed by the extent of his knowledge, gave him a pass mark. Some, however, were more lucid. Years later, one of his teachers described the young Mikhaël to her son:

> As a boy he was extremely intelligent and had exceptional inner strength. He was always surrounded by a little group of comrades who were very attached to him.

In spite of his dynamism and the influence he had on his schoolmates, Mikhaël did not try to put himself forward. On the contrary: he preferred to remain in the background and rarely intervened in group discussions. The most important aspects of his development were taking place inwardly. If it had not been for his integrity and his exceptional openness to others, no one would have noticed him.

World War I brought many changes at the school. When Bulgaria allied herself to Germany in 1915 in the hope of regaining her Macedonian territories, many of the teachers were called up, and those who replaced them did not always have the necessary competence. Three of these substitute teachers left a lasting impression on Mikhaël, each for a different reason.

The first, a math teacher, was incapable of maintaining discipline in his class. The boys laughed at his mannerisms and amused themselves by goading him into losing his temper. But Mikhaël felt sorry for him and refused to join in. He recognized that it was the man's sensitivity and lack of control over his own emotions that somehow caused his pupils to be so unruly. One day, when the teacher had stormed from the class, slamming the door behind him, Mikhaël spoke up in his defence, and because of their affection for this quiet boy from the back bench, his classmates promised to mend their ways. But their good resolutions lasted no more than a few days, and it was not long before the teacher gave up the unequal struggle and resigned.

He was replaced by a little man who, though outwardly insignificant, had a perfect grasp of his subject and was always completely calm. The discipline in his class was exemplary. The contrast between this teacher and his predecessor gave Mikhaël much food for thought. He began to realize that quite apart from the knowledge and competence of a teacher, it was something that emanated from him that made others react as they did. This teacher was no less sensitive than the first, but he won the respect of his pupils because of his inner strength and emotional control. Also, he had a quality of presence which the other had lacked.

The third teacher, a violinist, was a stiff and silent man, whose dry, authoritarian manner intimidated his pupils. One day, probably following a discussion about the rhythm of respiration, Mikhaël abandoned his usual reserve and talked to him about the Hindu breathing techniques that he had been practising for some time. To everyone's surprise, instead of snubbing him for his impertinence, the teacher relaxed visibly, questioned Mikhaël about his experiences, and accepted his offer to lend him a book on the subject.

Human behaviour was a topic that never failed to fascinate Mikhaël. At that time he was already beginning to formulate his ideas about will-power and about the self-mastery that enables one to keep control of one's emotions. In his view, sensitivity was very important: it was far better to be sensitive and to suffer than to be like a stone. Commenting on this later, he would say that the more one develops spiritually the more sensitive one becomes, but he always insisted on the importance of developing self-control and sensitivity in tandem.

At this period of Mikhaël's life, his ideal towered before him in the distance, like the glittering peak of a mountain. To reach that peak he would need tremendous will-power, of that he was convinced, and he set himself to reinforce his will in every way he could think of. In his family, his neighbourhood, or at school, the need for self-control arose many times a day, and he took every opportunity to practise it. At school, for instance, he drilled himself to endure the offensive behaviour of an arrogant youth who, believing himself to be a writer of genius, constantly heaped ridicule and sarcasm on those whom he considered less gifted. On one occasion, after humiliating some of his schoolmates in public, the bully turned his attentions on Mikhaël once again. Mikhaël's mysterious influence in the school was probably a source of envy to this boy, who hoped to provoke a reaction by insulting him, and for once, Mikhaël caught fire. Standing up, he looked his adversary in the eye and proceeded to describe his character as he read it in his face, until, completely deflated and speechless, the boy sat down. From that day on, his attitude toward Mikhaël changed radically and he began to seek his company. He who had been used to attacking others without risk of retaliation had finally come up against a strength that commanded his respect. He had discovered that silence and patience are not necessarily signs of weakness.

Mikhaël's friends could not help but realize that although his basic orientation was toward the spiritual life, there was not a trace of bigotry in him. He was as capable as they of youthful enthusiasm, and his fiery temperament made him eager for new experiences, always ready for ventures that kindled his interest. The only activities in which he systematically refused to take part were those that might wrong others. This did not prevent him from taking an interest in what was going on in his neighbourhood, where he saw several of his young comrades fast becoming delinquents. During his adolescence, he witnessed many tragic incidents, and although he rarely talked about them in later life, they remained vivid in his memory. One day he spoke of having seen some of those youths gunned down by the police as they tried to run away. Others had been caught and sent to prison.

Without going into detail, he declared that he had always retained a certain independence and freedom, and that the spiritual world had protected him from the difficult milieu in which he was growing up. He was already conscious in those days of a strong bond with the invisible beings that dwell in light.

5

The Aspirations of Adolescence

Adolescence, the age of noble sentiments, utopian dreams, and heroic decisions, was for Mikhaël a period in which to explore a variety of emotional and intellectual experiences. Like other youngsters, he dreamed beautiful dreams which faded one after the other. At the age of fifteen, it was time to make specific practical decisions about how he should work toward his ideal. What would he do in life? What field would he choose?

At one point his ambition was to be a scholar, a university professor. Later, he began to write mystical poems and tales, weaving spiritual truths into a tapestry of visions and prophecies. He put a stop to this phase when he realized with a lucidity beyond his years that much of the poetry he liked aroused hazy, melancholic sensations within him and made him hypersensitive and vulnerable. It debilitated him by imprisoning him in the world of feelings. He was already aware of the moon's influence on human beings and knew that the world of emotion was linked to the lunar cycle. Sensing intuitively that true poetry, the poetry that touches the most sensitive chords in the human heart, belongs to the higher, more spiritual planes, he resolved to linger no more in the world of the emotions, but to 'look for true poetry in the sun.' Although he continued to rank poetry above both music and painting, he no longer wrote it himself. He turned his attention instead to philosophy and science.

At this period his most cherished dream, that of becoming a true sage, was growing ever stronger and more insistent, pushing other ambitions into the background. He was spending more time in the practice of yoga and in meditation, and when not at school, he read for hours. His thirst for knowledge was fuelled by the works of the great authors of all time, available in translation in every good public library. Mikhaël perused all the major philosophical and spiritual works he could find and soon became familiar with the sacred scriptures of humanity's great religions. The spiritual teaching of Gautama Buddha had a special place in his heart, and he continued to read everything he could find on the subject. Among his favourite Western authors were Emerson, Berkeley, Steiner, Blavatsky, Spinoza, and Paracelsus.

One day, exploring the shelves of the library, he discovered a book on palmistry by the French author, A. Desbarolles, and became passionately interested in the art of divination by reading the lines of the hand. What first caught his attention, however, were the writer's comments on the nature of magic: 'Magic is a comparison between two worlds.' Until this moment Mikhaël had thought of magic as 'the ability to command the spirits and work miracles.' But pondering Desbarolle's statement in relation to his long-standing awareness of the importance of links, he realized that it expressed an important truth:

> You cannot compare two things unless there is a link between them. That is what a comparison is, therefore, first and foremost, a connection. True magic is the comparison between the divine and the physical worlds which is made possible by the link between them. Without this link there can be no magic. [...] The whole of my philosophy is based on this little thread, the fragile link between the two worlds.[7]

From his earliest youth Mikhaël had been interested in how two different realities can be linked. In later life he would give his disciples examples of formulas they could use to activate that link and harness the forces of the invisible world for their own benefit and the benefit of others. One might say, for instance: 'As the sun rises in the heavens, so may the sun of love rise in my heart...' He compared this link to a power line carrying an electric current which can be transformed into the diverse forms of light, heat, or movement. In the course of his life,

---

7. January 14th, 1968 (*Cosmic Moral Law*, p. 239).

as he penetrated the heart of this idea, the elements of nature became an integral part of his spiritual work.

At this time, wanting to understand what people hoped to find in the practice of magic, and having heard that spiritualistic seances were being held in a house in Varna, he decided to go and find out for himself. A few seances were enough to convince him that the participants were mainly seeking to satisfy their appetite for money, power, and sensual pleasures. It was not what he was looking for, and he returned to his books.

His interest in the art of palmistry having been triggered by Desbarolles' book, Mikhaël now began to study it seriously. Whenever his friends allowed it, he took an impression of their hands in plaster of Paris so that he could study them at leisure, making careful notes of his observations. If no plaster was available, he would sprinkle a little powdered charcoal on a person's palm and take a print on paper. His natural aptitude for clairvoyance was developing steadily, and after examining the prints he sometimes told his friends what he saw in their future. Years later, some of them were impressed to find his prophecies coming true. One in particular, a musician at the height of his career, was to say that he had been a shy, self-effacing adolescent when Mikhaël had foretold a brilliant future for him in music.

All these dreams, all this research led Mikhaël to a succession of choices, each of which brought him imperceptibly closer to the role he was to play in life. When he decided not to dedicate his life to science, it was because he understood the path he was destined to tread lay elsewhere, that his spiritual research was worth far more than a chair at the university. When he turned his back on the dangerous ambiguities of spiritism, it was to pursue the study of palmistry, an art which presented no such dangers. And when he gave up writing poetry, it was to turn to philosophy and also to music, for which he was developing an ever greater need.

This need was so intense, in fact, that he constantly regretted being unable to play an instrument himself. Seeing his more prosperous schoolmates arriving for music lessons with their guitars or violins only accentuated the feeling, for he knew that his family could never afford the violin he longed for. One day, however, he received an invitation which compensated in large part for this lack: the sister of one of his neighbours, an excellent pianist, invited him to come and listen while she played. After this, he spent hours, sitting cross-legged in a corner of her studio, learning to analyse the effect the music had on him and, above all, to use it to 'fill the sails of his meditation,' as the wind fills the sails of a boat. Often, he paid little attention to the music itself. It was simply a great force, an impetuous wind that lifted him and sped him toward the sublime regions to which his soul aspired.

*
*   *

The recent discovery of radio waves opened yet another field of spiritual reflection for Mikhaël. It is not clear whether this research began when he was fifteen or some years later, but crystal sets were already available in 1913, and at some point, Mikhaël, who could not afford to buy one, built one of his own. In order to tune in to a station, a needle had to be positioned on the surface of a lead crystal, and he was quick to see the symbolism of this detail and to apply it to his daily life. He noticed that he could pick up a program only if the needle was in contact with a 'live spot' on the crystal, and that there were days when it was impossible to find that spot. The correspondence between the crystal set and the spiritual life was obvious: countless messages and currents criss-cross the universe, and if human beings are incapable of tuning in to them, it is because their inner radio is not on the right wavelength. We must try to tune in to God in order to receive light, health, and happiness.

Music was not the only heaven-sent gift Mikhaël received at this period. A friend gave him a prism, and with a sense of wonder he discovered the splendour of the seven colours contained in sunlight. From this moment on, the thought of the seven rays was always with him, and that small piece of crystal became the starting point of a life-long reflection on light. He juggled with fascinating ideas: white light is one, but when passed through a three-sided prism, it is refracted into seven different colours. Similarly, every human being is a prism with three facets – heart, mind, and will – which, when correctly positioned in relation to light, receives all the wealth of the seven colours, symbols of the seven virtues.

In order to understand the physical phenomenon of the refraction of white light, he began to study scientific texts and conduct experiments which opened new horizons for him, but which also gained him a growing reputation as a very strange boy. One of his first experiments was to daub the window of his room with red paint and then to meditate in the coloured light that filtered through the glass. After studying the effect of this colour for a few days, he washed off the red and repeated the experience with orange, and so on through the spectrum. When it came to violet light, he found to his astonishment that flowers wilted and his friends fell asleep after being exposed for a time to the special atmosphere it created. As for himself, he soon found that violet light helped him disassociate from his physical body and 'fly away to other worlds.'

Intrigued by these discoveries, he went on to other experiments. He mounted sheets of coloured cellophane on a cardboard frame and spun it in the light of a powerful lamp, so that enchanting nuances of colour were projected on the walls. Seated in the lotus position, he contemplated all this beauty around and within him, as his soul soared and expanded in space. Through closed eyelids, he felt that he could actually see the brilliant light and colour in which he was sheathed. His heart overflowed with love, and his sole desire was to pour out his life for the good of all humanity.

One day while meditating, he was inspired to create a design that would be a visual representation of perfect harmony. After several attempts, he finally drew a circle, on the circumference of which he placed six circles of equal diameter, thus creating the stylized form of a rose. He then painted the figure with the colours of the spectrum. Intuitively he had rediscovered the ancient symbol of the Rosicrucians. Having written beneath the rosace the opening words of St John's Gospel, 'In the beginning was the Word,' he hung it on his wall. The contemplation of this perfect geometrical figure gave him an extraordinary sense of well-being. But he was still not satisfied, and to enhance its effect, he found a way of rotating it slowly on its axis.

His passion for beautiful colours led him to discover realities that astonished him, so far were they above those of the visible world. He had a clear perception, for instance, of the correspondence between the seven colours of the spectrum, the seven notes of the musical scale, the seven days of creation, the seven bodies of man, the seven heavens, and the seven archangels before the throne of God. As his intuitive perception of the link between colours and virtues became stronger he drew the logical conclusion: by being as pure as prisms, human beings allow divine light to enter them, thus becoming capable of developing the virtues that correspond to the seven colours. Every time Mikhaël gazed at his rosace, he was transported to a dazzling world of peace and happiness. With the passing months the symbol seemed to grow and blossom within his soul.

*
*   *

While all these spiritual experiences were a source of great joy to Mikhaël, they also led him to demand more and more of himself. He scrutinized his life, his behaviour, his activities, and concluded that what he saw was a disaster. Disgusted by his 'mediocrity', he resolved to replace it with something very great that would demand such striving that he would never have time to tire of his efforts. He began to implore the help of the invisible beings whose presence he sensed: 'What am I going to do? I'm feeble, stupid, mediocre, worthless... Do you really want me to be like this for the rest of my life?' He spoke as though to his spiritual parents:

> I can't go on living as I am now. Send some Angels to help me, send me all kinds of pure, noble, intelligent creatures. It will be to your advantage because, if you don't answer my prayer, I'll never do anything right [...]8

In the light of his desire for perfection, he judged himself severely, seeing only his weaknesses and failings. His sights were set so high that he could not be satisfied with what he had already achieved. In later years he often spoke of a very intense phase of spiritual work that began when he was fifteen, as though all that had gone before was totally negligible. And yet, judging from his own accounts, two years previously he had already realized the importance of regular meditation and conscious breath control in achieving inner equilibrium. He would one day tell his disciples that the practice of

---

8. August 6th, 1968 (*Cosmic Moral Law*, p. 83).

rhythmic breathing could be of incalculable benefit to one's intellectual, emotional, and psychic life, that it could help to balance one's sexual energies and even facilitate contact with the most exalted entities of invisible worlds.

It was at this time that Mikhaël left school in order to devote every minute to his spiritual exercises and research. His mind and heart were already steeped in the age-old truths of initiatic science, and he began now to study other texts treating of Hindu philosophy and ancient theosophy. But in spite of the inner peace that this work brought him, he was very much alone. He had barely known his father, and there was no one in his immediate surroundings to whom he could turn for guidance in his spiritual development. His mother was a constant presence of love and solid common sense, but no one knew enough to warn him of the danger of prolonged breathing exercises without the supervision of an experienced guide. His family, who witnessed his strange behaviour, sometimes wondered if he was not slightly deranged. Why did he not behave like other boys of his age? His experiments with colour, his unusual eating habits and frequent fasts seemed ridiculous.

At this stage of his adolescence, by strength of character alone, Mikhaël had already surmounted many of the difficulties inherent in the harsh conditions of the times. Progressively he had succeeded in harnessing his prodigious energy in the service of his spiritual ideal, and he was ready to sacrifice everything for that ideal. Little by little he demonstrated that he was afraid of nothing. And yet he was convinced that he needed a spiritual Master. Following his intuition, he began searching in earnest for the being who would help him to develop and channel both his spiritual impulses and his exceptional psychic powers.

His deep-felt need to put himself in the hands of a sage was the expression of a demanding conscience. In the East, a spiritual Master has always been considered the greatest treasure any human being can possess, and those who choose the spiritual path are capable of giving up all their worldly goods in order to find a true Master. Born at the frontier between East and West, imbued as he was with Hindu and Buddhist philosophy as well as the teaching of the Gospels, Mikhaël adopted this attitude wholeheartedly. All his life he would say that a spiritual Master inspires and stimulates, that he is a link with heaven, a path that leads to the summits. It is the mental image that a disciple forms of his Master which becomes his true inner Master, and it is this inner Master who opens the doors of the spiritual world to his disciple.

The models that Mikhaël chose at different ages corresponded to and answered the needs of each phase of his life. In his early years it was naturally to his mother that he turned. Later, Jesus and Buddha became his chosen models. At the age of seventeen, without in any way relinquishing his close bond with them on a higher plane, he strove to resemble Peter Deunov, the spiritual guide he was to find on the physical plane. Many years later, after the death of Peter Deunov, when he himself had disciples, he often spoke of a 'timeless being', the Master of all spiritual Masters, with whom he had had a special relationship since the age of twenty. Also, at the centre of his life there was always the sun, that unique model, dispenser of light, heat, and life. Often he would say: 'I want to be like the sun.' But above all it was the desire to resemble his heavenly Father that most consistently inspired his efforts.

At the age of fifteen, however, he was still searching fervently and sometimes with painful intensity for his first spiritual guide, and the words of the Austrian philosopher Rudolf Steiner were often in his mind: 'When you love an exceptional human being, that love creates a bond between you, and the qualities of that being enter you.' These words sparked a conviction that was to accompany him all his life: to model oneself on an exalted being is always to one's advantage, for that ideal spurs one on to greater heights.

In the hope of finding such an 'exalted being', Mikhaël began to attend the sermons of Orthodox priests and Protestant ministers, but he always returned home disappointed by what he had read on their faces while they commented on the Gospels. Refusing to be deterred by each successive disappointment, he listened to dozens of speakers. Finally he gave up and returned to his books, consoling himself with the biographies of exceptional beings, the great benefactors of humanity. What he read stimulated him and nourished his thirst for perfection and beauty, but the painful fact still remained: he found himself as alone as if he had been in a desert.

Family and friends ridiculed his quest and criticized his unusual behaviour, blaming him for his all-absorbing interest in the things of the spirit. The few with whom he sometimes spoke of what was closest to his heart showed only lukewarm enthusiasm for his ideas.

The general lack of approval, however, failed to turn him from his chosen path, and he continued to call on the higher beings in whose existence he firmly believed. The living, visible guide he longed for was still no more than a dream, and at one point his solitude became so acute that he felt the need for something concrete to cling to, some physical symbol of that unknown spiritual Master. He found an old armchair, which he carefully cleaned and set in a place of honour in his room. The empty chair represented for him both a promise and a sign that his Master would soon reveal himself.

One day, thanks to prolonged reflection and meditation, he had a flash of intuition, a certitude that somewhere in Tibet or India there existed a brotherhood of high initiates dedicated to helping humanity, to spreading the light. He had a strange but clear conviction that he had known and worked with these beings in the remote past, and that they would play an important role in his life. From this point on he considered them his spiritual companions and thought of them constantly, receiving from their presence an extraordinary mystical impetus. At the same time, the sun, source of light in the world, remained a constant inspiration to him.

Mikhaël was truly a solar being. Even as a young boy he seems to have understood that the mightiest and most perfect fire, the fire that is never extinguished, was the sun itself. And as his understanding of the vital importance of light grew, so did his love for it. For him, the sun would always be the most perfect image of God, the one great source of life, light, and warmth on earth. Already at this time, whenever he had the opportunity, he attended the sunrise and spent long hours meditating in the park, from where he had a view over the sea to the east.

6

Illumination

Mikhaël had reached a key period of his life. He had worked long and with single-mindedness to open his mind to wisdom, to purify his heart, and to strengthen his will. He had tirelessly implored God to come and dwell within him, and now he was ready to receive the Spirit. When he spoke in later life of the illumination he received at the age of fifteen and a half, he linked it to the mystical experience triggered by the Book of Proverbs at the age of nine. This later experience, he said, was the occasion on which he took possession of himself for the second time.

It was during this period that an essay entitled *The Over-Soul*, by the American philosopher Emerson, had an extremely powerful effect on him. At about the same time he came across a text which described the human aura and the splendours of the invisible world. The combined influence of these two books was to be decisive, but it was apparently the description of Buddha's aura that led him across the threshold of ecstasy.

One summer morning, as usual, he went to the sea shore to watch the sunrise, and climbing a slight rise, sat down in an orchard. He had been meditating for a little while when he sensed the presence of heavenly beings around him. Suddenly bathed in a nimbus of brilliant light, he was plunged into a state of ecstasy.

The sparse references he made to this illumination in later life evoked an image of dazzling beauty, but he clearly found it impossible to express the essential core of the experience. It could never be described or shared with others. We know only that he saw 'a mysterious being', one of those heavenly entities that manifest as pure light, the sight of which leaves such a profound impression that a mystic feels as though he had seen God. Later, he commented:

> I had never abandoned my desire to become like Buddha, like Jesus. This was still primordial in my mind… and it was so beautiful that I was beside myself. To see such a being, with all those colours, all that light! He was almost invisible in the extraordinary luminosity that surrounded him. I found myself flooded with light. I was in a state of bliss, of ecstasy so immense, so powerful, that I no longer knew where I was. It was a delirious joy; it was heaven; it was the universe! Ever since then I have felt that if God were not all beauty I could not believe in him. It is beauty that remains in my mind as the one essential: neither power, nor knowledge, nor wealth, nor glory. Only beauty![9]

The vision he had been granted was perhaps that of his higher self, that cosmic element that is an integral part of every human being and of the same nature as the divine spirit, a particle of God, a luminous quintessence. In a state of ecstasy, a mystic looks into the mirror of God and sees this part of himself which is divine. And it is when the identification of the two 'selves', inferior and superior, is achieved that he is united with the universal soul and attains true self-knowledge.

Immersed in an ocean of ineffable beauty, Mikhaël was beyond the common bounds of time and space. His whole being seemed to expand without limits. The illumination was so intense and the rapture so all-absorbing that he felt as though he were on fire. He felt his brain burning. His whole being seemed to have become a living flame. And just as this divine illumination became more than he could bear and he sensed that he was about to be reabsorbed into cosmic light, he lost consciousness. The loss of consciousness is a frequent corollary of ecstasy, a protective mechanism that the visionary must accept in order to avoid destruction. The intensity of the light and the expansion of being brought about by divine love is so great that the physical human envelope needs this protection when it reaches the limits of its capacity.

---

9. Unpublished talk, December 9th, 1968.

Did Mikhaël's illumination last a few minutes or a few hours? He never said. But when he recovered consciousness and found that the state of ecstasy had vanished, a sense of desolation swept over him. He felt like a dry, empty husk and strove in vain to recapture that exquisite joy, for he could not resign himself to living without it. After a mystical experience of such intensity, he felt that all that had gone before was mere heedlessness and mediocrity.

For days, he was barely aware of being on earth. His mind still absorbed in the contemplation of the splendours he had discovered, he could neither sleep nor eat. His only nourishment came from the divine forces that had filled his being, and his yearning for the beauty of the invisible world awoke in him the overwhelming desire to create the harmony of that world here on earth. Many years later, speaking to his disciples about certain spiritual experiences, he explained that in ecstasy all the wastes in one's organism are burned away, that the mystic's being is totally renewed and purified. His physical body is changed and transfigured; even the texture of the skin is transformed and the face illuminated. He added:

> In this contact with divine grace which clasps you in its arms and warms you through and through, you feel yourself inundated by an infinite sweetness, peace and happiness. This is the greatest privilege. You can only weep with pure, wonderful emotion. At that moment you are ready for any sacrifice; you glimpse eternal life; you see the greatness of God.[10]

Spontaneously, Mikhaël began to live in ever more conscious union with the brotherhood of glorious souls that he believed in. As though by a miracle, he found a book which confirmed his presentiment of the existence of a community of exalted beings who for centuries had gathered in the Himalayas to help and enlighten humanity. Deeply moved by this corroboration of his intuition, Mikhaël thought about them constantly, calling upon them and uniting himself with them in his mind, participating in their work of love and light. He contemplated the splendour of this brotherhood of glorious souls who, free of all hatred and rancour, dwelt in perfect

---

10. Unpublished talk, January 28th, 1951.

harmony and devoted themselves to the good of humanity. The revelations he received from them filled him with joy.

*
* *

Mikhaël was overflowing with such happiness that he had only one thought: to devote his life to helping others. In his eagerness to share his divine experience with his family and friends, to enable them to vibrate as he had vibrated, he described to them the beauty of a life lived in the light of the spirit. He was convinced that if they read the book that had so inspired him they too would be electrified, impelled to transform their mentality and their way of life.

We know from one of his teachers that although Mikhaël's friends had always been impressed by his intelligence and his knowledge, they remained sceptical about his spiritual practices. But now they became aware of a new, subtle quality that emanated from him. He was no longer the same. He seemed to be lit from within, to be incandescent. Hoping to achieve a similar fulfilment, some of them began to meditate, to study initiatic science, or to adopt a vegetarian diet, but although Mikhaël did his best to help and encourage them, he saw that they soon tired of their efforts.

'Why do you persist in nourishing your old mentality?' he exclaimed. 'Get rid of it! It is the cause of all your problems. Put something better in its place.'

But not one of them really understood him, and eventually he left them in peace. He was alone with his sublime ideal, and the realization that there were none to share it often distressed him deeply. How could these truths have such an effect on him and none at all on others, he wondered. When he saw their indifference to the beauty of the spiritual life, he felt so small and inadequate and blamed himself for not being intelligent enough to convince them.

In the long run, many of his comrades jeered at him and held him up to ridicule, for they could not feel at ease with his ideas. They found them too exalted and the demands he made on himself too stringent. They were unwilling to follow him on the steep slopes leading to the summit. But their derision did not deter him. His passion for the light continued to radiate from him. His whole life was now firmly founded on a certainty that would become the corner-stone of his mission.

Mikhaël did not owe his personal initiation to an earthly spiritual Master. His ardent efforts had been rewarded with the greatest gift a human being can receive from the spiritual world: he had already found the inner guide who would be always with him. It is clear that, like other great beings before him, the divine seal was upon him. This period of his life was one of profound inner initiation. Between the ages of fifteen and seventeen he was to know the joy of frequent mystical experiences, and by the time he met the spiritual guide who was to accompany him on the physical plane, he would have mustered all his forces, tested his capacities, and purified his whole being.

The irresistible impetus that drove him to seek the purest form of Christ-consciousness – that inner consciousness that links a highly advanced human being to the divine principle at work in creation – obliged him to distance himself to a certain extent from his family and close acquaintances. Henceforth nothing would stop him. Ceaselessly and single-mindedly he pursued his work, reaching such a state of physical exhaustion that, before the year was out, he would be overcome by a life-threatening illness.

*
* *

To say that Mikhaël was absorbed by his spiritual work to the exclusion of all else would be inaccurate. An unerring instinct always brought him back to the physical world and its countless possibilities. He enjoyed using his manual dexterity to draw, to do odd jobs, or to make something useful. Above all, mindful of the demands of family life and his responsibilities as the eldest son, he continued to take temporary work whenever he could find it. For two months in the summer of 1916, while World War I was still raging in Europe, he was hired as a secretary in a food rationing centre.

As always, he enjoyed watching those around him. The supervisor of his section was a tall, stout man with a loud voice, and Mikhaël noticed that it was easy for him to impose his opinion on the other employees, who never raised their voices. And yet he was very popular with them, for he was always cheerful and friendly. This made Mikhaël reflect on his own behaviour: he always spoke softly, with the result that he often had to wait before anyone paid attention to him.

We find here, not for the first time, one of the paradoxes of his temperament: in spite of his strength of character and all that he had already experienced, there were still times when he was paralysed by 'unbelievable shyness.' His friends may not have noticed it, but for Mikhaël it was a hidden sore. It irked him to have to walk up and down in front of a shop before he could summon the courage to go in, or to stutter and stammer when he had to speak to a stranger.

One day he decided to cure himself of this affliction by self-suggestion. In the evening, before going to bed, he focused on a bright spot placed in the centre of a circle and repeated to himself, over and over, that his shyness was cured. He pictured himself doing all the things that he was too shy to do in real life. He repeated the exercise more than once, and thanks to his powers of concentration, the results were remarkable. Several times he was able to induce in himself a state of hypnosis and fall into a deep sleep, and before long he found that he had rid himself completely of the problem that had caused him so much embarrassment. Talking in later years about this and other youthful experiments, however, he always emphasized that, at the time, he had not known of the danger to the nervous system of methods of this kind. He was always careful to warn his disciples against attempting such exercises without suitable preparation.

At some point during this period he began to frequent one of the principal book shops in Sofia. The capital was some 280 miles from Varna, and although at the time of Mikhaël's youth the journey by train cost nothing, the trip must have taken him most of the day and brought him home late at night. On his first visit to this shop, he was leafing through some books on the shelves when the owner, who had been watching him, picked up two or three booklets and handed them to him, saying:

'Look, this is what you should be reading.'

Mikhaël looked at them and wondered what could be so interesting about them. He had already read so many articles and brochures which had left him unsatisfied. Nevertheless, he smiled at the man gratefully, saying:

'I believe you sir. Thank you for showing me the best you have.'

Returning to his perusal of the shelves, he picked out several books by Rudolf Steiner, whose work he continued to study. How it happened he never knew, but on his way home he was disappointed to realize that he had lost his books. This was a great blow, for his contribution to the family expenses left him little money for his own intellectual nourishment. The pamphlets, however, were still in his satchel, and he began to read them.

They were like nothing he had ever read before. The plain, simple language spoke directly to his heart. At the same time, many of the questions in his mind found answers that were intellectually satisfying. The author of these booklets, Peter Deunov by name, lived in Sofia, and Mikhaël thought to himself: 'He is head and shoulders above all the others. How can I meet him?' In fact, he was not to meet him for several months, but his quest for a spiritual Master was finally drawing to a close. He had begun to glimpse a light at the end of the tunnel. It was still dim, still no more than a promise, but it was there. Later, he often returned to that shop in Sofia, whose owner lent him books and invited him to sit in his office, where he could read in peace. Mikhaël and the older man were soon fast friends.

*
* *

His burning thirst for knowledge, for all the knowledge of the universe, drove Mikhaël to read without pause from morning to evening and often late into the night. There were days when he devoured six or seven hundred pages, often reading while eating so as not to waste time. The flame that burned within him since his ecstasy was so intense that he went to extremes with his prayers, meditations, and breathing exercises, not noticing that he was seriously undermining his health.

Having become accustomed since the death of his father to frugal and insufficient meals, he often made do for the whole day with some raw cabbage or bits and pieces from his mother's store of pickled gherkins, peppers, and celery. He did not mind the sensation of weightlessness induced in him by this inadequate diet. On the contrary, he took advantage of it, for it made it easier to disassociate, but he grew thinner and thinner, and his face became deathly pale. And as he never had enough sleep, he often dozed off at the most inopportune moments. Not knowing how to improve the situation, he thought it was enough to force himself by will-power alone.

Mikhaël's mother watched all this with deep concern. Convinced that the evil came from his books which influenced his thinking and led him to extremes, she threatened to burn them. Mikhaël's only response was to lock himself in his room to avoid such a catastrophe. When she knocked on his door and pleaded with him to go to the park for some fresh air, he refused to give in. Repeating gently that she must not worry, that he would go later, he continued to do the only thing that seemed to him worth doing.

Dolia wept. She was at her wit's end. Her neighbours and the other members of the family kept repeating:

'You must not let him go on like that. He's going to die!'

One day, defeated by her own fears and the insistence of others, she threw Mikhaël's books into the fire. But even this did not deter him: he continued his spiritual exercises, his deep breathing, fasting, and meditations as before. Speaking many years later of the fire that consumed him at this time, he would say: 'It was such a flame, such a light… it was so exaggerated it was a kind of madness.'

Once again Mikhaël's family and friends were convinced that he had taken leave of his senses. They could not understand that he was simply wild with joy. They could not know that the ecstasy that had triggered this seeming folly was the culmination of a long maturing, the climax of the spiritual work he had accomplished since the age of twelve. Such excessiveness is almost inevitable in these forceful and determined beings who are destined to accomplish great things, but for their family and friends, the need for such extremes is hard to understand. They often cannot accept the seemingly outrageous discipline, the superhuman drive toward perfection of one who has grown up in their midst and whom they believe they know well.

*
*   *

In the period between his illumination and the first meeting with his long-sought Master, Mikhaël had other mystical experiences, but we do not know exactly when or in what order they occurred. About the most remarkable of these we know little. When he spoke of it, he said only that one day, while doing his deep breathing exercises, he felt a drop of fire enter his lungs and inflame his whole being. The sensation filled him with such inexpressible delight, such an exquisite sense of sweetness, that he could only weep for joy.

Later he understood that this fire had been a drop of ether, of prana, a particle of the cosmic spirit, of the fire that is capable of melting and transmuting obsolete forms and creating a new being. As usual, he spoke modestly and with detachment of this exceptional phenomenon, and yet it seems that what he experienced that day was a second birth, the birth in the Spirit by which a human being is consecrated for a sacred mission. This divine baptism, this pervasion of his being by the Christ-Spirit took place without witnesses; those he lived with saw no more than a pale reflection, a new radiance whose source remained a mystery.

Also in this period, he was snatched one day from his physical body and borne far away to the heart of the cosmos, where all is music. Suddenly he found himself as one with the universe, at once rock, tree, flower, mountain, and star. Vibrating in unison with the powerful currents that passed through him, he became acutely aware of the essence of all being:

> The whole world sang… the stars sang; plants, rocks, and trees sang. Everything sang. And the harmony was so glorious, so sublime that I felt myself expanding until I feared that I would die. …I wish you might all hear what I heard, if only for a few seconds. It would give you some point of comparison, some idea of the true nature of music.[11]

Mikhaël had achieved, that day, one of the rarest and most beautiful experiences it is possible for a human being to have. He had attained a truly exceptional level of vibration. But the human body is not built to withstand such stress for long, and the ecstasy lasted only a few seconds. If it had lasted any longer, it might well have put an end to his existence in this world,[12] and sensing that he was in danger of being pulverized, he interrupted it:

---

11. Unpublished talk, April 19th, 1945.

12. Everything in the universe moves and vibrates. Nothing is totally immobile. 'When an object reaches a certain level of vibration, its molecules disintegrate and decompose, returning to the original elements and atoms from which they came. These atoms, obeying the Law of Vibration, fall apart in their turn and become once more the countless corpuscles of which they were composed. Finally, when the corpuscles themselves disappear, we can say that the object is composed of Etheric Substance.' *Le Kybalion*, Bibliothèque eudiaque, Paris, 1917, p. 97 (Our translation).

It was fear that brought me back. Not the fear of death, but the fear of being unable to continue my work on earth. If you have been given a task to accomplish on earth, you have to go through with it. I could not simply abandon it.[13]

In the months and years that followed, his yearning for the joy of that precious experience was so great that he could not avoid a sense of regret at having put an end to it, a regret all the more poignant because he could never hear music to equal it on the physical plane. But the memory of those indescribable moments steeped in the music of the spheres would continue to give him courage in difficult times and serve as an absolute yardstick: his appreciation of a piece of music was never governed by the norms commonly accepted in society but by that measure alone. He was to say later that each planet has not only its own particular colour, but also its own note, and that the symphony of those notes varies with each hour of the day.

This intensely mystical period of Mikhaël's sixteenth year was, nevertheless, fraught with certain dangers. His ardent temperament led him sometimes to the edge of the abyss, and his prolonged exercises of pranayama nearly ended in disaster. Yogic breathing techniques are based on an ancient tradition of Hindu mysticism which attaches great importance to the role of the spinal column and its seven chakras or etheric force-centres. At the base of the spine lies the formidable force known as Kundalini, which has a close affinity with sexual energy. When aroused by the use of certain techniques, it can release tremendous psychic forces.

Mikhaël did not know enough to be on his guard against the danger of practising certain techniques without guidance. He probably did not know that the ancient Sanskrit treatises of pranayama were made intentionally obscure in order to prevent neophytes from experimenting with them without the supervision of a skilled teacher. One day, while engaged in rhythmic breathing, he was suddenly seized by an agonising pain and felt as though his brain

---

13. Unpublished talk, August 21st, 1954.

were about to explode. His whole being was on fire. Appalling currents flowed through him, and he suffered atrociously. Sensing that he was in mortal danger, he was gripped by terrible fear and made a tremendous effort to subdue the Kundalini-force and oblige it to retreat. Summoning all the strength of which he was capable, he concentrated his thoughts and called on the powers of the invisible world to save him, and at last succeeded in putting this extraordinary force to sleep again.

Had Mikhaël not escaped this destructive power, he might well have lost his mind or died in terrible torment. And yet this trial by fire was something he had to go through; without doubt, it belonged to the body of knowledge and wisdom he needed in order to teach the great truths of initiatic science. Later, when he had disciples of his own, he never encouraged them to awaken the Kundalini-force. On the contrary, he always emphasised that the best way of furthering one's evolution was to purify oneself, to work patiently and with perseverance to perfect oneself. The virtues and psychic gifts and powers would come quite naturally, he maintained, when one was ready for them and capable of controlling and using them in the service of light.

*
* *

Early in 1917, worn out by his frequent fasts and excessive spiritual exercises, Mikhaël fell seriously ill. He had recently become interested in the methods of hydrotherapy with which the German therapist Sebastien Kneipp obtained many cures. In the hope of purifying his system and regaining his physical energy, Mikhaël decided to try the Kneipp method. For several weeks he took his baths in the old stable that still served him as a laboratory, but the unheated building with its floor of packed earth was so cold that he ended by catching a chill. He became so ill and sank so rapidly into a state of deep torpor that his mother, fearing the worst, called in a doctor who diagnosed typhoid fever and put the household in quarantine. Dolia nursed her son night and day, watching over him while his condition gradually worsened. Burning with fever and racked by fierce headaches, Mikhaël alternated between a state of delirium and longer periods of total prostration.

For a whole month he hovered between life and death. In his periods of delirium he clamoured for books. He wanted nothing else, only books. He did not think about getting better or even about the possibility that he might die. He was interested only in learning, in knowing everything there was to know, in reading all the books in the world. Restless and tormented by a burning thirst, he continued to ask for philosophical, spiritual, and scientific works. In particular, he begged for those of Spinoza, one of his favourite philosophers. In their anxiety, his parents did their best to satisfy him. Somehow finding those precious books, they brought them to him and laid them on his bed. Mikhaël, barely conscious, would thank them and clasp the books lovingly for a few moments before putting them by his pillow, with the feeling that he was getting better. But when the fever brought back the delirium, he begged for still more books.

At one point the tiny flame of life burned so low that it seemed certain to fail altogether. Dolia, in tears, was afraid that he was going to die.

But Mikhaël was not yet destined to leave this world. Throughout his illness something had continually been at watch within him. In his lucid moments he had often been aware that it was within his power to work mentally to cure himself. He was far too weak to concentrate for long, but whenever possible he willed with all his might to accept the suffering in every fibre of his being and allow it to purify his organism. Years later he made a strange but certainly true comment about his recovery: 'I cured myself through suffering.' When at last he was out of danger and his strength was slowly returning, his craving for books had disappeared. He continued to read, but never in the same way.

Mikhaël's 'terrible illness of purification', as he called it, seems to have been an integral part of this intensely mystical phase. It was also the prelude to a vision that made a deep impression on him. One evening, when in the state of somnolence that lends itself particularly well to such phenomena, he had a vision of a tall, arrogant being splendidly clad in black. Looking at the dark eyes in which a terrible intent smouldered, Mikhaël sensed that this being, whose whole demeanour spoke of power and authority, wished to possess him and communicate that power to him.

Almost immediately there appeared a second figure in stark contrast to the first. Dressed all in white, he was radiant with light and inexpressibly beautiful. His eyes spoke only of love and benevolence. In a flash of intuition Mikhaël understood that he was being given a choice. Fascinated though he was by the might of the dark being and the powers he seemed to promise, deep in his heart he was fearful of something terrible that emanated from that sombre visage. Suddenly he understood: the forces of darkness and destruction were trying to win him over to their side and use him for their own ends. Turning back to the second apparition, he was enraptured by the beauty that shone in his face, 'the very face of Christ, the image of sweetness, goodness, and self-sacrifice.' There was no possible hesitation, and the instant his choice was made, the being of darkness vanished, while the being of light gazed at him for a moment with an expression of infinite sweetness before disappearing in his turn. It was the splendour of this being that he was to describe in later years. 'I can never forget it,' he said. 'I was dazzled by his beauty. It was the beauty which captivated me.'

This vision constituted a milestone in Mikhaël's life. He sensed that he had been absolutely free: free to choose between putting his considerable psychic powers at the service of his personal satisfaction or at the service of light. That night he made up his mind that he would use those powers only in the pursuit of a selfless spiritual goal.

Other choices he made at this period were equally unequivocal. He was deeply impressed, for instance, by a text of Paracelsus in which he stated that the loss of a man's semen is a loss of life. Mikhaël would say later that his encounter with this statement played a decisive role in his life, that it led him to reflect at length on the question of sexuality and to make an important decision. A decision that was possible only because he already shared the conviction of Paracelsus. Resolving not to give physical expression to his sexual energies but to sublimate them in the service of a mystical goal, he would use them throughout his life as one uses hydraulic pressure to raise water to the top floor of a building, the 'top floor' being a symbol of the mind, the brain, the seat of the 'thousand-petalled crown chakra.' Without repudiating or stifling these energies, he would gradually develop a balanced philosophy of sexuality deeply respectful of human beings and their evolution.

*
* *

During his long convalescence in the winter of 1917, Mikhaël began to hear talk of Peter Deunov, the author of the booklets his friend at the book shop had given him. He was said to be a spiritual Master, a clairvoyant and musician, who had a great many disciples. On the insistence of Church authorities, who disapproved of a teaching which drew not only on the Gospels but also on the ancient tenets of initiatic science, Peter Deunov had been expelled from Sofia and was now living in Varna. He had taken a room in the Hotel Londres, not far from where Mikhaël lived.

One day while Mikhaël was taking some gentle exercise out of doors, he saw a man of medium height and vigorous appearance coming rapidly toward him. In an instant he had passed, but not before Mikhaël had glimpsed his face. Moved to the depths of his being, he murmured to himself: 'That must be he!' The face he had seen expressed such nobility that it could belong only to Peter Deunov. Incapable of thinking of anything else, he made inquiries which confirmed his intuition. It was truly Peter Deunov. Without hesitation, Mikhaël set out for the hotel to make the acquaintance of the author whose writings had so inspired him. When he was shown into his room, he saw a grey-haired man whom he recognized instantly as the one who had passed him in the street. He was sitting at a table, playing the violin, while the person with him sang softly in accompaniment.

'When you knocked,' said Peter Deunov, 'we were singing a song that I am composing. You can sing with us.'

A little taken aback by this unexpected greeting, Mikhaël obediently sat down and tried to sing with them, but his vocal cords refused to make a sound. Peter Deunov continued to play his violin, humming the melody with the young woman, who was a member of the brotherhood he had founded. Gradually Mikhaël recovered his composure and began to sing with them. When the song was complete and written down, Peter Deunov laid his violin on the table, turned to his guest, and engaged him in a lengthy conversation.

From time to time he picked up the Bible, read a passage, and commented on it. Mikhaël's hunger for clear and honest explanations was at last satisfied, and he would say years later that from the first time he met Peter Deunov there had been an 'inexplicable bond' between them. It was as though they had recognized each other.

Mikhaël was eager to learn Peter Deunov's opinion on many subjects, particularly on the question of clairvoyance. By then he already knew a good deal about spiritual, extra-sensory, and occult phenomena and was familiar with the philosophy of several initiatic schools of both East and West. But here, at last, was a man reputed to be a great clairvoyant, who could speak from personal experience.

Mikhaël's first question, 'How can I become clairvoyant?' received an answer that surprised him. Instead of explaining a method, Peter Deunov simply said:

'Through love. You must develop your love. Your clairvoyance will be far greater if you work in this way.'

Mikhaël was touched to the quick. On reflection he realized that until then he had been looking for 'great mysteries, for things that transcend concrete realities.' That very day he decided he would never make a deliberate effort to develop the gift of clairvoyance, but would work only by means of love. The ability to see invisible realities on a higher plane would grow within him naturally, without any special exercises or conscious effort. He knew that although certain methods are effective, they can also be dangerous, for they can destroy a person's inner equilibrium. From that day on, he 'worked to understand the truth and to sense the beauty hidden in all things, in trees, in flowers, in fruit.' In his eyes this was the highest form of clairvoyance.

After this first meeting, Mikhaël often saw Peter Deunov at dawn, as he walked through the park on his way to the sunrise. At this early hour the *Morskata Gradina* was deserted, and Peter Deunov would gravely lift his hat to this lad of seventeen who went out so early each morning to contemplate the rising sun.

Part Two :

The Disciple

The true order of going to the things of love, whether we travel alone or are led by another, is to begin from the beauties of earth and mount upwards until one arrives at the notion of absolute beauty and at last knows what the essence of beauty is.

Plato, *The Symposium*

7

The Beginning of a New Life

In the course of history, Bulgaria, the homeland of Orpheus, was variously known as Thrace and Moesia before receiving its present name. A land of ancient myths lying at the frontier between East and West, it was particularly well placed to serve as one of the principal cradles of the esoteric tradition in Medieval Europe.

Omraam Mikhaël Aïvanhov sometimes said that the Mysteries, taught for thousands of years in the temples of Egypt and India, had also been faithfully preserved in an initiatic centre deep in the heart of Bulgaria's Rila massif, known only to true adepts. One of these ancient adepts, the mysterious Magus Boyan who had developed great psychic powers in the course of his initiation in India, was at the origin of a charismatic religious movement in Bulgaria known as the Bogomils. The spiritual renewal inspired by this movement, however, was short-lived, for the Bogomils boldly condemned those in high places for their dissolute way of life, with the result that many were exiled or burnt at the stake. Some, fleeing the torment in Bulgaria, settled in other European countries where their ideas influenced such initiatic movements as the Knights Templar and the Cathars.

It is in the spiritual tradition of initiates such as the Magus Boyan that Peter Deunov takes his place. His teaching rested on the key elements that were those of the Bogomils – the light, self-mastery, and purity – but had none of their austerity. Neither did he teach that the physical world was created by the powers of evil, as did the Bogomils and Cathars. In his turn, Omraam Mikhaël Aïvanhov would say that the Cathars' yearning for liberation was based on their perception of life on earth as a terrible misfortune, and this, he insisted, was an error: our task is to work here in the physical world, to realize the kingdom of heaven on earth.

Peter Deunov, born in the region of Varna in 1864, was the son of an Orthodox priest. After studying theology and medicine in the United States, he had returned to Bulgaria in 1895. There he undertook an intensive and wide-ranging study of phrenology, travelling to towns and villages throughout Bulgaria to study the relationship between human character and temperament and the shape of the skull. It seems that he also devoted much time to meditation, laying the groundwork for a spiritual brotherhood. It was in 1900, at about the time of Mikhaël's birth, that he began to give public lectures, and nine years later, with a good number of disciples at his side, he organized the first in a series of summer conventions for his followers near the small town of Ternovo, half-way between Sofia and Varna.

Peter Deunov's explanations of the esoteric meaning of biblical texts breathed new life into traditional Christian doctrines, but it was not long before his work met with strong opposition. The rapid rise of this spiritual movement that drew inspiration not only from the Judeo-Christian tradition but also from ancient initiatic teachings was a source of concern to religious authorities. A teaching based on light and the notion of cosmic justice implicit in the doctrine of reincarnation seemed to be a condemnation of their own teaching and way of life. In 1917, the government yielded to pressure exerted by the Bishops and expelled Peter Deunov from Sofia.

Hardly had the exile settled in Varna – a town he knew well, having spent part of his youth there – than he began to give public lectures. He was now fifty-three and recognized by many as an authentic spiritual Master. His talks soon attracted a large following, for his words manifested a vision of reality which was both original and profound and spoke to a deep need in his contemporaries. His style, however, was unusual: he sometimes interrupted his discourse to hum a melody that had suddenly come to him. Gradually, he developed and refined it and asked his audience to sing with him. He was also an accomplished violinist, and composed over the years a great many mystical songs for his fraternity.

Mikhaël soon became one of Peter Deunov's most devoted followers, but Dolia cried when she learned that he was following a teaching that was not sponsored by the Church. As a fervent member of the Orthodox community she had difficulty in understanding her son's enthusiasm for the brotherhood. In an attempt to allay her concern, Mikhaël tried to interest her in the spiritual philosophy that was becoming so important to him and invited her to attend some of Peter Deunov's talks with him. To please him, Dolia finally agreed, but her first contact with the brotherhood was not a success. Peter Deunov continued to be harassed by the religious authorities, and some of his enemies had followed him to Varna, where they attempted to hinder his spiritual work by hiring hooligans to create disturbances during his talks. It was a veritable persecution, and Dolia wanted no part of it. 'Don't worry, Mother,' Mikhaël tried to reassure her; 'the Master has said that the police will be there next time to protect us.'

The protection materialized as promised: several policemen were stationed in the back of the hall before the lecture began, and Peter Deunov spoke to his disciples without interruption. However, this was not enough to convince Dolia to attend any more meetings. Her path was not that of her son, but she respected his options. 'If this is what is right for you,' she told him, 'then I am with you.'

Deeply grateful for the freedom she gave him, Mikhaël lived in a permanent state of joy and enthusiasm. At last he had found what he had sought for so long: a spiritual Master who knew how to link himself with the divine world, a sage whose life was devoted to the enlightenment of humanity. And this sage dispensed a teaching whose source lay in the highest spheres of the invisible world, a teaching which had been preserved for centuries in the ancient temples of the world. As Peter Deunov once said to his disciples:

> Do not say that the doctrine I teach was invented by someone called Deunov. Say that it is the teaching of the Fellowship of Light. Tomorrow someone else will appear, with another name. The greatness of all those who have come into the world lies in their transmission of the truth just as it was given to them by God.[14]

---

14. *L'Enseignement du Maître Deunov*, p. 62. (Our translation)

For Mikhaël, it was the beginning of a new life; his quest for perfection was now channelled in a more definite direction. He felt extraordinarily rich to have found one of the most precious treasures a human being can have: a spiritual Master. He realized that this new teaching confirmed and brought into perspective all that he had discovered and practised in the last few years, and this gave him great joy, for by now he was aware of the dangers inherent in his excessive exercises. Convinced that he needed a guide in order to progress in the spiritual world, he looked to Peter Deunov for advice and instruction in the methods he should use. Peter Deunov recognized this need, and often invited Mikhaël to visit him at his hotel.

The young man always arrived for those interviews with a series of questions, and as the answers he received were often abstract and symbolic, he was obliged to reflect at length in order to understand their hidden meaning. To help him to remember what he had heard, he developed a method all his own. Instead of taking notes during the interview, he tried simply to become a receptacle, to absorb what was said not with his intellect but with his heart, in order to grasp the beauty and the spiritual dimension of Peter Deunov's words. Back in his own room, he concentrated on what had passed between them, reviewing the whole conversation in his mind over and over again, until he remembered every word, every detail. Only then did horizons open before him that he could not have imagined during the meeting. Convinced that whatever he received through the intermediary of Peter Deunov was precious beyond words, he practised this method faithfully for many years.

In one corner of Peter Deunov's room stood a large incense-burner and in cold weather he would revive the fire by stirring the coals with a small poker. As Mikhaël watched, captivated by the grace of his movements, he reflected that the subtle harmony of his gestures could not fail to have a profound influence on those around him. But if the young Mikhaël was a skilled observer, he soon saw that Peter Deunov was as well. When he walked to the door at the end of an interview and turned to say good-bye, he saw that his way of walking and of opening the door were being closely observed. Struck by this, he began to scrutinize his own gestures and correct anything that did not seem aesthetically pleasing.

Mikhaël's desire for perfection frequently led him to the Master in search of advice. One day, knowing his skill as a phrenologist, he asked him to analyse his features and tell him how to correct the faults they revealed. Peter Deunov complied, and his comments seem to have impressed the young Mikhaël deeply:

'Your forehead,' he told him; 'was designed in accordance with the musical laws of divine harmony.'

He added that his chin expressed stability, and then gave him some advice about how to correct the aspects that were not perfectly balanced.

When Mikhaël said that he too would like to study phrenology, Peter Deunov smiled and replied:

'You already have that science within you.'

This response may have seemed surprising, but as Mikhaël was to say later, he had begun to realize that while the Master was answering a question he often knew the answer already, and that Peter Deunov was simply bringing to the surface truths that lay hidden within him.

After his long and lonely quest in the world of books, Mikhaël found great comfort in the burgeoning community that had become his spiritual family. The teaching he was studying so ardently fulfilled his aspirations, for it embraced not only initiatic science and philosophy, but also meditation, prayer, music, methods of breath control, and even rhythmic physical exercises designed to harmonize the whole being. In this teaching he found light, wisdom, and brotherly love.

'This is the new life,' he said to himself, 'a life that is all giving, not taking.' But what could he give? Certainly not money. His only wealth lay in his love and his thoughts, and these he dedicated whole-heartedly to the Master Deunov and his spiritual mission. Every morning, he devoted himself to this work, picturing Peter Deunov as inexpressibly beautiful, surrounding him with a wealth of magnificent colours, projecting on to him every imaginable quality and virtue. His passion for subtle links urged him to unite mentally with this spiritual Master at every possible moment, for in his eyes he was a vital link in the ascending chain of highly evolved beings that binds us to the Creator. By uniting with him, thereby forging a bond with the most sublime hierarchies, he received an abundance of spiritual benefits which both fuelled and intensified his hunger for perfection, his quest for God.

*
*   *

But Mikhaël was not to enjoy this ideal situation for long. Toward the end of 1917 the time came for him to do his military service. He was devastated. The very idea of being a soldier horrified him, for he wanted no part in any form of human violence. He, whose ideal was one of love, sharing, and mutual support, had already spent his whole life in a world ravaged by wars and insurrections, a world of terror and brutality. And now, with the First World War in full spate, the Balkans were tragically affected by the conflict.

As soon as he received his conscription papers, he went to tell Peter Deunov. 'I was crying,' he said later. 'I did so want to stay with him and continue going to the sunrise.'

This reaction is revealing. Of all the sacrifices military service would demand of him, the most difficult to accept was the separation from his spiritual Master and the impossibility of practising the 'yoga of the sun.' To his surprise, Peter Deunov's response was to laugh, and Mikhaël, hurt by this apparent indifference, fell silent. But then he thought to himself: 'I cannot expect a great Master to share in the sorrows of a little disciple like me.' As he was to learn later, Peter Deunov often assumed an air of gaiety in the face of his disciples' sadness in order to dissipate their negative vibrations and induce a more positive reaction. After a few moments, however, his expression changed completely, and looking at Mikhaël with the love of a father, he said:

'Don't worry! You will soon be freed in an extraordinary way. You have no idea what heaven has in store for you.'

In truth, Mikhaël's military service was brief. Shortly after his arrival in camp he fell ill with jaundice and was transferred to the infirmary, where he was treated by a sergeant whose medical competence was limited to the use of tincture of iodine. Peter Deunov's prediction soon came true: Mikhaël was declared unfit for military service and sent home to recuperate. When he was better, although still pale and thin, he went to see Peter Deunov, who told him:

'Your liver has been damaged.'

'What should I do to get better?'

'Every morning before eating, you must drink a cup of water. Drink it slowly, chewing each mouthful and concentrating on what you are doing. You must also talk to the water. Tell it, "Dear water, we are going to work together to repair what is wrong in my body."'

Perplexed, Mikhaël thought to himself: 'Water? That is his remedy?' Without really believing in it he nevertheless obeyed, for he was convinced that it would always be to his benefit to follow his Master's advice, even if it were mistaken. For, while he knew that genuine Masters who work with the forces of white light never demanded submission from their disciples, he also knew that obedience was very beneficial, for it could help one to acquire humility.

Mikhaël began his treatment and with the first mouthful experienced an extraordinary sensation: it was as though he were tasting water for the first time. It was an elixir on his tongue. As an agreeable light-headedness took hold of him, his consciousness seemed to expand and become keener and more receptive. While his thoughts focused on the pure water, his whole being responded to the mysterious properties of this element he loved so well. Before long, he felt his strength returning, and the extreme exhaustion resulting from his recent illness was soon a thing of the past.

But Mikhaël was still not satisfied and began to look for ways of improving his health further. Meditating on the unity indispensable to a human body, he thought to himself, 'The organs function well only if they obey a higher authority that regulates their activity. How can I make contact and communicate with that authority? How can I enable it to take possession of its inner kingdom?' He thought of the cells and organs of the body as a realm that was governed very imperfectly by its human owner, and he pondered how to communicate with the true king of that realm.

By means of fervent meditation he succeeded in raising his mind to the level of his higher self, that omniscient element that dwells in every human being, and it was then that the existence of an extremely potent point at the back of his head was revealed to him. He began to concentrate on this spot and permeate it with all the light he could imagine. Years later he would give his disciples different exercises to help them to communicate with their higher self, so that it might infuse new energy into their cells. Speaking of this one day, he added:

> Or there is another exercise that you can use: it consists in concentrating on the occiput, the region at the back of your skull. Try it for a few minutes and you will notice that something begins to happen: your whole body begins to vibrate and you feel as though sparks were coursing through you. But this is not an exercise that should be continued for long: as soon as you feel a tension, a tingling, as though you had touched a nerve centre that made your whole body vibrate, it is time to stop. The first few times you must be very careful and be sure not to go on for too long.[15]

Gradually, thanks to his regular efforts, the poor state of health he had suffered for years disappeared.

From this point on, although he now had a spiritual Master with whom he intended to work for many years to come, Mikhaël knew that he would continue to make important discoveries on his own, almost independently of Peter Deunov's influence. His later comments on this period of his youth are revealing: all his experiences and discoveries sprang from an inner dynamic, not from any external stimulus. Since his illumination, his invisible guide had been continually present within him, and it was he who inspired his spiritual work, while Peter Deunov was the touchstone of his progress, the sage in whose presence he gained perspective on many things and learned to confirm his intuitions and discoveries. Peter Deunov's role seems to have been to provide occasional concise explanations that served as a leaven for the ideas already taking shape in Mikhaël's mind, and to guide him with care toward that which he needed to learn. He was the Master on the visible plane who was leading Mikhaël toward an unknown Master from another dimension.

In the spring of 1918, Peter Deunov offered Mikhaël the occasion for a very special spiritual experience: by teaching him to use the technique of disassociation more effectively, he led him for the first time to the causal plane, one of the higher planes of being, each of which has its specific vibratory field and which together constitute

---

15. January 17th, 1971 ('*Know Thyself*' – *Jnana Yoga I*, p. 147).

the different levels of energy in the cosmos. At the time, Peter Deunov was a guest in the home of a disciple who lived among the vineyards to the north of Varna. One day when Mikhaël went to see him there, the Master invited him to return early the next morning, saying that he wanted to take him up into the hills for the sunrise.

Peter Deunov attributed great importance in his teaching to the sun, and encouraged his disciples to attend the sunrise during the spring and summer. He taught them to assimilate the sunlight in order to transform it into virtue and communicate it to others. It is clear that he did not teach them to consider the sun as a sort of God or object of worship, but simply to nourish themselves with its light at the moment when its energies were most beneficial.

At the prospect of this excursion Mikhaël hardly slept that night and arose long before dawn, anxious to be at their meeting place in good time. They reached the highest slopes just before sunrise. The red disk of the sun rose through the mists, glowing with such pure intensity that Mikhaël longed to drink its light. After completing their breathing exercises, Peter Deunov said:

'Now we are going to lie down.'

He stretched out on the grass with his back exposed to the sun's rays and Mikhaël, overcoming his first surprise, did the same and soon felt the heat of the sun warming his skin through his clothes. His back became a great battery charged with solar energy, and pervaded by a deep sense of well-being, he sank into a state that closely resembled sleep. When he came to himself, he had the impression that Peter Deunov had returned at the same moment. While he had no clear memory of what he had seen, he sensed that he had experienced something exceptional; his whole being reverberated with a mysterious bliss. Peter Deunov, smiling at him, asked:

'Do you know where we were?'

'No, Master,' replied Mikhaël; 'I should be glad if you would tell me.'

'We went to visit the causal plane, but the entities that received us told me that you must not be allowed to remember what you had seen. That is why I was obliged to draw a veil before your eyes. But you can feel, can you not, that something happened?'

'Yes, Master. Yes!'

Mikhaël knew that what he had experienced was important for his soul. It seemed to him that the very air was filled with vibrations from the higher planes, that the whole of nature was enchanted. After a moment of silence, the spell was broken when Peter Deunov took some food from his knapsack and they ate together before going down to the town. For the rest of that day, Mikhaël lived in the memory of the morning's experience, and from then on, he often accompanied Peter Deunov to the sunrise. After a long meditation they disassociated, and the Master guided his young disciple with extraordinary love and attention, giving him the opportunity to learn 'the realities of the invisible world.'

*
* *

While it was given to Mikhaël to learn the realities of worlds unknown to most human beings, he was not allowed to remain in ignorance of the realities of the physical world in which he lived. At the age of eighteen he was called on to make one of the important decisions that his future mission required of him. The occasion was provided by a man who had been a consul in the United States and who had recently returned to Bulgaria after travelling about the world. Author of several books about spiritism and passionately interested in magic, he had brought back from his travels all kinds of fetishes, magic mirrors, and ritual robes which he intended to use in his experiments. Once he became president of a group of spiritists, however, he had been obliged to admit that his psychic abilities were meagre, and he was looking for a young man gifted in this way to help him implement his plans.

One day Mikhaël received an invitation to the ex-consul's home in a fashionable neighbourhood of Varna and a dazzling proposal was put to him: in exchange for his services, he was offered a good salary, free room and board, and the use of a library well supplied with books on the occult sciences, magic, and extra-sensory phenomena...

'And whatever else you want,' added the consul.

Word of the abilities, the purity, and the spirituality of this exceptional young man had reached his ears, and with his assistance he could foresee extremely interesting prospects in terms of communications with the spirit world. He was prepared to pay a good deal for his collaboration. For Mikhaël, this was the classic temptation of wealth and power: unrestricted access to an excellent library, the freedom to experiment with extra-sensory phenomena, and the money that would enable him to help his mother and live at ease himself. His first reaction, however, was to consult Peter Deunov and to do as he advised. When Peter Deunov counselled him in no uncertain terms to have nothing to do with the ex-consul or with magic of any kind, he was not surprised; he had already arrived at the conclusion that the truly magical element in the ascent toward perfection was the presence of a spiritual Master, and that psychic accomplishments were of secondary importance:

> I did not know much about human nature, about the cupidity and perversion of men or the fascination of danger. Fortunately, as I did not want to be led astray, I never did anything without consulting my Master, Peter Deunov. [...] There are a great many different ways of selling one's soul to the devil! You do not need to make the kind of pact with the devil that is described in books on witchcraft; you only need to obey the dictates of your own selfishness and greed. Each time you do so your soul loses some of its light.[16]

At the age of sixteen Mikhaël had chosen between the two beings who had appeared to him in a vision. But that did not dispense him from the successive choices that all human beings have to make to reinforce an initial decision, however firm. Free will remains, and our options must constantly be renewed. Fortified by Peter Deunov's wisdom, he persevered with his spiritual exercises, working continually to purify his motivations.

Speaking later of his psychic powers and in particular of his clairvoyance, he said that at that period he had sensed a great inner effervescence, and that he often had revelations about people's past lives. Whenever possible, he asked Peter Deunov to verify the truth of those revelations. But before long he realized that to reveal such things could be dangerous, that he had no right to lift the veil that divine wisdom draws over the memory of human beings: 'If they

---

16. *Youth: Creators of the Future*, p. 20f.

knew what terrible things they had done to each other in the past, how would they react today?'

Mikhaël's dearest wish was to help his friends to advance, and he adopted the habit of denying his gift of clairvoyance. It is evident, however, that he perceived emanations and the aura surrounding each human being, an aura which cannot lie, for its colours express the physical and spiritual state of health of the individual. Occasionally he could even see the luminescence of Peter Deunov's aura and capture the fragrance of the spiritual perfume that emanated from him.

Peter Deunov, aware of Mikhaël's decision in respect to his clairvoyance and knowing his interest in the art of divination by chiromancy, warned him that it was an extremely subtle science which was very difficult to master.

'If you want to understand what a hand reveals,' he explained, 'palmistry alone is not enough. You also have to use phrenology, which studies the shape of the skull, and physiognomy, which enables you to know a person's character as indicated by his facial features.'

Mikhaël thus began to study the three disciplines together, and not long after this, Peter Deunov held out his hand for him to read. Deeply moved, Mikhaël took his hand and examining it in silence was immediately struck by the length of the line of Saturn. Then he noticed a line which started at the Mount of Venus and, crossing the life line, the head line, and the line of Saturn, ended on the other side of the palm. The Master, who had been watching Mikhaël's expression, asked:

'Do you see that line? What does it mean?'

'It is the line of great ordeals,' replied Mikhaël without hesitation. Then, instinctively looking at his own hand, he saw the same line. For a moment he was speechless. So that was it! Peter Deunov knew that he had the same line. He had only shown Mikhaël his hand to help him to understand something important: he too would have to endure great ordeals.

'For the time being you will have the best possible conditions, and receive the help you need to advance,' said Peter Deunov. 'Heaven will give you many blessings. But a time will come when the forces of darkness will put obstacles in your way and try to prevent you from advancing.'

'It should be possible to get by,' said Mikhaël with a smile, unable to grasp all that those words of warning implied.

The Master then decided to reveal further aspects of the ordeals that he would have to face later, and after listening attentively, Mikhaël asked when these trials would take place.

'In the twenty-sixth year,' replied Peter Deunov.

'In my twenty-sixth year,' thought Mikhaël to himself. But he was mistaken. He was then eighteen, and Peter Deunov's ambiguous answer meant that his worst ordeals would begin twenty-six years later. And, in fact, it was in 1944 that the descent into hell began and continued until he touched the depths in 1948. Not wanting to impose too heavy a burden on Mikhaël, Peter Deunov had been deliberately vague.

*
* *

In the meantime, the fraternity was growing rapidly and counted several hundred members who thought of themselves as brothers and sisters. In this they were heirs to an age-old tradition of mankind, for human beings have always had the nostalgic dream of one great family in which all lived together in a spirit of love and mutual support. Throughout the ages, many such fraternities have seen the light of day in different countries, different social classes, and different religions. The members of Peter Deunov's brotherhood strove to express this ideal through the harmony of their life together, and as a reminder in times of difficulty that they all belonged to the same family, they addressed each other as 'brother' or 'sister'.

By 1919, the summer conventions at Ternovo had been a regular feature for ten years. The site of the gathering lay among the vineyards on the outskirts of the town, and as there was only one small house, the participants camped in tents and held their activities in the open air. This year Peter Deunov had arranged for Mikhaël and one of his friends to join them, and when they arrived from Varna they found several hundred participants already gathered from the four corners of Bulgaria. Mikhaël and his friend, at nineteen years old, were the youngest.

During this convention Peter Deunov talked at length about light. He asserted that the science of light and colour would be the dominant science of the future, and that light, seemingly so inoffensive, was in reality the greatest force in creation.

That summer was a time of great happiness for Mikhaël: he was happy to be with his spiritual family again, and above all he was happy because of his relationship with Peter Deunov. One day, in conversation with a woman who often acted as Peter Deunov's secretary when he travelled, Mikhaël spoke of the Master's kindness, affection, and consideration. In return he received a warning which opened his eyes to other aspects of the life of a disciple and prepared him for what was to come. The woman exclaimed:

'Brother Mikhaël, you will see later on! He is like that with all his disciples in the beginning, but after a while he becomes much more severe. That it how it was with me, and I thank Heaven that he shakes me up from time to time. You do not yet know what a Master is.'

In effect, it was this same summer that Peter Deunov began to treat his young disciple differently. One day, while he was gathering tools and materials to pave a walk in front of the house, Peter Deunov arrived and started laying out the path himself. Mikhaël helped enthusiastically, until, in a severe tone of voice, the Master said:

'Your work is not well done. The flagstones are uneven.'

Mikhaël laid them again, with greater care. But each time Peter Deunov looked at his work he found fault with it, and each time, the young man patiently began again. While he was working Peter Deunov said nothing, but as soon as he had finished, the criticisms fell thick and fast. Mikhaël, who had always taken care to work with accuracy and an economy of movement, said to himself that he must have been mistaken in thinking that his work was well done. 'I need the Master,' he thought, trying to understand the hidden meaning of the incident; 'I need him to point out my mistakes and show me the way.'

8

Retreat in Ternovo

Ternovo, one of the ancient capitals of Bulgaria, is built on a cluster of steep rugged hills through which winds the river Iantra. Mikhaël liked the picturesque little town, but he loved even more the beautiful countryside all around. That year, after the summer convention, he decided to remain there with one of his friends and devote all his time to spiritual work in this peaceful natural setting.

The two youths were lent an empty villa belonging to a member of Mikhaël's family. Surrounded by trees, the house stood in the middle of vineyards not far from the town. On entering the house they immediately tried to open the window of one of the rooms, only to find the space between shutter and window filled with honeycombs, and a swarm of bees at work. Fascinated by the spectacle, they watched for a long time and agreed not to disturb them. From then on, Mikhaël lived in that room as though in a hive, observing the different phases of the bees' communal life. The delicious, heady perfume that filled the room helped him to meditate. Ever after, he had a special affection for these tiny creatures who 'give us a magnificent example of an advanced form of society.'

This two-year retreat in Ternovo was an important phase in Mikhaël's life. He read and meditated to his heart's content, often into the small hours. Without fear of interruption, and with the concentrated scent produced by the bees to help him to disassociate, he was free to multiply his out-of-body experiences and explore space – as he called the regions to which he travelled in his astral body – in order to understand the structure of the universe and see how all its different elements hang together. Utterly fearless, he attached little importance to his life and succeeded in reaching the loftiest spheres of the invisible world. As he would say later, he explored the higher worlds of ideas and archetypes, the laws and principles that govern creation.

> For years and years I worked with only one idea in mind: to contemplate and comprehend the structure of the universe. For years, it was the only thing that interested me. I spent days and nights out of my body, striving for a clear vision of that structure, of the bonds that tie all the disparate elements together. I knew that everything else was unimportant. The only thing that mattered was to see the overall structure.[17]

At one point he began to concentrate on the distant past of humanity. To go millions of years into the past was a terrifying experience, for he found himself in front of nothing. After many other experiments he attempted to project himself billions of years into the future, and once again was seized with dread. When he spoke about this second experiment later he did not explain the reason for his fear. He simply concluded by saying that eternity is not a temporal reality, it is a state of mind, and that we all have the potential to change a great deal in our present state by concentrating on the future; that through concentration, 'you can touch a nerve-centre of eternity that is capable of sweeping away all that exists.'

Although his experiments were sometimes terrifying, he did not let this deter him. His thirst for knowledge of the invisible world continually urged him on. During this period he talked to Peter Deunov about one of his first experiments at the age of seventeen. He had left his body and launched into space in search of the cosmic archives, the *Akasha Chronica*, that subtle form of matter that fills the cosmos and bears the record of all that happens in the universe: every thought, word, and action. Having succeeded in leaving the physical world far behind, he found himself on the threshold of the unknown, and was seized by such terror that he could go no farther. He was never to forget this fear; a fear that had nothing in common with that of the earthly plane. He was seized by the conviction that

---

17. August 10th, 1968 (*Cosmic Moral Law*, p. 104).

he would be pulverized by the power of the vibrations in which he was immersed. Incapable of going forward, he had great difficulty in returning to his physical body, and succeeded only after great efforts. When he heard this, Peter Deunov explained:

'You had reached the initiatic abyss, and as you were not ready for the experience, you were not allowed to continue.'

Conscious of his excessive nature which led him to explore the most dangerous paths of initiatic science, Mikhaël became more cautious and reasonable in his experiments. The failure of his first attempt to penetrate the most sacred regions of the universe incited him to ponder and weigh things more carefully.

But all these perceptions, ecstasies, and discoveries were part of the inner initiation that had been working within him ever since his illumination. The perfection of the symbols he saw and described so vividly is a clear indication of the spiritual maturity he had already attained. He would explain one day that if one meditates for a long time on an idea, a geometrical symbol will gradually take shape in one's subconscious – or superconscious – a symbol corresponding exactly to the idea on which one is meditating.

*
*   *

Mikhaël was capable of tuning in to the wavelengths of higher worlds, of vibrating on a very high plane, but he had not lost his love of mischief and was also likely to do something spectacular just for the fun of it.

One fine day he was climbing Mount Musala with some friends when a thick fog suddenly blanketed the area. The lakes and peaks of Rila were lost to view as completely as though they had never existed. Cautiously, keeping close together for fear of losing each other in the dense cloud, the young men continued to climb. They were used to sudden changes in the weather at this altitude, but they were nevertheless disappointed to be unable to see the countryside. Suddenly it occurred to Mikhaël that to console them – and also for the sheer joy of it – he could disperse the fog and reveal the view.

'If you like,' he said, 'I can give you a glimpse of the countryside.'

At this, one of the boys asked to see the third lake. After a moment of concentration, Mikhaël stretched out his hand and the fog drew back like the curtain of a theatre, revealing the lake like an immense moonstone framed in the billowing white clouds. His companions exclaimed in astonishment, Mikhaël lowered his hand, and gradually the fog rolled in again.

'Show us the mountains of Macedonia,' said one of the boys, wanting to be sure that what they had witnessed had not been pure chance.

Once again Mikhaël stretched out his hand, the mass of clouds scattered, and the mountains appeared on the horizon, gilded by the rays of an invisible sun. Finally, Mikhaël dispersed the remaining clouds that hid the sun. Referring to this incident in later years, he insisted that if it is possible to act on external clouds it is even easier to work on those that obscure our inner world. By mentally focusing rays of light on them, one can disperse them and regain inner peace and joy. 'What I have told you is absolutely true,' he added gravely; 'I know that the invisible world is listening to me, and I cannot lie to you.'

In spite of the intensity of his researches, Mikhaël was never satisfied. Conscious of the importance of continual purification to allow the currents of divine life to flow freely within him, he decided to fast for ten days. After two or three days he experienced a thirst which continued to increase as the days went by. He was obsessed by water. All his dreams were of springs and rivers at which he drank without ever quenching his thirst. On the seventh day he picked up a piece of fruit and sensed that when he breathed in its perfume he received a subtle nourishment that satisfied him completely. It was then that he understood more profoundly than ever a truth that he would refer to all his life: fruit – indeed, all plants – contain subtle, etheric elements that can nourish us if we are not too satiated to assimilate them. For the last three days of his fast, before gradually resuming a normal diet and his usual rhythm of life, he continued to nourish himself solely on the emanations of fruit.

At this period of his life Mikhaël often continued his spiritual exercises far into the night, with the result that he was sometimes too tired to awake in time for the sunrise. Although he regretted this, it seems that he could not resign himself to working less. One fine day, however, something happened that enchanted him: at dawn a small bird alighted on his window-sill and began tapping on the glass with its beak. The following morning and every day after that, the bird returned and took up its tapping, and Mikhaël responded as to a friend:

'All right. I'm getting up at once!'

Then he put some bread-crumbs on the window ledge and the bird, singing merrily, flew off in search of others to join in the feast, while Mikhaël thanked heaven with all his heart for this gift of joy from the kingdom of the air.

Mikhaël always had this special relationship with birds. Throughout his life, they often served as messengers from the invisible world to bring him answers he was waiting for. At one time or another, most of his friends witnessed such incidents which pointed to a rare harmony between a human being and the natural world.

*

* *

Mikhaël had many friends, but he would say later that in Bulgaria he had always remained in the background, and those who knew him confirm this. Yet there is ample evidence that he had remarkable influence on his contemporaries. According to his family and friends he was much sought after and people were always coming to ask his advice. He attracted them like a magnet. With the fire that burned within him and his radiant energy drawn from the higher planes, he was a being who led others irresistibly toward new horizons. One might think that people would have been uneasy in the presence of such intensity, but his high spirits and unfailing sense of humour always gave it balance. Also, his affection for his friends was so genuine and warm that they easily forgot the supernatural and almost intimidating aspects of his behaviour, his research, and his work.

At one point, several young friends went to live with Mikhaël in Ternovo to pursue their spiritual work in a favourable atmosphere, and gradually the house became a focal point of spiritual life in which other young friends found encouragement and support. They spent their days reading, meditating, and working in the house and garden.

One day they were surprised to see a youth, dressed in rags and with every appearance of being a fugitive, emerge timidly from among the vines. Without hesitation, they welcomed him and offered him something to eat. The fugitive was trembling with fear, but gradually, reassured by their attitude, he told them that his name was Dimitri and he was being hunted by the police. He had belonged to a group of anarchists of which only he had escaped death; all his comrades had been executed. Mikhaël and his friends invited Dimitri to stay with them as long as he wished. It was a courageous gesture, since at the time, two years after the end of World War I, violence was rife in the country and the political situation was increasingly unstable. Groups of agrarians, communists, fascists, anarchists, and Macedonian revolutionaries all contributed to the general unrest, which was even further intensified by the presence of thousands of refugees from the devastated war zones.

Dimitri had long conversations with these young men whose ways astonished him: they were vegetarians, they meditated, they loved to watch the sun rise, and they lived in an atmosphere of harmony. It was the integrity of his own character that had first led him to rebel against the injustices of society and join the anarchists in the hope of building a better world through violence. But bitter experience had opened his eyes, and he was spontaneously drawn to the philosophy of love and peace that inspired his new friends. Yet it was difficult for him to believe in this sudden reversal of his fortunes. To hide or flee at the first sign of danger had become second nature to him, and the adaptation to a life of peace did not come easily. Mikhaël, observing him with affection, thought to himself: 'It is as though he missed the torments of the past.' Gradually, however, Dimitri's native qualities reasserted themselves and blossomed in the friendly atmosphere of the group. He became particularly attached to Mikhaël and remained ever after a faithful friend.

In the meantime, Peter Deunov had received permission to return to Sofia, and was now giving lectures in his own home. In many ways, however, his work was becoming increasingly difficult. In the past he had often had to take a stand against those who wanted him to make life easier for them or who sought his protection and hoped for miracles. In their anger and disappointment some of them turned against him and began to spread criticism and false rumours about him, and he was now faced with a difficulty that confronts almost all spiritual guides: the bitter recriminations of one-time disciples.

Several young brothers, worried by these negative rumours, went to consult Mikhaël, who was vehement in defence of Peter Deunov. He had far too much respect and affection for the Master to believe such criticisms or to question his decisions. But this time of difficulty for Peter Deunov was also a period of trial for Mikhaël. He was nineteen, and the young men with whom he lived often turned to him, confident that he could enlighten them and give them good advice. It was not a role that he chose for himself. On the contrary, he had stayed in Ternovo in order to devote himself to a life of contemplation. But in spite of his desire to remain in the background, he could not hide the fire that burned within and shone from him. And it was here that another test awaited him.

Just as he had known the lure of power at the age of sixteen, it was inevitable that he should now be tempted by the exercise of authority. Later, he spoke with the utmost simplicity of how, during his second year as a disciple of Peter Deunov, he had once spoken 'as a Master' to some members of the brotherhood. As soon as he had spoken, he realized that he was in danger of seeking glory for himself, just as three years earlier he had been in danger of using his powers for his own ends. He reproached himself bitterly for having abandoned his habitual discretion and self-effacement. It was at this point that Peter Deunov's attitude, for reasons known only to himself, changed radically. From then on, he ignored Mikhaël completely. Commenting later on the Master's reaction, Mikhaël said: 'If you only knew how I suffered! How I regretted what I had done!' Adding that, in reality, it had been no more than a childish mistake, but that Peter Deunov must have seen it as the sign of a danger from which he wanted to protect him.

Mikhaël's inner strength coupled with his deliberate self-effacement aroused admiration in some and envy in others. When the latter spread the rumour that the Master was displeased with his decision to live in Ternovo with his friends, Mikhaël became the object of criticism and denigration. He also suffered greatly from the change in his relationship with Peter Deunov, and for years puzzled over his apparent coldness. He could not know that the Master had decided to keep him in the background until it was time to entrust him with his unique mission: to carry his teaching to France.

Occasionally, however, Mikhaël was deeply moved by a rare and unexpected gesture of approval and support on the part of Peter Deunov. One day, his close friend Ivan told him:

'Mikhaël, I was just talking about you with the Master. He said you had one of the keenest minds he had ever met; that your intelligence was as fine as a thread of silk, capable of penetrating everything.'

Mikhaël understood the message, which seems to have had special significance for him at this stage of his life. Peter Deunov must have known that what he said to Ivan would be passed on. The attitude of indifference he had adopted towards his young disciple was probably intended to fortify him in preparation for his future work. He knew how much Mikhaël loved him. He also knew both his extreme sensitivity and his exceptional inner strength, and apparently had decided to deprive him of the consolations of an affective relationship. His attitude toward Mikhaël was often enigmatic. The explanations or advice he gave were not easy to understand, often no more than a glimpse of light through a half-opened door, for he knew that nothing would deter Mikhaël from exploring new horizons, that he was capable of finding for himself all that his soul needed. Peter Deunov was leaving him free to advance alone so that he might reach his full potential more rapidly.

Mikhaël thus went forward alone but never in isolation. As often as possible he participated in the three- or four-day excursions Peter Deunov organized to Mount Vitosha, a 7,500 ft summit to the south of Sofia. The Master would set out in the middle of the night accompanied by the most courageous of his disciples, thereby giving them an occasion to fortify their will and powers of endurance. The ascent lasted several hours, taking them first through a thick forest criss-crossed by a confusion of streams and torrents, and then, once above the tree line, to a desolate landscape of gigantic boulders which streamed down the slopes like great petrified rivers. From the summit, an immense, level cirque strewn with enormous rocks, they contemplated the grandiose spectacle of the rising sun.

In addition to these excursions, Mikhaël joined the other members of the brotherhood for the meetings in Peter Deunov's house as often as possible. He would slip in quietly and take a chair at the back, or if the room was full, remain standing by the door.

When the Master entered, those present greeted him by raising their right hand, palm forward, to the level of the forehead. As the Master responded in kind to this beautiful, ancient greeting, his face seemed to glow and become radiant. Mikhaël, who had sometimes wondered why his expression changed at this moment, realized that the ambience born of the respect and love of his disciples was an inspiration for him, a stimulus which manifested as light on his face.

While listening attentively to what the Master was saying, Mikhaël often watched the expressions on the faces of those present. The spontaneous exchange between speaker and audience always fascinated him. In his eyes, every teacher was a medium, and it was the ambience created by the audience that enabled him to communicate the message dictated by the spirit.

Paradoxically, it was Mikhaël's desire to come as close as possible to Peter Deunov's thought that led him to remain in the back of the hall. The physical distance stimulated the powers of perception not only of his eyes, but also of his soul and his mind. After a talk, he listened silently to the discussions between the Master and his audience, remarking that some of the disciples presumed to give Peter Deunov advice publicly. The Master listened to them, sometimes putting them in their place, but more often than not smiling at their vanity and letting them have their say. As for Mikhaël, in the course of these discussions he did not try to attract attention or display his knowledge. If he had once been tempted to assume an attitude of authority, he had since renounced it completely.

*
* *

In the school of Pythagoras, one of the ordeals least expected by new students was the flood of scorn and unfair criticism to which they were subjected, sometimes for a long time. Very few were able to endure the corrosive effect of such treatment, but those who did so were admitted to initiation.

Instinctively, from the first moment of his relationship with the Master he had sought for so long, Mikhaël longed to undergo ordeals that would purify his heart and strengthen his character. In the course of these first two years, he often begged Peter Deunov to chastise him, to put him through the seven retorts, the traditional vessels of the alchemists in which mercury is separated from amalgam or other impurities by volatilization. He repeated that he was willing to be ground to powder and put through fire in order to be purified and become an exceptional being. Each time he spoke in this way, the Master listened attentively and smiled without speaking. For months, Mikhaël wondered: 'Does he agree? Will he do what I ask?'

And then the time came for him to be put through the first retort. Peter Deunov's attitude of indifference was already painful to Mikhaël, but something more painful still had to be faced. One day, probably in 1920 during a convention of the brotherhood at Ternovo, he was put to the test in a way that affected that most sensitive part of his being: his attachment to his spiritual Master. After speaking to the disciples gathered around him in the open air, Peter Deunov suddenly turned on Mikhaël and one of his friends in bitter condemnation. Feeling himself the target of all eyes, Mikhaël was paralysed with shock. While the Master rebuked him, it was all he could do to maintain a calm expression that revealed nothing of the deep hurt caused by the harsh words and pitiless tone of voice.

Later, as the participants silently dispersed, most of them shunned this disciple who had been so publicly denounced. His own reaction was to withdraw to reflect and fast. In the days that followed Mikhaël told himself repeatedly that Peter Deunov must certainly have had a reason for lashing out at him in this way. With all his might, he worked to purify himself with the light. Then, pale and thin, but with his soul 'reaching toward the heavens' he returned to see the Master. As he entered his room, his whole being expressed the respect and trust which had never faltered, and he spoke as a child to his father:

'Master, purify me. In your great wisdom, root out all that is useless and bad in me. I want only to be like you.'

The light within Mikhaël was so bright and the fire so intense after those days of purification and fasting that he had a sensation of burning, as though flames were darting from his mouth. Speechless, Peter Deunov gazed at him in astonishment.

This phenomenon in which flames blaze from the face of a mystic in a state of spiritual concentration is well known to those who have studied the lives of great saints and visionaries. An intense work of purification floods the face with light, and the mystic experiences a burst of light streaming from the centre of the forehead, between the eyebrows. Mikhaël was aware both of what was happening to him and of Peter Deunov's amazement.

Suddenly, the Master's face was transfigured. Smiling lovingly at his young disciple, he shook hands with him, and the smile and the grip of his hand expressed something quite out of the ordinary. But he did not say a word, and Mikhaël, who never expected any favours, accepted his silence.

This exchange, sober though it was, sufficed; the message he read in it was all the recompense he needed. He already knew that initiation, which once took place in a temple, was now given in everyday life when it was least expected. It was this realization that spurred him on to fortify his will so that he would be capable of accepting whatever vexations and humiliations came his way. Instinctively, he learned to use the fire that had burned within him since the age of fifteen to propel himself ever forward on his chosen path. Peter Deunov saw this clearly, and during this same period at Ternovo, he said:

'Mikhaël, part of your fire has become light.'

*
* *

His public ordeal, however, had serious consequences. In the fraternity, many of the brothers and sisters avoided him, convinced that one thus stigmatised by the Master must be wholly contemptible. Some even became his sworn enemies and in the future would do him great wrong. They may well have had reasons of their own for their antagonism: the integrity with which Mikhaël expressed his opinions and his absolute frankness were often disconcerting and inconvenient; his habit of analysing everything in the light in order to discern and discard all impurities left no room for complacency. Whatever their reasons, Mikhaël sensed that, from now on, if he was to preserve his integrity and be faithful to the unerring intuition that he called 'the God within', he would have to accept that most of the brotherhood disapproved of him. Keeping a firm grip on his sensibilities, he bore in silence every manifestation of enmity and derision, every petty vexation. But he received with gratitude the occasional encouragement of those who came to tell him, alluding to the classical ordeals of initiation:

'Be glad, brother Mikhaël, for the Master loves you very deeply.'

It was only much later that he himself felt sure of that love. In the meantime he was determined to bear whatever came, to accept every ordeal and every demand Peter Deunov made of him. To his mind, true love consisted in striving, come what may, to be as radiant as the sun.

The year 1920 was an important one in Mikhaël's life. Apart from the ordeal at Ternovo, he would speak later of 'an extraordinary event' that had occurred in this period. Without giving details, he later alluded more than once to 'a great Being' who had accompanied and guided him since that time. It is possible that this event took place in the mountains in the region of Rila or on Mount Musala, where he had known several mystical experiences about which he said very little.

More is known, however, about one experience he had at the age of twenty, for he described it later to his disciples. It occurred during his first camp at Rila with the brotherhood. One of the most beautiful parts of the massif, 7,500 feet in altitude, known as the Seven Lakes, was a region greatly loved by Peter Deunov. From 1920 on, he often camped up there for a few days with groups of disciples. Toward the middle of summer the snow had melted from the highest peaks and the mountains revealed themselves in their stark majesty. This splendid region with its steep slopes and tumbled masses of boulders was well chosen, for while it demanded considerable physical exertion on the part of the campers, it also provided an ideal setting for meditation and contemplation.

Those who took part in the first camp were both exalted and much tried by the experience. In the first place they were poorly equipped, having neither tents nor sleeping bags. In addition, the weather was bad throughout their stay. On these summits, even in summer, the climate is harsh. The noontime sun is uncomfortably hot, while the nights are icy. The campers could not sleep for the bitter cold and the gusts of rain sweeping over them as they lay shivering in their blankets.

One morning, an elderly sister asked Mikhaël to accompany her to a higher altitude. After climbing for a long time they eventually reached a place in which nature seemed to have retained its pristine beauty of eternal purity and youth. The silence seemed as fragile as a crystal that the slightest sound would shatter into a thousand fragments.

Settling down on a large rock, Mikhaël began to meditate. The slopes all around were covered in a deep carpet of moss, scattered here and there with great boulders. Suddenly Mikhaël thought he was hallucinating as the landscape became wondrously animated before his eyes. The life that pulsated gently in the nature around him gave to each element its own subtle light. Every stone, every blade of grass glowed with a mysterious radiance, and Mikhaël understood in a flash that every created thing, from the grains of sand on the beach to the stars in the heavens, is made of light. Spellbound, transported by wonder, he was unable to take his eyes from the indescribable beauty before him, a beauty hidden from human beings until they are given the privilege of seeing it.

It is easy to understand why, after experiencing such ecstasy in the light, Mikhaël continually sought to contemplate the splendour of the rising sun. Mount Musala, the highest peak of the Rila massif, which was a long way from the camp site, drew him like a magnet; at times he spent the night at the summit from where he could watch the dawn coming up and catch the first rays of the sun as it rose over the surrounding peaks. Ever since his first childhood meditations high in the poplars of his home village, he had dreamed of the summits. In his eyes, the true temple of God is nature, at the centre of which the sun, the giver of life, is the celebrant. He understood that a country's highest peak represents its causal body, that subtle body that dwells on the higher planes of the invisible world. He also knew that the forces and powers necessary to the materialization of ideas on the physical plane are to be found on the causal plane, where the obstacles encountered on the physical plane do not exist.

Ever since his first excursion to Musala two or three years earlier, in response to a profound intuition about his future, he was in the habit of linking himself in a special way with France. Creating an association in his mind between the highest peak of his own country and Mont Blanc, he called down light and heavenly blessings on the people of France. Strangely, he dreamed of taking to the French the teaching that filled him with such joy, never suspecting that Peter Deunov would one day entrust him with this very mission.

9

Back to School

At the end of that summer, Peter Deunov called Mikhaël to him and told him:

'Mikhaël, you must go back to school and finish your studies.'

Thunderstruck, Mikhaël could only stare at him in silence. He had left school five years before. He was now nearly twenty-one, and Peter Deunov was asking him to go back to the classroom with boys of fifteen. It would take three years to get his baccalaureate. Above all, in this period of intense spiritual and intellectual development, his most urgent need was to continue the work that had become the mainstay of his life. For a young man of Mikhaël's calibre, experienced in the mystical life and able to communicate with the subtle realms of the spirit, to return to the routine of school would be a great trial. But it was a trial that Peter Deunov deemed necessary in order to help him to moderate his spiritual experiments and follow the development of every normal human being of his day.

In fact, it would have been possible for Mikhaël to study at home and apply only for the examinations, but Peter Deunov was adamant: he must attend classes. As always, Mikhaël bowed to the decision of the one whom he had chosen as his spiritual Master and, leaving Ternovo, returned to his family in Varna.

For his mother the return of her eldest son was a great joy: it was a comfort to her to be able to count on his presence again. For the two boys and two little girls, here was their big brother, home again as an adult after a two-year absence, during which he had endured many painful ordeals and known spiritual experiences more intense than ever. For his friends he was still someone out of the ordinary, still capable of stimulating them, infecting them with his enthusiasm or exasperating them beyond endurance.

Mikhaël's first weeks at school were uncomfortable. For one thing he was obliged to wear a uniform, and Dolia, knowing how ridiculous it made him feel, found an old greatcoat of his father's to wear over it. At the Lycée the boys laughed at this young man who was old enough to shave and yet shared the school bench with them. They were forever pulling his hair and playing all kinds of tricks on him. Fortunately, Mikhaël's sense of humour had not forsaken him. Later, when he recounted some of the amusing incidents of this period, it was obvious that he had not taken the chaffing too seriously. His generous smile and friendly ways soon won over his young classmates, and many of them accompanied him after school, questioning him about all kinds of things. He readily adapted himself to their level and, calling on his imagination and his gifts as a story-teller, used the opportunity to open their minds to realities they had never before envisaged.

All in all, these years at school in Varna seem to have been profitable for Mikhaël, who took the opportunity to ponder and arrive at a more profound understanding of all that Peter Deunov's teaching had awakened within him. Also, his close relationship with Jesus led him to delve deeper into the Gospels in an attempt to grasp their hidden meaning, for he had never found a commentary that really satisfied him. Seated in the lotus position in his little room overlooking the nearby roofs, he meditated for hours, until one day a revelation came to him: the only way to understand the true meaning of Jesus' words was to enter his mind. He set to work immediately, concentrating his mental powers on losing all consciousness of himself and the world he lived in. In his mind he was in Palestine in the time of Jesus, walking on the shores of the Jordan and Lake Gennesaret, entering the cities of Capernaum and Jerusalem. Repeating aloud the very words that Jesus had said to his disciples, he concentrated on penetrating his consciousness, on seeing and thinking as though he were one with him.

Gradually, this work became more and more important to him. Whenever he had a moment he returned to it, and little by little the true meaning of Jesus' words was revealed to him. Naturally, his efforts were not always successful. There were days when he was disappointed with the meagre results, but he persevered, refusing to be discouraged. At other times his labours were richly rewarded: a dazzling light flooded his being and everything became crystal clear. Transcending all earthly contingencies, a true communication between two spirits was gradually taking shape, thanks to which Mikhaël was able later to give such authentic and inspired commentaries on the Gospels. Those he would give in Paris in 1938 cast a dazzling new light on the Parables which was deeply moving.

In later years he often spoke of having been profoundly influenced not only by Jesus, but also by the Buddha, the two great luminaries of his youth. He must have striven to enter the mind of the Buddha as he had with Jesus, since he would say later that he had succeeded in communicating with him at the age of twenty-two or -three.

In the solitude of his little room, eager to draw upon every source that spoke of God and the perfection of the created universe, he studied a wide range of spiritual philosophies. He was already familiar with the Cabbalah, whose definition of the structure of the subtle worlds satisfied him deeply. He found great inspiration in The Tree of Life, with its depiction of the different levels of creation, and in the six-pointed Seal of Solomon with its symbolic representation of Good and Evil. This impressive symbol, composed of two interlaced triangles, contains a representation of the glorious countenance of God in the higher part of the upright triangle. In the inverted triangle below is a representation of the devil, a distorted reflection of the divine countenance. At the intersection of the two triangles, a horizontal line separates the air above from the waters below, and across this line, God's hands have a firm grasp on the hands of the Devil. In Mikhaël's eyes, this representation of good and evil was an excellent and unequivocal expression of all creation as a reflection of God, who makes use of both positive and negative forces.

For one in whom the spirit of mysticism is highly developed, every philosophical discovery seems to lead directly to a spiritual experience; it is an 'event' that triggers an inner change, however minute. One day, reading the Zohar, the principal book of the Cabbalah, Mikhaël was extraordinarily moved by the text, '*Seven lights are there in the highest, and therein dwells the Ancient of Ancients, the Hidden of the Hidden Ones, the Mystery of Mysteries, Ain Soph.*'

> When I recited these words everything within me started to vibrate and quiver. Those seven lights are the seven colours, and each one corresponds to a particular virtue or quality: purple corresponds to sacrifice, blue to truth, green to hope, yellow to wisdom, orange to sanctity and red to love.[18]

Conscious of the influence of colours on a human being, Mikhaël continued to work with them – and his strange experiments continued to astonish those around him. A friend who had always admired his spirituality and his intellectual gifts often visited him in his room. One day he was amazed to see that Mikhaël had covered the walls with red paper.

'Have you gone mad?' he exclaimed.

Mikhaël laughed and explained that it was Tuesday, the day of the planet Mars and therefore of red, the colour of love, vitality, and energy. For some time he had been working in this way, surrounding himself with the colour that, according to the books he had been reading, corresponded to the day of the week. At the age of fifteen, when he first started experimenting with colours, he had noticed that one extreme triggers its opposite. Thus, if he switched his gaze to a white surface after staring at something red, he saw the same form in green. The phenomenon, which is well known to painters, had opened interesting avenues of spiritual exploration for him.

The symbolism of the planets began to be of practical importance: thus the red planet Mars, symbol of strength and war, calls forth green Venus, the symbol of love, and vice versa. Mikhaël worked

---

18. *Light is a Living Spirit*, p. 67.

with the characteristic of each colour and made use of their complementarity: the dynamic vitality of fire symbolized by red; the peaceful life of nature symbolized by green; the spirituality of violet, and the wisdom and science of yellow.

Every spare moment was used to consolidate the discoveries of his adolescence and to reflect, among other things, on the meaning of nutrition. In order to be consciously in union with the hidden forces of food he ate frugally and preferably alone. Very often, after his meditation, he took a mouthful of food and let it dissolve in his mouth until it had completely disappeared. This sufficed for the whole day.

*
* *

Thanks to Mikhaël's dynamic, creative temperament, many everyday objects or circumstances served to stimulate his spiritual centres or chakras. This was the case with roses. It is well known that Bulgarian roses are unique. They are cultivated for their precious aromatic oil in the Valley of Roses, a vast expanse bordered by mountains to the south of Ternovo. In summer, when the flowers are in full bloom, the fields stretch for miles like an immense, glowing carpet of colour.

One day, Mikhaël picked up a rose and breathed in its scent, and his reflections, stimulated by the perfume and emanations of the flower, became as light as air. Imperceptibly, his meditation became contemplation, a profound spiritual experience with its own special complexion, different from any he had known before, and one that he often repeated in the years that followed. He had long since learned to use earthly objects as channels of communication with spiritual realities, and he sensed that a rose enabled him to draw upon the most spiritual form of love. 'This exercise can even lead to ecstasy,' he was to say later.

To the casual observer, one flower is much the same as any other, and yet, like human beings, each has its own countenance and is inhabited by its own specific energies. Mikhaël knew this, and when he went to the flower market to buy a rose, he chose one for its colour, perfume, form, and freshness. Back in his room, he began simply by looking at it with great love, treating it as a living being, 'an exquisite young maiden from heaven, who has sacrificed herself to show us the path that leads to the virtues that are hers.' Each time he repeated this exercise, he experienced an indescribable state of consciousness and his mind floated far above earthly realities. When he said that it could lead to ecstasy, he was certainly speaking from experience.

In the meantime, however, every morning meant a return to school, to the tiresome uniform and boring lessons, and yet, all things considered, the effort and discipline was as good as any yoga or other exercise for the development of his will.

One day, toward the end of his studies in Varna, someone who knew his dream of playing the violin gave him an instrument. His delight knew no bounds, and he enrolled at the Musical Academy, where he gave himself with passion to the study of music, determined to become a true virtuoso capable of awakening the most noble sentiments in his audience:

> When I thought of God or of something beautiful, I could only envisage a perfect, harmonious music, and this thought awakened certain spiritual centres within me. Sometimes it left me in tears.[19]

In the years that followed he was never without his violin. He took it everywhere, even to the mountains, where he delighted in playing in the open air with his friends. Music was as necessary to him as the air he breathed, and song in particular, was an instrument of magic, a potent weapon which he used to dissipate negative feelings, attain certain spiritual states, or express gratitude. In the fraternity he was always happy to sing with his brothers and sisters, and when Peter Deunov composed the sacred song *Fir fur fen*, he was transported by the power of its vibrations. In his mind's eye he saw processions of angels advancing, driving the darkness before them.

On warm summer evenings in Varna, his need for music often drew him to the *Morskata Gradina*, where a good orchestra gave concerts or played waltzes for public dancing. Without lingering in the Garden, he went down the long flight of steps to the beach and sat on the sand. Over his head, the myriad diamonds of the Milky

---

19. Unpublished talk, November 1st, 1966.

Way formed a great river in the night sky. He often stayed for hours, listening to the music and contemplating the stars.

*
* *

During this period of his life Mikhaël experienced some difficult moments. He confessed later that as a disciple he had known 'moments of real pessimism'. Whether this pessimism was triggered by Peter Deunov's apparent rejection or by the ostracism he suffered in the brotherhood is difficult to say. From adolescence he had had to learn to pursue his own course without worrying about what others thought of him. At nineteen, after the public rebuff at the hands of Peter Deunov, he had had to armour himself further against the malicious lies that continued to distress him. Seeking to protect himself without closing his heart to others, he strove to master his sensitivity and transform his difficulties into 'precious stones' for the soul, using pain as a springboard. In order to vault upwards toward the joy of the spirit, he first sank to the depths of despondency, sometimes deliberately feigning extreme sadness in order to spark the opposite reaction. He realized, however, that to remain in a state of sadness for a long time could be dangerous unless one's consciousness was fully awake and in control.

He applied the same principle to his spiritual life. Having experienced 'periods of exaggerated ecstasy' followed by periods of drought, he came to the conclusion that moderation was indispensable in facing the storms of life. This practice of moderation, which helped him to rise above difficulties and trials, would serve him all his life.

At one point he began to make a rigorous annual review of his life. For three days he called to mind and analysed everything he did, examining the interwoven threads of his existence, judging and evaluating each one in order to discern 'those that came from God and those that did not.'

As for his relationship with Peter Deunov, he did everything in his power to restore it to its former cordiality, but this was not easy. 'My will was strained to the utmost, my heart was on fire, and he saw nothing!' he would say later, adding that Peter Deunov's attitude was certainly intended to test his ability to persevere and rise above his difficulties. He knew that the only thing that really mattered was to remain in contact with Peter Deunov's soul, and he continued to work mentally for him and to speak of him with the innate reverence he had for all great beings.

On the other hand, as he said himself, his secret was to continue his work in silence. If he felt unhappy, as sometimes happened, he noticed that there was someone within him who looked on and laughed, who even enjoyed the situation. He recognized this being as the one known in India as 'the Silent One'.

One day, however, in the most unexpected way and in full view of many of his disciples, Peter Deunov took Mikhaël's side. It happened at Rila. A young man who had formerly been a good friend but who now held a grudge against Mikhaël following a misunderstanding, had taken to insulting him and trying to belittle him at every opportunity. Unable to change the situation, Mikhaël remained patient and unruffled. But one evening, faced with his ceaseless insults, he said to himself: 'Humility, restraint, and non-violence will not cure him; he will go on being abusive,' and he made up his mind to respond.

Before he knew it, he was fending off his adversary's blows and very quickly, although not as tall or as strong as the other, he managed to get the better of him. Thinking that that would be the end of it, Mikhaël relaxed his hold, whereupon the other flung himself at him a second time. Once again, without knowing how, Mikhaël got the advantage and he was still holding his assailant down when Peter Deunov appeared. At once, the two brothers sprang to their feet. To Mikhaël's amazement, the Master told him:

'Stand aside. Leave him to me!'

Then he began to chastise the young man severely until, after a moment, the latter managed to slip away. He did not dare to show his face again that evening. Mikhaël could not get over his astonishment. 'How could the Master know who was in the wrong?' he wondered. 'It was the other who was on the ground and needed help, and yet he sided with me!' The next day the attitude of his persecutor was completely transformed, and Mikhaël told himself that he should have tackled him long ago.

Throughout these years Peter Deunov remained extremely reserved toward Mikhaël when others were present, but during the summer camp at Rila in 1922, he did much to dissipate the negative repercussions of the ordeal he had imposed on him two years earlier. One evening, several hundred people were gathered near the second lake under the pure transparent blue of the evening sky. A huge bonfire, fed by dead branches brought up from the forests below, threw a fantastic light all around. The only sound was the crackling of the flames. After a long silence, Peter Deunov turned toward Mikhaël and said in solemn tones:

'You do not yet know who Mikhaël is.'

All eyes were on the startled Mikhaël who thought to himself: 'Does this mean another ordeal?' But while he braced himself for what was to come, Peter Deunov continued:

'No, you do not yet know Brother Mikhaël. At the moment he is disguised, but one day you will know him. You will see who he truly is.'

All the escapades of his youth surged into Mikhaël's mind as he waited in alarm for what would follow. But as the silence lengthened, his first emotion faded, and he realized that this time Peter Deunov's voice conveyed no harshness. Their eyes met. Flooded with an overwhelming sense of gratitude, Mikhaël saw that the Master's face was suffused with love. His remark had implied nothing negative, rather the contrary.

In fact, Peter Deunov had publicly shown his esteem and appreciation of Mikhaël. Most of his disciples understood the message and hastened to apologise for their past attitude, but it did not occur to Mikhaël to take advantage of this public endorsement. He remained in the background and continued his work in silence. Unfortunately, however, the melee between him and the other brother was to become a cause of scandal. Some members of the brotherhood used it to discredit him, for they could not understand Peter Deunov's attitude toward this disciple. Sometimes he put him through terrible ordeals; at other times he defended him or made mysterious pronouncements about him; most of the time he seemed to ignore him, and yet he continued to receive him for long hours at a time.

*
* *

Mikhaël's relief was great when he finally received his baccalaureate. He thought he would once again be free to devote all his time to his spiritual work, but when he went to see Peter Deunov in Sofia, the first thing the Master said was:

'You must go on with your studies at the university.'

Mikhaël knew that this meant renewed sacrifices, but his faith in Peter Deunov's wisdom never faltered. After taking leave of his mother in Varna, he returned to Sofia, where he registered at the faculty of Physics and Mathematics. Upon his arrival in the capital, some friends offered him the use of a room in their home. He still had to find work to pay for courses and food, however, and whenever his money ran out he took a temporary job on a building site as bricklayer, carpenter, painter, or odd job man. The wages were meagre, and for years he lived in extreme poverty. His room was scantily furnished with a bed and some blankets received from his family, a bookcase from Peter Deunov, and a small table on which he kept his violin. He wrote on his knees, sitting cross-legged on the floor. His clothes were threadbare; a scarf concealed the absence of a tie, and for a long time his only footwear was a single pair of sandals that served in summer and winter alike. As he remarked with a smile in later years, although he had many friends in Sofia, they did not invite him to their elegant receptions, but rather to informal meals in the intimacy of the family.

At the beginning of the 20th century, the University of Sofia consisted of six or seven faculties housed in several old buildings. Another institution, the Bulgarian Academy, offered additional faculties, and it was here that Mikhaël registered for courses in mathematics, a discipline which gave him great satisfaction for it corresponded so well to his sense of order and perfection. He also studied astronomy, drawn by its close relationship with mathematics, and spent hours striving to decipher the correspondences between the two disciplines. But his memory for figures was not good, and he too easily forgot the formulae he needed. Less than a year later, realizing that he had little hope of passing his exams, he abandoned mathematics and transferred to a different faculty.

This time, he chose the faculty of History and Linguistics, where he took courses in philosophy, education, and psychology. His thirst for knowledge was as lively as ever. He read a great deal and studied sufficiently to pass his exams, but in fact he spent little time at the university. In his eyes, the true university was that of Peter Deunov, for it was there that one learned the essential truths valid for all eternity. All his spare time was devoted to meditation and contemplation. 'For me,' he would say later, 'it was a question of life or death.' But he kept all this inner work to himself. He never even told Peter Deunov what he was doing.

Throughout his years of higher studies, it was the great philosophical tenets of initiatic science that guided him. The sun was his guarantor of life, light was his shield and only weapon, for in his eyes light was a living spirit.

At the same time, the mountains continued to attract him irresistibly. He could never ignore the siren-song of the summits, and when the call became too insistent, he threw books, food, and a few warm clothes into a satchel and left the town. Free as air, he would spend a few days on Mount Vitosha or even a few weeks at Rila. His love of trees had never diminished and the long climb through the forests gave him profound joy.

Mikhaël's unusual behaviour irritated his professors who censured him severely. One of them, hostile to Peter Deunov's disciples on principle, excluded him from his lectures and barred him from the examinations. Fortunately, he soon repented this decision, which would have prevented Mikhaël from completing his studies, and authorised him to appear before the examiners.

Mikhaël, well aware of the importance of a degree, passed his exams and chose for the subject of his thesis, the aspirations of the young. His research led him to interview a great many students who readily confided in him their hopes and plans for the future. Listening with interest to what they told him, he noticed that very few wished to serve God or work for the good of humanity.

After receiving diplomas in philosophy, psychology, and education Mikhaël continued to frequent the university. Stimulated by curiosity he moved freely from one faculty to another, exploring the different disciplines, following courses in medicine, chemistry, and physics. He spent so many years at the university that his friends nicknamed him 'the eternal student.'

*
*   *

During those student years, as always, the events that assumed the greatest importance in Mikhaël's eyes concerned his life as a disciple. One such event stood out among others. Soon after his return to Sofia, Peter Deunov gave him a special test that he reserved for the boldest of his disciples: the ascent of Mount Musala alone on a moonless night, without a lantern.

'The experience will help you to understand many things,' said the Master.

Mikhaël waited for a night without a moon before setting out. The dense darkness and the quality of silence created an atmosphere of dread as he groped his way through the forest, hoping not to lose his way. Aware of the danger from wild boars, bears, and wolves, he was also constantly mindful of the steep ravine that bordered the trail. One false step and he would fall. Suddenly he sensed that he had strayed from the path. Poignantly conscious of his vulnerability and his isolation, he paused to catch his breath, and in answer to his ardent prayer, a mysterious light appeared, extending about two yards in front of him. His heart overflowing with gratitude, he walked on, singing joyfully.

After climbing for several hours, he came to a sudden halt as he heard the deep baying of dogs. How could he defend himself with only a stick against enraged dogs? To retreat would only incite them to attack. Standing perfectly still, he listened to them coming nearer and fixed his mind on thoughts of light and the powers of the invisible world. Never one to remain long in a state of indecision or fear, he told himself, 'What must happen will happen!' and advanced resolutely toward the increasingly ferocious barking. What happened next was over in seconds. Suddenly he saw two mastiffs the size of small donkeys bounding toward him. Summoning every ounce of strength and will-power, he thrust his right hand forward with extraordinary energy, the two first fingers pointing straight at them. At the same moment he felt an electrical current surge from his whole being, and sensed the presence of invisible entities all around. The dogs gave one agonised howl as they were picked up and thrown to the ground by a terrifying force, and cowered where they fell, their eyes fixed on the ground.

Once he had regained his breath, Mikhaël spoke soothingly to the dogs, and when he felt sure that they would no longer try to attack him, he relaxed with renewed gratitude and joy. But suddenly, he felt terribly tired, as though all his strength had drained away through his right hand. Laboriously, he started to walk again, only to stop moments later, unable to continue. He sat down on a rock to pray and thank out loud the invisible entities whose presence he sensed and who had accompanied and protected him. After a short rest he slowly set off again, emerged at last from the forest, climbed the stony slopes, and reached the summit just as the sun was rising. There, on the highest spot in the country, with the innumerable peaks all around, he thanked God with his whole soul.

> That experience taught me that a great many of the trials and tribulations of life are sent by the invisible world with the purpose of teaching us to rely on our inner spiritual strength.[20]

This ordeal was not the only one Peter Deunov imposed on Mikhaël in those years. He gave him all kinds of harsh tasks. On several occasions he sent him to work in remote hamlets that could only be reached on foot. More than once, as Mikhaël approached a village, he was attacked by fierce dogs. The peasants, often so uncouth and ignorant that they did not even know how to make bread, would let him sleep in a hut or in a corner of a stable or barn. His mission was to live with them for a time, to talk to them and teach them things that would help them to evolve. Little by little he became their friend, their brother. Sometimes, the relationships became so close that people who had seemed incapable of emotion were moved to tears as they confided in him.

In spite of the great distances, Mikhaël continued to attend Peter Deunov's talks in Sofia. Even in winter, braving rain or snow, with only sandals on his feet, he trudged miles through forests infested by wolves and wild boars.

One day, Peter Deunov manifested his satisfaction with him, saying:

'You have changed your skin.'

Although he ignored Mikhaël in public, Peter Deunov continued to give him an occasional precious indication, an expression of

---

20. March 12th, 1938 (*The Second Birth*, p. 211).

approval or support. Each time he made one of his laconic remarks, Mikhaël had to ponder it at length to discern the hidden meaning. On this occasion the allusion was to an inner transformation, a purification that expressed itself in a visible radiance. Despite the undemonstrative nature of their relationship, the mysterious and precious bond that had existed from their first encounter was still there. Mikhaël was extremely sensitive to Peter Deunov's reactions, and it seems that this was fully reciprocated. Imperceptible though it was, the Master was never indifferent to Mikhaël; nothing that he said or did went unnoticed.

10

The Seven Lakes of Rila

Although the summer camps in the Rila mountains were called 'holiday camps', the activities had little in common with the ordinary idea of a holiday. It is true that the participants were there for a refreshing break from the work and worries of everyday life, but their primary motive was to continue their apprenticeship with their spiritual Master in the ideal conditions of the mountains. As the years passed, the duration of these camps was extended from a few days to several weeks. After a month or two in the mountains, the campers returned home renewed and purified.

In later years, Mikhaël evoked with enthusiasm the special ambience that reigned in these camps. Gathering in the village of Samokov at the foot of the mountains, the campers strapped on their knapsacks and began the long ascent to the Seven Lakes, while a train of mules transported tents and kitchen equipment. Seven or eight hours of hiking and climbing through forests of evergreens and up steep slopes strewn with boulders, brought them to the first lake at an altitude of 7,500 feet. A little higher, near the second lake, they pitched their tents among the clumps of dwarf pines called *kleks*, the only shrubs to survive at this height.

For the contemplation of the sunrise, Peter Deunov had chosen a craggy spur of rock above the camp which he named the Summit of Prayer. Under a translucent dawn sky it seemed to thrust out its mass like the prow of some great ship silhouetted in space. Every morning at daybreak, awoken by the music of a violin, the campers arose in silence and washed and dressed in the icy air of their tents or by the lake. As the sky grew lighter, they climbed up among the enormous boulders to the Summit where they settled down to meditate and wait for the sunrise. At first glimpse of the rising sun, they sang very softly one of Peter Deunov's songs in praise of light. The Master then talked quietly to them as the sun climbed slowly into the sky.

These days in the mountains were very full. The campers did a great deal of arduous walking, climbing endlessly up and down the steep slopes among the boulders and the twisted branches of the dwarf conifers. They thought nothing of hiking for an hour or two every day to reach the level ground near one of the higher lakes, where they practised the movements of a symbolic dance called the 'Paneurythmy.'

The Paneurythmy, created by Peter Deunov, is a round, which, turning slowly to the sound of music, evokes the great round of the universe in which is manifested the ebb and flow of life. The simple, beautiful movements are designed to unite the dancers alternately with heavenly and terrestrial energies. Peter Deunov defined the dance as 'a conscious exchange between man and the forces of nature.' Every morning, accompanied by a small group of musicians, he positioned himself in the centre of an immense circle formed by the hundreds of dancers. Here and there voices could be heard singing with the orchestra in spontaneous harmonizations that rose and fell in rhythm with the dance.

After the Paneurythmy, they returned to camp for the communal meal, serving themselves from the enormous cauldrons steaming in the shelter of the makeshift kitchen. During the rest of the day, every spare moment was taken up with physical work, much of it very strenuous: meals had to be prepared for the whole camp, food supplies fetched from the village below, newcomers met halfway and guided to the camp. The men built a stone shelter roofed with slate; piled up slabs of stone to serve as tables or as benches overlooking the lake that Peter Deunov had named the Lake of Contemplation. Evening found the campers exhausted, but the mountains had a mysterious hold on them and filled their hearts with such profound joy that fatigue and discomfort were forgotten. They had eyes only for the beauty of the light that transfigured the summits.

Peter Deunov often led the campers on excursion to one of the surrounding peaks, and at least once each summer to the summit of

Mount Musala. Before leaving, he explained how to walk all day without tiring, then, at the head of the group, he set out at such a pace that those behind were hard put to it to keep up.

In this notoriously unstable mountain climate, menacing clouds often began to gather just as the hikers were ready to leave, and although those who were fearful of being soaked to the skin sometimes protested, Peter Deunov rarely heeded their complaints. In rain, snow, or squalls, after only a few hours' sleep, they set off for the summits. There were days when the lightning fell all around, the rain streamed from them, and the electricity in the air became almost unbearable, but their guide strode on without faltering. His disciples, accepting it as a trial of endurance, followed him stoically. And as most of these excursions lasted from ten to fourteen hours, they were constantly called on to surpass their own limits. Once back in camp, exhausted but happy, they gratefully quenched their thirst with hot water that had been prepared in the great cauldrons and samovars. In the mountains, hot water was of great importance, a panacea for colds, fevers, and every kind of malaise.

The task of making tea was entrusted to a brother called Tseko. Every now and then, the campers were startled by the sudden whistling of a samovar, and turning saw this brother climbing the hillside, the lighted samovar on his back. Tseko had the face of a brute and a heart of gold. Although he was almost illiterate, he dreamed of being a poet, and sometimes recited his compositions before the entire camp. His verses were often so ridiculous that they were greeted with laughter, but one could not help loving this man so full of gentle goodness. Surprisingly, after several years of persevering efforts to compose poems about the sun, the birds, the spring, he became a true poet. Mikhaël, who loved and understood him, told how, at the end of an evening around the fire, Tseko once stood up, and much to the amusement of the campers, sang one of his compositions. Most of them were so used to his eccentricities that they were deaf to the beauty of his song. But the next day the mountains resounded to the sound of that song, for it had remained in the memory of all who had heard it.

*
* *

We have not forgotten Mikhaël's passion for springs. To contemplate the water of a spring bubbling from the ground still gave him great happiness, and he was overjoyed to find that Peter Deunov shared his enthusiasm. The Master often asked some of the men to clear away the dead leaves and grass blocking the mountain springs so that the music of the crystal-clear water could be heard flowing freely. He also asked them to build stone bridges over the many small streams. Few understood why they were asked to do this kind of work, and were often surprised at the sense of satisfaction it gave them. 'In reality,' Mikhaël explained later, 'the Master was clearing debris from his disciples as well as from the springs, and building bridges between the brothers.'

One of these springs was the main source of water for the camp. A constant stream of campers drank from it or filled their buckets and saucepans. In one of those significant gestures he occasionally made toward Mikhaël, Peter Deunov asked him to design a symbol to be carved and put in place as a channel for the water. The resulting sculpture is a symbol of Aquarius: a white stone channel representing two hands, from which, to this day, flows the pure spring water.

Fire, like water, had a vital role to play in life in the mountains. Each evening, the campers gathered around a paved area where the camp fire blazed. Warmed by the fire, their faces lit by the leaping flames, they sang, told of their personal experiences, recited poems, or gave little concerts.

> Later, we would go to sleep beneath the starlit sky until it was time to get up, very early in the morning, to communicate with another fire, the fire of the sun. We went to sleep by the fire, we woke to fire, the whole day was a feast of fire, and our lives were illuminated.[21]

In the evenings around the fire – as during meals or while out on an excursion – Peter Deunov often closed his eyes and meditated for a

---

21. August 18th, 1962 (*The Fruits of the Tree of Life*, p. 121).

long time, sometimes for an hour or more, to accustom his disciples to do the same. Before withdrawing into his own meditation, Mikhaël often looked at the Master and asked himself: 'Where is he? What is he thinking about?' Realizing that Peter Deunov never put the whole of his knowledge into words, Mikhaël tried to capture the thoughts that illuminated his glance, to see people and things from his point of view. Using the exercises he had developed earlier to penetrate the minds of Jesus, Buddha, and Hermes Trismegistus, he now attempted to penetrate the mind of Peter Deunov. When in his presence he listened attentively to what he was saying, and afterwards, when he was alone, continued to imagine that he was 'in Peter Deunov's head': gradually he was discovering his thought processes.

*
* *

Judging from what Mikhaël would say later about these mountain camps, it is obvious that they were the scene of some unforgettable moments in his life. For him, mountains represented a link between heaven and earth. Everything he did in this setting – walking, climbing, immersing himself in a lake – had repercussions in his inner life and created a bond between himself and the beings of subtler planes.

In the region of the Seven Lakes, high above the camp, he had found a spot he particularly loved for meditation. For someone so susceptible to cold, it must have required great will-power and endurance to continue his spiritual exercises in all weathers, at an altitude of more than 8,000 ft. He often spent the night up there under the stars, sometimes alone, sometimes with a friend. As darkness fell, he settled down between the dwarf trees on a makeshift bed of pine needles, and warmly wrapped in his blankets stretched out to contemplate the stars until a deep peace filled his whole being. The memory of his grandmother often came back to him: she had helped so many sick people to regain their health, not only by treating them with herbal infusions, but also by exposing them to the light of the stars.

What was the effect of starlight on the human body? At this altitude, the countless points of light shining in the dark velvety sky were indescribably pure. Contemplating them, Mikhaël sought answers from them. Intoxicated by their beauty, he linked himself to

An excursion at Rila. Mikhaël is on Peter Deunov's right.

the cosmic forces and entities whose presence he felt so strongly. Recalling these moments in later years, he often spoke in the name of his companions as well as his own, perhaps because of the intense communion that united them. 'There were nights,' he once said, 'when we were out of our minds with ecstasy and wonder!' At the same time, he added, their great joy had made them almost sad because they could not share it with the whole world.

One night, enraptured by all this splendour, an idea occurred to Mikhaël: he imagined that the stars had declared war on each other, a magnificent, glorious war in which they were spraying each other with bullets of light. This notion suggested a new spiritual exercise, and he spent hours mentally pouring light into the world, until he fell into the untroubled sleep of a child. At times he was caught up in ecstasy and experienced divine sensations that bore him far from the earth. Often, after a night on the mountainside, he awakened at dawn to find himself covered with snow. Chilled but happy, he jumped up, collected his blankets and hurried down to the camp in time for the sunrise.

One day he decided to attempt an extremely difficult ascent on a seemingly inaccessible summit: he wanted to see whether, in the course of an arduous exercise of this kind, he would find within himself something that would warn him not to continue, the something that we call intuition. For this experiment he chose a particularly beautiful peak formed of a multitude of smooth, vertical ridges. No footholds were visible, and yet, inching his way from one knife-edge to the next, he always managed to find some slight crack or irregularity to hold on to. As he clung to the rock face, he prayed, linked himself to God, and listened to his intuition. Slowly and laboriously he climbed, searching the surface for every tiny asperity, and moving foot or hand forward only when he heard the inner voice telling him to advance. Thus, at last, he reached the top.

The audacity that was such a notable part of Mikhaël's temperament was always suggesting new experiments, always urging him to devise new and more difficult tests for himself designed to lead to self-knowledge and self-mastery. Some comments he made later about one such experience were very revealing:

> There is a way out of every situation, and we have to look for it. It is a magnificent thing to venture out, to throw oneself into action. Spiritual people are often hesitant and indecisive. They keep asking themselves: 'Is this right? Is this the way?' They spend years hesitating, not daring to enjoy the splendours of the new life. Did you know that in ancient times initiation was given not to those whose hearts were full of goodness, but to the audacious? Those who were not daring were told that they were not ready for initiation.[22]

Mikhaël's constant excursions to the mountain heights were symbolic of his aspirations to attain the heights of the spiritual life. In the twenty years of his discipleship he climbed Mount Musala nineteen times, often in difficult circumstances and always with the specific idea of doing a spiritual work on the highest peak of the Balkans. It was here as nowhere else that his contemplative soul

---

22. Unpublished talk, May 9th, 1944.

could open and expand, that he was conscious of the presence of powerful invisible entities that stimulated and sustained him. It was here on the mountain heights that he found a deep sense of peace. Here he understood that the only truly important thing in life was to be one with the cosmic Spirit.

His years of spiritual work often rewarded him with gifts straight from heaven: stones became animated and luminous; a fruit was transformed into a receptacle for divine forces. This was the case one summer morning on Mount Musala.

It was a glorious day in August, and Mikhaël and his friend Svezdinski (the name means 'son of the stars') had decided to climb Mount Musala before joining the camp at Rila. Striding along energetically, they felt young, vigorous, and full of joy. After walking for several hours in heat that was becoming increasingly intense, they paused to rest and refresh themselves. Taking a pear each from their knapsacks, they sat down and began to eat slowly, savouring it as long as possible. Ordinary though it was, the action triggered in Mikhaël's soul an ecstatic communion with nature. Later, speaking for both his companion and himself, he said that thanks to the fruit they had been transported to paradise and the experience had opened immense horizons to them. His consciousness, he said, was awakened, and he was filled with all the light of the cosmos.

Often, throughout his life, Mikhaël spoke of an awakening of his consciousness as though it had been sleeping until then. The fact is that when he examined his state of consciousness he was never satisfied. For him, true love, peace, and initiation were all states of consciousness, and he was insatiable, always thirsting for God to pervade and possess his whole being. He worked tirelessly to replace in himself all that was old and worn, and become one with the divine beings whom he called on ceaselessly.

11

The Wondrous Powers of Thought and Word

In the winter of 1925 or 1926, Mikhaël found work as a mason to pay for his courses and help his family. His crew was assigned to the site of a new building which was still open and exposed to bitter winter winds. Wearing only a thin wind-breaker and trousers with a large rent at the knee, Mikhaël felt his leg gradually becoming numb under the bite of the icy wind. By the end of the day, one knee was so swollen that he could no longer walk, and had to be helped home.

Finding himself obliged to stay in bed, he decided to take advantage of his forced immobility to turn to his favourite occupations. The days slipped by unnoticed, gradually becoming weeks, as he immersed himself in an in-depth study of astrology. Once he felt that he had sufficient knowledge, he drew up his own chart, and it was here that a painful surprise awaited him: his horoscope depicted a crude, mediocre human being whose character had nothing in common with his own. Whereas the quest for God had characterised him from childhood, his chart showed no hint of spiritual aspirations, no trace of the ecstasies or spiritual revelations he had already known. The fact is that he had forgotten something important: when he and his mother had arrived in Varna in 1907, he had been registered as one year older than his true age, so that he would be accepted at the school. This made it impossible to calculate his true horoscope.

Not before he was fifty years old did he learn from his mother that he was a year younger than he had thought. Even then, the details were indefinite, for his mother was not sure of the exact time of his birth. She remembered only that it had been some time after midnight on January 31st, 1900. The circumstances of Mikhaël's birth, in fact, have always been somewhat obscure, due to the conditions in the country, the mentality of its inhabitants and the burning of his village, during which all official documents were destroyed. Also, at the beginning of the 20th century in the mountain villages of Macedonia, years and days were reckoned according to the weather or the seasons. Marriages, births, and deaths were dated by natural events rather than by the calendar. It is as though Omraam Mikhaël Aïvanhov was not destined to be circumscribed by time or defined by astrological analysis.

At the age of twenty-six, however, the negative implications of this false horoscope constituted a new challenge for him. Much as he was drawn to this science, to its view of the universe and the web of relations between individual creatures and creation as a whole, he could not help but doubt its reliability when he attempted to draw up his own birth-chart. For a serious astrologer – especially one who studies spiritual or holistic astrology – a birth-chart is a basic tool, a composite frame of reference through which to view one's life and gain spiritual understanding. Mikhaël eventually found some consolation in the idea that he had perhaps managed to neutralize the negative aspects of his birth-chart by his intense spiritual work. In any event, he continued to study astrology and to meditate on the great laws on which it is based until, ten years later, he was considered the foremost specialist in the country, and was consulted by several prominent persons.

In the meantime, his knee was not getting better. One day, some friends who often came to visit him decided that he should take a more active part in his situation.

'Why don't you try to heal yourself?' they asked.

'How can I?' Mikhaël responded.

'By the power of thought! You are perfectly capable.'

'I should have to concentrate for a very long time,' replied Mikhaël; 'and I am too busy.'

The fact was that his knee was painful only when he tried to walk, and, deeply absorbed in his study of astrology, he was quite happy to stay in his room and work. Also, in what he thought to be his birth-chart he found an indication of a health problem that would prevent him from walking, and this motivated him to devote hours to prayer and meditation in a desire to purify himself. But after a month of being confined to his room, he decided he had had enough. His knee was still purple and badly swollen, and he resolved to try to heal it 'by the power of thought, by love, by the spirit.'

Summoning all his mental resources, he created a beam of brilliant light and focused it on the swollen knee. After concentrating for a long time, he gradually began to feel a gentle warmth followed by the burning sensation of light penetrating his knee. He continued in this way until at last he sensed a movement, a tremendous influx of force in his very bones. Within a few minutes he fell asleep and awoke next morning to find his leg completely healed. Surprisingly, he himself was astonished by his success even though this was not the first time he had experienced something of the kind; he had often achieved spectacular results through the powers of thought. But for him everything was always new. He never became blasé, or considered himself an expert.

All evidence indicates that this period of his life was one of immense, dynamic energy. His whole being was expanding and he was continually discovering new possibilities within himself. At one point he discovered that he had the same gift of healing as his mother and grandmother. And when he read a biography of François Schlater, an Alsatian who had healed people by touching their hands, he was so moved that he almost aspired to imitate him. But in fact, the means he already used with great conviction was thought. For him, thought was the most powerful of all instruments.

When a friend told him about a young man who had hurt his leg and whose wound was so badly ulcerated that nothing seemed to do any good, Mikhaël made up his mind to try and help him. Filling a bottle with spring water, he concentrated on instilling into it the healing elements present in nature and then gave it to the young man to drink. The following day the ulcerated leg was completely healed, without so much as a scar.

Each time Mikhaël discovered new gifts or powers in himself he was faced with the same choice: whether to use those powers for his own purposes or to dedicate them unconditionally to the service of God. Peter Deunov, who was well aware of this, probably intended to give him one more occasion to make that choice when he showed him how to make a dowsing instrument equipped with a small copper rod with which to find gold in the ground. Mikhaël used it once, when he was dining in the home of some wealthy friends. His host hid some gold coins in different places throughout the house, and to the amazement of the family and their guests, he found them all.

The discovery of such a possibility was enough to turn many heads, but Mikhaël never used it again. What purpose could it serve except to exploit and dominate his fellow human beings? Had he not already renounced such use of his psychic powers at the age of eighteen, when he had refused the offer of the retired consul? His exceptional gifts could easily have assured him a brilliant career as healer, clairvoyant, or astrologer, but he knew that his role in life lay in a different direction. As soon as he sensed that a particular discipline would not enable him to help others to free themselves and overcome their difficulties, he abandoned it.

It was with sadness that he observed one of his fellow-workers, an exceptional young man who had discovered a natural gift for healing through iridology and used it to become rich and seduce girls and young women who came to him for treatment. For Mikhaël, it was not one's gifts and talents that mattered – however spectacular and lucrative – but the way one lived. The only way to help and enlighten others was to be kind, loving, and generous. When he saw that a friend needed help, he often suggested simple but effective methods.

It was in this spirit that he suggested that several of them might do well to take a new name, in order to trigger an inner transformation. He had long been interested in the meaning of proper names and in the influence of their vibrations, which, it seemed to him, could be as powerful as the vibrations of colours. A few years later he was struck by the results. One of his friends in particular, a violent person whose original name had a very negative meaning, was gradually transformed after adopting a new one.

Eventually, however, Mikhaël began to realize that by taking the responsibility of giving someone a new name he was perhaps linking himself too closely to their destiny and making some of their problems his own, and he abandoned the practice. It was only many years later, having disciples of his own, that he occasionally gave someone a new name for a specific reason. Similarly, he decided to do no more Tarot readings for anybody but himself, for, as he was to say later, such methods were too easy. They might be helpful for a time, but it was not the way to transform people; on the contrary, only their own efforts could help them to advance and perfect themselves.

*
* *

In Varna, Mikhaël's mother had always been the confidant and consoler of her neighbours, the person they instinctively turned to for help in their troubles. Many of those who were destitute or bed-ridden were cheered by a visit from Dolia, who arrived with a gift of bread or a cake hidden under her apron. One day she did something that was the talk of the neighbourhood for a long time after. One of her neighbours, a married man with a growing family, needed to add on a room to his house but was unable to pay for the building

permit. The room was almost finished when the police got wind of the affair, and news went around that they were on their way to demolish it.

Filled with compassion for the unfortunate family, Dolia quickly decided to champion their cause. Collecting all the children she could find, she gathered them around her in the room, hung a photograph of King Boris on the wall, and waited. When the police burst in, they found themselves confronted by this little woman surrounded by a crowd of laughing children.

'Madam,' they said; 'we have a warrant.'

'We're not moving from here,' replied Dolia calmly. 'Will you have the courage to pull the room down around us?'

Embarrassed, the men looked at each other sheepishly and after a moment the officer motioned for them to leave. Once outside they did their best to conceal their discomfiture from the crowd that had gathered in the street. After this defeat the matter was dropped, for the police, knowing Dolia's devotion to her neighbours and the affection and respect they had for her, had no desire to stir up unrest in the Turkish quarter.

Mikhaël's occasional visits were a great comfort to his mother, for she missed him very much. She did not really understand why he continued to be Peter Deunov's disciple, but to her family and friends she continued to say:

'That's where he belongs. He's happy there.'

For his part, when he arrived in Varna and saw her tired and preoccupied by so many difficulties, he often scolded her gently and told her not to take everybody's problems so much to heart.

The friends of Mikhaël's sisters were always much impressed by this serious young man of twenty-six who turned up from time to time with his violin tucked under his arm. He knew so many fascinating things about physiognomy, music, or the influence of nature on human beings. Seventy years later, one of them confided:

> I was fifteen when I saw Mikhaël for the first time. He was so sunburned that I thought he looked like a Hindu. He had a beautiful, mellow voice. I was studying a theorem about a triangle, and for something to say, I talked to him about it, whereupon he explained the symbolic meaning of the triangles he saw on my face, full-face and profile. That day I learned a good deal about myself and my character!

Mikhaël also played the violin with great feeling, and although his family admitted that he was not a virtuoso, they say that there was so much love in the way he played that he healed several people by playing a melody chosen especially for them.

*
* *

In Sofia, Mikhaël still lived with the friends who had given him a room when he first arrived. As earlier in Varna, he found here the possibility of integrating music into his spiritual work, for a member of the family, a professional pianist, invited him to listen to her playing whenever he liked. He had long thought of music as a great wind capable of bearing him to higher planes, and here was

a golden opportunity to learn to use it more intensely than ever. As
he listened, his eyes closed, he tried to discern the specific force
emanating from each piece:

> When we listen to a piece of music, we must first of all know
> whether it is a force for good or for ill; what it represents and what
> comparison it suggests. Is it like the wind or like thunder? Is it like a
> cataract or a waterfall tumbling down the mountainside? Is it like
> electricity? Or heat? Whatever the energy it emits you must learn to
> use it. If it suggests the wind, you can imagine that you are on a ship
> in full sail. If it suggests electricity, you can use it to set in motion
> your spiritual 'appliances', and so on.[23]

He often joined other friends who were musicians as well, and
spent hours listening to them. The friendships of his youth were
without doubt extremely important to him. Speaking in later years
of some of these profound and sincere relationships, he would not
hesitate to say, 'We had great love for each other.' One of his friends,
Ivan, was exceptionally gifted and his improvisations on the guitar
were often a source of inspiration to Mikhaël. Thanks to the subtle
affinity, the mysterious current that unites two beings, Ivan's music
had the power to propel Mikhaël to the world of the spirit. For this
he was always grateful and for the rest of his life he had a special
affection for the guitar because of the mystical experiences it had
inspired in his youth.

The two young men, both disciples of Peter Deunov, certainly
had a great deal in common. Their spiritual aspirations and the
similarity of their tastes were a bond between them, and in addition
to making music together they often experimented with telepathic
communication. Unfortunately their friendship lasted only a few
years, for Ivan died young, and his premature death was one of the
great sadnesses of Mikhaël's youth. He was to say fifty years later:
'He is still with me.'

Mikhaël continued his music lessons at the Conservatoire for
several years. If truth be told, he was both happy and unhappy about
his studies, for he was well aware of the flaws in his playing and

---

23. July 20th, 1965 (*'Know Thyself'- Jnana Yoga II*, p. 215).

knew that his fingers would never acquire the necessary agility. If only he had been able to learn as a child! Would he ever be a really good violinist? After a few years, recognizing that he would never be a virtuoso, he regretfully gave up his music lessons. He kept his violin and continued to play, but never in the same way.

His role in life was not that of a musician. Indeed, he had known for a long time that the higher beings who guided him put one obstacle after another in his way on the physical plane in order to help him to grow on other planes. Just as they had barred the route to a specialization in mathematics, so they now made it clear that the world of musicians was not for him. In his mind he heard them murmuring: 'You cannot lead people to the ultimate goal by means of music. We will show you another realm, a realm in which there will also be music; a realm in which you can act effectively.' As soon as he acquiesced he felt a powerful urge to turn to inner realities; he was learning to recognize the music concealed in all things, animate and inanimate; everything became music.

Above all, he understood that he must learn to play as perfectly as possible on the instrument of his own being. One day, this resolve received an unexpected stimulus. On a fine summer evening he was in his room, reading, when he suddenly heard the pure, limpid notes of a violin. Laying aside his book, he listened to a music so beautiful that it seemed to come from another, higher world. Intrigued, Mikhaël went out to see who was playing and found all the neighbours on their balconies, listening to a ragged old gypsy playing like an angel on a strange-looking instrument. In the awed silence that followed the last notes, Mikhaël went up to the old man and asked him where his violin had come from:

'I carved it myself, with my pocket knife,' replied the gypsy.

Mikhaël asked to look at it more closely and found that it was a roughly made wooden box, with the strings stretched on its crooked bridge. How could any musician draw the pure sounds he had heard from such a strange instrument? It defied belief.

'Would you consider selling it to me?' asked Mikhaël.

'Oh, no!' the old man insisted; 'Never! I'll never sell it!' And he told Mikhaël at great length how he had made it, and how a professional musician had once tried to buy it from him.

Mikhaël returned to his room thinking: 'How astonished Stradivarius would have been by such an instrument!' But reflecting on this incident, he realized that it was not necessarily the perfection of an instrument that counted. It depended on who played it. Even if his own instrument – he himself – was far from perfect, he should be able to make music with it. 'What counts,' he thought to himself, 'is to use my difficulties to produce something good.' He had learned long before not to count on external conditions for success, but that day the gypsy had strengthened the overriding desire of his life, the desire to be useful to others, to help, console and comfort his fellow human beings.

*
*   *

In the life and mission of Omraam Mikhaël Aïvanhov thought was an instrument capable of tremendous realizations; silence was both a need and a medium of communication; a look was a mysteriously potent means of exchange. But it was perhaps his use of speech, the power of words, that was the most important. He never consciously cultivated a talent. Instead, he put all his efforts into working with words, for 'words can achieve wonders.' The advice he gave always cut straight to the heart of a problem. We see an example of this in the way he helped a wealthy young friend who always looked sad. Meeting him in the street one day, Mikhaël greeted him warmly, whereupon his friend exclaimed:

'You're looking very joyful. What has happened?'

'Oh, nothing much,' replied Mikhaël; 'I have just bought some joy. And it cost very little.'

Puzzled, his friend looked at him in silence. He knew that Mikhaël had almost nothing in the world, and yet he always seemed to be in a state of supernatural joy. It was incomprehensible. On the other hand, he knew him well enough to know that he was not teasing. With a sigh, the young man complained that he had spent a lot of money in his life without receiving any joy in return. Wordlessly, Mikhaël beckoned to him to come with him, and pausing some distance from a poor man selling buttons, shoe-laces, and string, he murmured:

'Look! There's someone who sells joy. He stands there for hours in the cold, the wind, and the rain, waiting for customers. Go up to him and buy something, shoe-laces for instance. Ask him how much they are, and if he says they are ten leva, give him fifty and tell him to keep the change. When he hears that he will think: "Ah, there are still good people in the world." His faith will be strengthened, and his joy will be yours too. It will reverberate within you all day long, and it will have cost you only a few cents.'

Thoughtfully, the young man looked at the peddler and suddenly a smile lit up his face. Mikhaël added:

'You can also pay a visit to someone who is ill. Take him some little gift. Tell him that all will be well; that God is merciful. If you comfort others and give them joy, you yourself will become joyful. But when you want to give joy to someone you must choose carefully, for not everybody is ready to accept it.'

Mikhaël always spoke simply with words that went straight to people's hearts. His methods were those of all white magicians who, having mastered and refined their own faculties and feelings, are capable of using the power of words to great effect. For him, words were powerful instruments capable of eliciting vivifying reactions.

One summer, before joining the brotherhood camp, he spent a few days with a friend in the little town of Dupnitza to the west of Rila. One day, as he was on his way to join his friend for a picnic in the hills outside the town, he heard that two murderers were thought to have taken refuge there. Deciding that he ought to go and warn his friend, he walked on, never dreaming that the shirt he was wearing was similar to those of the assassins and would give rise to a serious misunderstanding. Hardly had he reached the hill when he found himself surrounded by a crowd of armed civilians and policemen who pointed their guns at him and ordered him to stop. He guessed from the expression on their faces that they had taken him for one of the fugitives. Standing still, he waited for them to come closer before saying anything. And what he said was surprising:

'You have arms, but the one I have is better.'

The police, taken aback, looked at him suspiciously, and taking advantage of their hesitation, Mikhaël took a New Testament from his pocket, saying:

'There you are. This is my weapon, and it is more powerful than yours.'

At once it was as though a tableau, frozen in time, came back to life as the tension went out of all those threatening countenances. The police asked what he was doing on the hill and ordered him to accompany them to the station. As he walked along quietly, an inner voice kept repeating: 'Don't worry! Everything is going to be all right.' An hour later, his friend, who had been arrested and then released, came to fetch him and stopped in the doorway in amazement to see Mikhaël sitting in the middle of a group of police, explaining a passage of the Gospels.

As they left the police station together, the two young men were greeted by the crowd that was waiting for news of the arrests. Learning that the 'assassin' was a visitor in the home of an honest citizen, they burst into applause. Mikhaël's popularity was assured, and in the days that followed there occurred a phenomenon that was often repeated in his life: his radiance and spontaneous kindness drew people to him, and suddenly everybody wanted to confide in him and ask his advice. For several days, his friend's house was besieged by people who seemed never to tire of listening to this young man whose eyes expressed such light and goodness, and who gave such clear and practical answers to their questions.

When he left Dupnitza to join the camp at Rila, some of these new friends went to find him there to continue their questions and talk about their problems. Every year after that, whenever Mikhaël was at the camp near the Seven Lakes, his friends from Dupnitza hiked up to see him.

No one who had anything to do with Mikhaël ever suffered from boredom. In his eagerness to stimulate the flow of life within them, he was not afraid to irritate them or even when necessary to arouse their anger. One day he had just reached the top of Mount Musala, when a Protestant pastor arrived and sat down beside him. Almost numb with cold, the man still managed to pull a Bible from his pocket saying:

'Do you know the Bible? Do you read it?'

Without more ado he started to preach. For him, nothing was more important than the written word. The spirit seemed to have been forgotten, and he did his best to convert Mikhaël to his own narrow views. After listening to him for a few minutes, Mikhaël lost patience and decided to shake him up a little and try to get him to reflect beyond the rigid limits of his militant theories. At one point, insisting that human beings were more important than books, even a book inspired by God, he said:

'Books can be destroyed, but they can always be written again, because the knowledge in them will always exist. I could throw this magnificent book into the ravine, but I would never throw you there. You are more important.'

The pastor could not help but see his point. How often in history men had killed each other in the name of religion, in the name of a holy book! Fanaticism has always led to destruction. More and more, Mikhaël talked about the importance of turning to the universal principle that is the source of all religions, and to his mind it was the sun that was the visible representation of this vital principle. The language of light is universal; all human beings can understand it. It is the language of life.

12

A Look is Enough

The estate known as Izgrev (Rising Sun) was an extensive property recently acquired by the fraternity of Peter Deunov. It lay on the outskirts of Sofia near Boris Gardens, one of the largest parks of the city. By the entrance was a white house with a lecture hall on the ground floor, and on the floor above a private room for Peter Deunov.

Over the years, as more and more disciples wished to live together in a fraternal setting, several smaller houses had been built on the grounds. Each had a small flower garden, and the absence of fences or hedges preserved the overall impression of one large park. As the years passed the fraternity at Izgrev expanded, and more and more visitors came, sometimes from afar, to see this experiment in collective living and meet the Master whose influence was so great.

When Mikhaël approached Izgrev after a forty-five minute tram ride through the city, he could always tell whether Peter Deunov was there or not. When he was there, the very air seemed to vibrate, the enthusiasm that animated the community was palpable. When he was absent it was as though the sun had disappeared from the sky. Mikhaël, struck by these observations, concluded that the presence of a Master kindles a more intense life in the hearts of his disciples.

Mikhaël himself did not live with the community. He had his room in the city, spent a good deal of time in the mountains, and only went to Izgrev to attend meetings and lectures. He came and went quietly without drawing attention to himself. Unlike many disciples who were invited to luncheons or dinners to talk about the teaching, he never spoke in public. When Peter Deunov gave him a

Mikhaël aged 30 on excursion with friends at Rila

private interview, Mikhaël always had many questions for him, and as they talked he rejoiced in the power and love emanating from the Master. He was now thirty; he knew the true nature of Peter Deunov's feelings towards him, and he continued to listen to every word he uttered with the loving attention he had shown at seventeen. His only desire was to deepen his understanding of the great truths of initiatic science.

Certainly, if he had lived in the brotherhood at this time, it would have been difficult for him to give so much time to the spiritual exercises that constituted the framework of his daily life. But it was not this that had determined his decision: he had sensed that Peter Deunov wished him to remain at a distance. He would understand the reason for this only much later, but in the meantime he was convinced that it was best.

Each time he returned to Izgrev, his joy in the Master's presence was renewed. Perhaps, he thought, he had been a little too possessive when he was younger, in his first enthusiasm at having found the Master he had sought for so long. Years later he frankly admitted that he had often taken up too much of Peter Deunov's time. He remembered that in his passionate desire to advance as quickly as possible, to correct his defects, and endure ordeals of purification, he had very often gone to him to ask his advice. He had ceaselessly implored him:

'Make me useful to the whole world.'

Indeed, the Master had imposed many ordeals on him, each more arduous than the last, but he had also let him see that he was satisfied with his work. Not many years later it was Mikhaël he would choose from among thousands to carry his teaching to France.

One day, at about this time, Peter Deunov gratified Mikhaël with another public expression of approval. In the middle of a lecture, he suddenly said:

'Brother Guirev is tuned to long waves, while brother Mikhaël operates on short waves.'

Brother Guirev was an intellectual, a veritable encyclopaedia, who liked to show off his learning. In referring to the longer wavelength of red, the colour of materialistic science, in contrast to the short waves of violet, which represent the spiritual world, Peter Deunov had described the most prominent and the most self-effacing members of the fraternity. The message was addressed to both, and having uttered it, he went on with his talk.

Violet light, that with the shortest wavelength and the highest frequency in the solar spectrum, was a constant source of inspiration for Mikhaël. But two of the most important means he used to open his soul and spirit to the spiritual world were fasting and silence. More than once, while still a young man in Bulgaria, he followed a practice much recommended by Hindu Masters and spent thirty days in silent retreat.

In India, where such methods are used by those seeking inner revelations, the practice of silence requires great self-control. How much more so in a country where few understand the meaning of such a thing! Mikhaël had to muster all his inner strength and discipline. People questioned him, trying to get him to talk; children laughed and teased him. But the rewards of his silence must have been very precious, for he repeated the experience more than once during his twenty years with Peter Deunov.

*
* *

Mikhaël's friends, recognizing his wisdom and his experience in the spiritual life, often sought his advice. Although he never hesitated to help them, to remind them of the aspects of the teaching most likely to enlighten and encourage them, it was always to Peter Deunov that he directed them. Determined not to assume the role of teacher, probably even mistrusting himself in this respect, he remained in the background, for in his mind, humility was essential to evolution.

His whole life was orientated toward something very special and unusual. As an adolescent, he had already decided not to give physical expression to his sexual energies but to sublimate them and use them in a work of spiritual maturation. Since then he had sought inspiration only in beauty, in the subtler dimensions of life. His attitude toward the opposite sex was unequivocal, and his companions knew he had chosen to live in chastity. During much of his youth, however, he had had to endure the purifying fire of criticism and derision. His close friends knew how he spent his time and respected and admired him. But others, unable to understand how anyone could sacrifice the things to which most people aspire, openly sneered at his options which seemed to them too radical.

Like all the great beings who had travelled this path before him, Mikhaël certainly had his own inner struggles, but never in his long life would he deny the reality of the human body created by God or its innate impulses, which are either good or evil depending on how they are used. He would say, later, that in his youth he had been filled with a great effervescence which had sometimes frightened him, but that when he had discovered its profound meaning he could only thank heaven for all he had received. Several years earlier, Peter Deunov, who was well aware of this, had told him:

'For you, Mikhaël, a look is enough.'

He had not explained his remark, and Mikhaël had reflected at length on the meaning.

The Master had seen the roots, the structure, of my deepest nature and had summed it up in a single phrase: I need only a glance, a look. Later on, I often used a glance and I discovered some important laws or, to be more accurate, I discovered how to look in such a way as to sanctify oneself, how to be filled with wonder, to feel elated and fulfilled with only a single glance.[24]

For his part, Peter Deunov was well aware of Mikhaël's detachment, of the stability of his conduct, and in particular of his frank and unambiguous attitude toward women. A few years earlier in the garden at Ternovo he had witnessed a minor but revealing incident: Mikhaël, perched on top of a ladder that was leaning against the branch of a tree, was lost in the contemplation of nature, when a girl approached and climbed half-way up the ladder to talk to him. Peter Deunov knew that the two young people were very fond of each other, and although he could not hear what they were saying, he could see that they were both enjoying their conversation. Finally the girl climbed down, beckoning to Mikhaël to follow. Peter Deunov had noted with interest that Mikhaël remained on the ladder and went back to his meditation. The incident was so significant in his eyes that he mentioned it to Mikhaël several years later.

To Mikhaël's way of thinking, true purity was God himself, and in a human being it was one of the most important virtues. When his friends talked to him of their problems, of their sexual desires or obsessions, he was not afraid to tell them to face them squarely and see them as blessings, as a starting point for a meditation on beauty. Ever since he had contemplated the spring in the village of his childhood, he had constantly striven for purity. But never would he reject the sexual energies created by God. Never would he approve the renunciations of certain narrow-minded spiritualists. On the contrary, in later years he taught his disciples to use those energies to fuel their ascent to the divine regions for which all human beings are destined.

At the time of his youth, however, it had not always been easy for him to make his contemporaries understand his position. His

---

24. January 2nd, 1967 (*Love and Sexuality I*, p.157).

radiance was such that more than once he had been obliged to resist the advances of young women in the fraternity who were in love with him. Far from being indifferent to feminine beauty, he always looked on it with admiration and delight, and never attempted to ignore it. With astonishing strength of mind, he succeeded in working exclusively with the eyes, and his efforts were sometimes rewarded by unexpected gifts from subtler regions. During the night, he was often awakened by the presence of unreal creatures of extraordinary beauty.

> They were all round me, looking at me in such a way that I felt myself melting in indescribable love. They did not touch me, just stayed there, looking at me, and all their power was in their eyes. I have never yet seen such an expression in the eyes of a human being. It seemed to come from a great distance and a great height. The experience lasted for hours. I learned, later, that these creatures were devas and I understood that they had visited me in order to show me that there existed in nature a beauty beyond anything one could imagine.[25]

Through their absolute purity, light, and radiance, these creatures opened up a new world in Mikhaël's soul. He received from them 'revelations about true love, the love that needs no physical manifestation.'

---

25. January 2nd, 1967 (*Love and Sexuality I*, p.156).

13

I Will Give You a Precious Stone

By 1930 or 1931, Mikhaël was no longer attending lectures at the university. He remarked later that much of what he had studied had been a waste of time, that it had drawn a veil between reality and his life, and was best forgotten.

In Bulgaria, before qualifying for a teaching position in Sofia or other major city, three years of experience in a village school were required. For his first school term, Mikhaël was employed in a high school not far from the capital. It is probably here that he lived in the bungalow that he once described as 'so small that two people could not be in it at the same time.' In the classroom, applying educational methods that owed little to prevailing customs, he soon obtained results that surpassed his most optimistic expectations.

Mikhaël had noticed that delinquency had been on the rise in the country following a popular series of plays about the bandit Zigomar. This confirmed his conviction that the power of suggestion exerted by theatre and cinema has a stronger influence on people's minds and behaviour than church, school, or even family. With this in mind, he organized and produced several short plays with his pupils. One of them in particular, the adaptation of a Tolstoy legend about a grain of wheat, was a great favourite with the parents. Seeking to awaken his pupils' minds and hearts to new ideas, he explained the lines they recited and helped them to discover the beauty in them. At home the children talked about this new teacher who was so unlike those they had known before, and their grateful parents began to pay him frequent visits.

Three or four years later, Mikhaël was appointed director of a college, and during the few months of this charge he was busier than ever. His methods, based on a pedagogical principle of love and patience, created once again a sincere and dynamic relationship between himself and the students. Their parents, not knowing how else to thank him, brought him cheese, nuts, and fruit. His office was often fragrant with the scent of their gifts. At the same time, however, he attracted the envy and resentment of some of the other teachers, who, unwilling to change their attitude toward their students, opposed him in different ways.

Jealousy always came as a surprise to Mikhaël. He found it difficult to realize just how powerful and tenacious it could be. But in spite of his new responsibilities and endless problems of this kind, he was always full of energy, and undertook to give a series of spiritual talks for the peasant population of the region, who attended in great numbers. They loved this new director who used such colourful imagery and expressive gestures, and who spoke with such humour, peppering his talks with anecdotes to illustrate his meaning.

*
* *

The time was drawing near when Mikhaël would be called on to leave his country for ever. Peter Deunov had kept him in the background for years, and most of the members of the brotherhood had forgotten the mysterious remark he had made one day by the shores of the second lake of Rila: 'You do not yet know brother Mikhaël; at the moment he is disguised, but one day you will know him.'

In the thirties, Peter Deunov had begun to reveal certain things to Mikhaël in order to prepare him more directly for his future task. One of these revelations was in the language of allegory:

'I have in my possession a precious stone. It is as big as an egg and valuable beyond words. I intend to give it to someone to take to another country, but as he will have to travel through a dense forest teeming with bandits and savage beasts, I will coat it with mud. Later, when it is washed, it will shine in all its splendour.'

It was a prediction that was to be fulfilled ten years later, but at the time Mikhaël was not able to decipher the hermetic language in which his future was described. He was to be the bearer of the teaching,

Peter Deunov   *Mikhaël*

symbolized by the precious stone, and he was to be soiled in the same way as the gem. Since Peter Deunov had prophesied in 1917 that the forces of darkness would oppose him, Mikhaël had known that he was destined to endure great ordeals, but the meaning of this allegory of the gem that had to be soiled in order to be protected became clear to him only when those ordeals were imminent. Even if Peter Deunov knew the nature of the tribulations that awaited Mikhaël, to have revealed them would only have made things more difficult for him. Thus this veiled allusion to the mission he would entrust to him a few years hence and to the need for concealment.

He told him, also:

'When you have passed through the "narrow gate" you will be so transformed that you will not recognize yourself. You will shine like the sun, and the whole world will be drawn to you.'

On another occasion he made an astonishing statement:

'You must realize that in the world above you were free. Before incarnating you signed a contract in front of an assembly of all the greatest spirits. You agreed to accomplish a certain task here below, and you must now fulfil your promise.'

Peter Deunov sometimes told his disciples that before their present incarnation they had had to agree to carry out a specific task on earth. To Mikhaël he spoke of the signature of a free being, of one who did not need to reincarnate in order to achieve perfection and who could be entrusted with a special mission by the great assembly of spirits only if he consented. He did not elaborate, knowing no doubt that Mikhaël would one day understand all the implications. Human beings are not permitted to know their future; even high initiates and great Masters are subject to this rule. Their mission is revealed to them only progressively in the course of their life.

Peter Deunov had also said: 'You came to bear witness to truth,' and Mikhaël often pondered those words. To bear witness to truth, he reflected, every fibre of one's being would have to vibrate in unison with truth; one would have to have the flawless purity of a diamond that bears witness to the transparency of all diamonds. One day, it occurred to him to ask the Master:

'When were you best pleased with me as a disciple?'

Mikhaël was then thirty-four. In the seventeen years Peter Deunov had known him, he had tried and tested him in different ways and followed his progress closely. He knew that Mikhaël was an exceptional being who never drew attention to himself. Destined to enlighten and console, he was a being of integrity, courage, and steadfastness beyond question. Over and over he had proved capable of sacrificing his own tranquillity to support and defend his brothers and sisters. All this Peter Deunov knew, and yet he chose to speak of the apparently insignificant incident in the garden at Ternovo, many years before:

'You were in deep meditation when that girl, who had great affection for you, and you for her, came looking for you. But when she descended the ladder and asked you to do the same, you remained up there and continued your meditation. That was the moment when I was best pleased with you.'

'But, Master,' exclaimed Mikhaël in astonishment; 'does that mean that it was the symbolic and perhaps prophetic aspect of what you saw that pleased you? It seems to me it was nothing much.'

Peter Deunov smiled and said nothing. The image of the ladder was indeed symbolic. He had been pleased to see that Mikhaël remained faithful to the divine world, to his ideal, to the mission of those who renounce marriage and procreation in order to devote themselves totally to the realization of the kingdom of God on earth. But he certainly knew also that Mikhaël's unconditional options, his frankness and honesty sometimes caused resentment. Eventually, even that young girl in the garden at Ternovo who had loved him, would be subjugated by an unscrupulous man, whom Mikhaël could not accept as a friend, and who would become one of his worst enemies.

*
* *

It was during these years that Peter Deunov made several important revelations to Mikhaël about his future, predictions he had deciphered in the *Akasha Chronica*. While he spoke of these things his expression took on extraordinary intensity, his features were transformed and radiant. Mikhaël would never forget those moments, the beauty that suffused the Master's face and the accent of truth in his words. Progressively, in the three years that followed, Peter Deunov revealed to Mikhaël many things about himself, in particular that books he had written in a past incarnation in India had been a source of instruction for the whole world. He told him that he had been especially destined for a work of spiritual assistance to women, and that he would one day converse with the great archangels, rulers of the planets. These revelations and promises came as a confirmation and consecration of all that Mikhaël had already accomplished.

During this period Peter Deunov was especially close to Mikhaël who had worked so humbly by his side for twenty years and who was already, without doubt, an exceptional spiritual guide. The Master could now allow himself to show his love for him. Mysteriously, he sometimes called him *Iacchoi*, a name that was unfamiliar to Mikhaël. It was only many years later that Mikhaël would encounter it in a book about the Dionysian Mysteries. There he learned that for the alchemists, the name *Iacchus* was synonymous with the sun. It also designated Dionysus, Apollo, and Osiris. In the Mysteries, the plural form, Iacchoi, was the name given to androgynes, those perfect beings who possess both the masculine and feminine principles within themselves. The Master's use of this name was once more an enigmatic reference that gave Mikhaël matter for deep reflection and meditation, but at the time he understood only that a whole program of work was being put before him.

In these years Peter Deunov was very much alive to the threat that the rise of Communism posed for the fraternity. In 1937, he invited Mikhaël to his house one last time, and entrusted him with the mission to make his teaching known in France. To prepare the way for him, he gave him three letters that he had dictated to his secretary, Boyan Boëv. The first stated that Mikhaël was leaving on a specific mission to which his whole life was dedicated. The second was addressed to a Polish woman who was in a position to introduce him to interesting people in Paris. The third, dated June 12th, and signed by brother Boëv, was addressed to a Bulgarian brother, Anastassi, who also lived in the French capital. It said:

> One of our brothers, Mikhaël Ivanov, is leaving for Paris. He is being sent by the Master. As you know, he is one of the very advanced disciples. He is deeply knowledgeable and totally dedicated, living and working only for God's work.

The official reason for Mikhaël's departure for France was to visit the Paris World Fair: Peter Deunov never disclosed to his other disciples that he had entrusted him with a mission. Knowing that his choice would inevitably arouse envious reactions on the part of those who thought themselves better equipped for such a task, he chose to say nothing.

On July 18th, 1937, after bidding farewell to his family, Mikhaël boarded the train that was to take him to Paris. A small crowd of friends and many of his pupils and their parents were at the station to see him off. Many wept when he left, sensing perhaps that they would never see him again. Mikhaël could only look at them, his heart torn. For years, he thought often of those children he had loved and of the brothers and sisters who had come to wish him Godspeed.

He was thirty-seven and was giving up everything, family, friends, and the country in which he had been born, for the sake of this new mission. Symbolically, he was selling all he possessed in order to carry the precious stone to a distant land.

Part Three:
Brother Mikhaël

Praised be you my Lord with all your creatures, especially Sir Brother Sun, who is the day through whom you give us light. He is beautiful and radiant with great splendour. Of you Most High, he bears the likeness.

Francis of Assisi

14

Paris

The train from Sofia, crowded with passengers bound for the 1937 World Fair, made a two day stop-over in Venice and reached Paris on July 22nd. A Bulgarian brother who had been told of his arrival by Peter Deunov gave Mikhaël a room in his apartment, but when he tried to contact the Polish woman who was to introduce him to various spiritual movements in Paris, she was away from home and her neighbours had no idea when she would return.

While waiting for her to appear, Mikhaël set out to discover Paris. For days, he explored the different *quartiers*, visiting churches, museums, the famous gardens, and the second-hand book stalls on the banks of the Seine. Gazing down the majestic sweep of the Champs-Elysées for the first time, he remembered with amusement the naïve idea he had had of it at the age of seventeen, when the name evoked for him the mythical 'Elysian Fields, the marvellous abode of the great spirits of the past.' In dusty old book shops in the Latin Quarter, he browsed through rare texts on alchemy. He also spent many fascinating hours at the Palais des Découvertes, where visitors may observe demonstrations of scientific experiments.

He used this time also to improve his rudimentary French by frequenting the cinema, the theatre, and the opera. During the performances he continued as in the past to note the effect of the instruments and voices on himself and others, attempting to understand how the different sounds activated the spiritual energy centres within.

Back in his friend's apartment in the evening, Mikhaël retired to his room. There, listening to the children at play, their cries echoing in the narrow street below, he pondered his situation. His visitor's visa would soon expire and if he failed to get in touch with the person Peter Deunov had written to, he would be obliged to return to Bulgaria. The days sped by, and on the eve of his departure he tried one last time to reach her. Miraculously, the telephone rang as she opened the door of her apartment, having just returned from Warsaw. Without hesitation she invited him to come and see her, and began at once to take steps to prolong his visa. After interminable telephone conversations with the immigration authorities, she was finally successful. Toward the end of the day Mikhaël was still with her when the doorbell rang, and his hostess introduced him to Stella Bellemin, a woman in her fifties who was to be one of the most faithful disciples of the new teaching he had brought to France.

Stella had also just returned from a vacation. She had been to Bulgaria and spent a few days at the Seven Lakes of Rila where she had met Peter Deunov. After about ten days with the Bulgarian brotherhood, she had asked Peter Deunov, in the presence of his secretary, Brother Boëv, how she could help to make his teaching known in France. His reply was:

'When you meet the person you are destined to work with, you will recognize him immediately.'

Many years later when the validity of Mikhaël's work was being contested, Stella remembered that although Peter Deunov had not named Mikhaël explicitly there was no doubt that he had been referring to him, and that his secretary, who had been present at the time, understood this perfectly. She would also recall that, during those ten days in Bulgaria, nobody had so much as mentioned a brother who had recently left for France. But that evening in her friend's apartment, Peter Deunov's prediction was fulfilled: as soon as she saw the visitor in the sitting room, she knew without a shadow of doubt that he was the one Peter Deunov had spoken of. And when she learned that he had come to France to make known the teaching she herself had recently discovered, her decision was immediate: she would collaborate in his work by putting all her resources at his disposal. Without hesitation – and with a total disregard for convention – she offered Mikhaël a room in her apartment and promised him all the help he needed. Mikhaël did not accept immediately: he needed time to consider the question in private, but the next day he accepted her offer and moved to her apartment in the rue des Princes, where she had set aside a small room with an easterly view for him from which he could see the sunrise.

Stella was an astronomer, attached to the Bibliothèque Nationale de Paris. Every morning she left for the office and returned home only in the evening. Before long many of her friends heard that one of Peter Deunov's disciples was staying in her apartment and came to make his acquaintance. With attention and the utmost patience, 'Brother Mikhaël', as he began to be called, listened to his visitors and responded to their questions. And as they came in increasing numbers, seeking advice, instruction, and consolation, there were days when the apartment hummed like a beehive. On weekends when Stella was free, he devoted many hours to instructing her in the teaching Peter Deunov had entrusted to him.

For her part, Stella observed her guest closely and could not help but be deeply affected by his extraordinary radiance. Drawn to the spiritual life since childhood, she was also an intellectual who had gained considerable authority in her field. She was not easily impressed, but in later years she would often speak of the deep impression Brother Mikhaël had made on her. Time and again she saw people who were harassed and irritable melting visibly under the effect of his smile. He instilled such rare kindness into a few simple words that their attitude was often completely transformed.

*
*   *

Toward the end of 1937 the social and political situation in France was deeply troubled. The threat of war hung over Europe and dominated every conversation. That autumn the French government passed a law severely restricting the right of foreign visitors to the World Fair to remain in the country, and Mikhaël, who had left Bulgaria with only a temporary permit to visit the Fair, was now faced with the necessity of renewing it every week. But neither the long hours of waiting nor the harassment, suspicion, and arrogance with which he was treated exhausted his patience. With tireless regularity, he renewed the legal formalities, and was so often obliged to be photographed that a great number of photographs from that period still exist.

One day, an official warned Stella that Mikhaël was a spy in the pay of the Soviet Union. She defended him vigorously, but each week, because of misunderstandings of this kind, he had to find additional people of influence to back his request for an extension of his permit. It was two years before he obtained a visa which had to be renewed only every three months, and it was many more years before the restrictions on him were further relaxed. But he was never to have citizenship in any one country. He would always be a citizen of the world.

In the meantime, he remained serene, counting as always on the unfailing support of his friends in the invisible world. It seemed that his prayers were always answered. More than once, at the last minute and under unusual circumstances, he met someone who was in a position to get his papers renewed. Sometimes it was the Bulgarian legation that put obstacles in his way; sometimes it was the French authorities. One day, just two hours before his visa expired, the French police demanded that his application be countersigned by ten French male citizens with substantial financial means. Half an hour later, ten 'solid citizens' arrived almost simultaneously at the apartment. All were among his regular visitors and all, without a word to the others, had decided to leave work earlier than usual and go to see Brother Mikhaël. Together they accompanied him to police headquarters.

His friends were constantly astonished by the unusual events they witnessed, and even the most sceptical were impressed. They could not help but recognize that he was surrounded by invisible beings who assisted him so that his work could go forward. Their support even extended to seemingly insignificant details: he received an unexpected gift of money that exactly matched the price of a small radio he needed; he found at his door a Japanese tea service that he had admired in a shop window, thinking that he could use it to offer his guests a cup of tea. Incidents of this kind were frequent, but in spite of his faith, Brother Mikhaël never seemed to take them for granted. Each time, he was as astonished and delighted as a child.

*
* *

As Brother Mikhaël's popularity increased, the visitors to Stella's apartment in the rue des Princes became more and more numerous. Once a week a score of people gathered for an evening meeting, but before long the apartment became too small and meetings were held in the more spacious home of her Polish friend, near the rue du Bac.

Peter Deunov was not unknown in the French capital at the time; in fact, several of his disciples in Paris claimed to be there at his behest, but Brother Mikhaël made no such claim. He was simply a Bulgarian living in France, one among a number of Peter Deunov's disciples. Without professing to represent Peter Deunov or to possess any special expertise, he talked quite simply about the major themes of this teaching which constituted the warp and woof of his life.

Although Brother Mikhaël's knowledge of French was improving rapidly, it was far from perfect. His audience, however, found little to complain about, for his lively humour and vivid imagery more than compensated for any shortcomings. But there were occasions when his imperfect knowledge of the language was a handicap: some of those who came to hear him were writers, astrologers, and alchemists, and occasionally, mistaking his limited means of expression for a lack of knowledge, one of them would presume to give him advice.

Many considered themselves to be initiates, a cut above ordinary mortals, and they sometimes held forth at such length that Brother Mikhaël could hardly utter a word. Without attempting to correct their perception of him, he simply listened patiently as they described how they had passed the 'second or third degree of initiation.' For his part, he was completely indifferent to these so-called degrees and had no intention of establishing them in the brotherhood. More than once he said that he had never known what degree he had reached; that the brotherhood was not interested in titles and there were no 'pundits' among the members. In his view, each time someone experienced an expansion of consciousness it meant that they had reached a higher degree of initiation.

One day Stella invited a friend, who was an engineer as well as a seasoned astrologer, to meet Brother Mikhaël. They had hardly been introduced when the visitor, full of his own importance, began to question Brother Mikhaël as though he were one of his students:

'Do you have some notion of astrology?'

'Yes, a little,' replied Brother Mikhaël – who had been known in his own country as one of the foremost experts on the subject.

The engineer then mentioned the titles of several books and advised him to study this fascinating science which would open undreamed-of avenues for him. Not in the least perturbed, Brother Mikhaël thanked him for the information and made a note of the books. One evening a few months later, intrigued by talk of Brother Mikhaël's brilliant interpretations of the major astrological themes, the engineer returned to hear him talk, and was astounded by the extent of his knowledge and the natural authority with which he spoke. From that moment on, his attitude changed completely. In a long letter of apology he expressed shame at the arrogance of his behaviour and signed it, 'Your worthless disciple.'

With his profound understanding of spiritual astrology, Brother Mikhaël was able to speak of the great laws that sustain the universe in ways that enhanced his audience's understanding of the world around them. Several well-known astrologers attended his talks regularly, drawing from them a wealth of new and vivifying ideas. In general, however, astrology was not a frequent topic of his talks; he referred to it only occasionally in order to illustrate or emphasize a point of the teaching.

During all this time, Stella, who never tired of listening to Brother Mikhaël and observing his reactions, did her best to fathom the secret of his behaviour. Many years later, she wrote that his actions had often amazed her; his code of conduct seemed so different from that of most people.

He was always natural, humble, unpretentious, and sometimes seemingly ignorant, and this astonished me very much. I still could not understand why he so consistently concealed every hint of his exceptional nature and true worth of which I had received such a clear indication from the very first moment we had met. [...] On first meeting him, the thing that struck one above all else was the intense light that radiated from him, a light that was imbued with tenderness and pure, impersonal love.[26]

---

26. Svezda (*nom de plume* of Stella Bellemin), *Vie et enseignement du Maître Omraam Mikhaël Aïvanhov en France*, p. 35f (Our translation).

In her desire to understand the wellsprings of his action, she observed every detail: the harmony of his gestures, so different from the abruptness of most people; the kindness that often cloaked his exceptional inner strength; and the way he looked at each person with an affection that laid no obligation on them. Stella could find no discrepancy between his teaching and his life.

15

The First Public Talks

Five months after Brother Mikhaël's arrival in France, his students asked him to address a wider public, assuring him that his French was perfectly adequate for the purpose. He finally agreed, and on the evening of January 29th, 1938, gave his first public talk in the Luxembourg Hall, Place de la Sorbonne.

On the morning of the talk, Stella's apartment was without water. Unable to get water from the wash basin in his room, Brother Mikhaël tried the kitchen tap but forgot to turn it off before going out. When Stella returned from work that evening, she was horrified to find her guest in the kitchen, mopping up the flood. At the sight of her expression, Brother Mikhaël could not help laughing. For him, the meaning of the incident was clear: in his eyes, the water, symbol of fertility, abundance, and life, was a message from the invisible world. With enthusiasm he explained:

'Don't you see what a wonderful sign it is? It is an outpouring, a torrent of love! My talk this evening will be a success. The audience will be fully satisfied.'

In fact, the reality surpassed the portent. His talk, entitled 'The Second Birth,' turned out to be the first in a series of more than five thousand. That evening, he surprised his listeners with the unexpected precision and aptness of his French, and the eloquence of his gestures contributed in no small part to his success. From time to time, at a loss for a specific word, he delighted them by asking them to supply it. Very often, after hearing their suggestions, he found the elusive word for himself, and the audience was charmed by his informality.

This first talk was rich in themes central to his philosophy: the symbolism of fire and water, the subtler forms of nourishment; the relationship between the twelve signs of the zodiac and the four elements; the spiritual significance of a triangular prism; the symbolism of colours and their influence on human beings:

He who has been born for the second time is like a living fountain of pure water which gives birth to a new and thriving civilization. His religion is the true religion of divine love and wisdom. For him, the only true temple of God is the universe, the sun is High Priest in this temple and the stars are its votive lights. He who has been born a second time is one who has opened his secret, innermost channels so that they may be filled with love and wisdom. He is the perfect prism that distributes the seven beneficial forces throughout his own being and projects them outwards for the benefit of all around him.[27]

Throughout his life, Brother Mikhaël spoke of light as the 'celestial water' that flows from the world above. His great desire was to foster the upsurge of life by ensuring the constant flow of this 'water'. His first public talk, then, was the initial outpouring of the fountainhead from which flowed his mission. At the same time, it inaugurated a ten-year period during which he would lay the foundations in France of Peter Deunov's teaching, and prepare to bring it to fruition.

After the success of this first experience, he continued to give weekly talks in a rented hall. Before long, his audience grew in numbers until they overflowed on to the podium, and a more spacious meeting place had to be found. The new assembly room quickly became inadequate as well, and people were often obliged to stand outside and listen as best they could.

The style Brother Mikhaël adopted for his talks was similar to that of Peter Deunov, and corresponded well with his own temperament. Rather than composing a discourse in advance, he prepared himself by spending some time in meditation. On entering the hall, he greeted his audience, his right hand raised in the salute that had become customary in the Bulgarian brotherhood. The gesture had

---

27. January 29th, 1938 (*The Second Birth*, p. 53f).

real significance for him. He saw it as an instrument, a means by which to communicate energy, colours, and life-giving vibrations. He often said: 'When you salute each other, the gesture should be a true communion; it should be powerful, harmonious, and alive.'

After the salutation, he remained in silence for a few moments sensing the state of mind of his audience. And when he spoke, whatever his theme, he always seemed to address the problems of each one and to offer the lucid, practical solutions they needed. A period of meditation invariably followed his talk, but the pattern of the gatherings never became routine; they were full of life, exuberance and surprise, for Brother Mikhaël maintained that routine 'leads to sluggishness and death.'

To relax his audience or stimulate their attention, he frequently interspersed his talks with jokes and anecdotes, and his laughter was contagious. Like the legendary story-tellers of the Orient, he peppered his discourse with tales that were both amusing and instructive. Particularly fond of Turkish folk-tales about Mullah Nashrudin learned in childhood, he was equally at home with the stories of Alexandre Dumas, the *Fables* of La Fontaine, or the *Tales of a Thousand and One Nights*. These stories were often a way of summing up an aspect of his teaching, but they also served to ease tensions he himself had created in his audience. He liked to say that laughter keeps the brain flexible, and that the brotherhood was a school for laughter.

Brother Mikhaël found constant inspiration in the everyday events of life. For him, they were a reflection of invisible realities, and he used them as examples to illustrate a point of his teaching. One day, some friends took him to Luna Park, in which one of the attractions was the Rotor, or 'butter dish'. This was a large circular platform, and as it spun faster and faster, those standing near the outside edge lost their balance and were thrown to the ground, while those who stood close to the central axis remained unaffected. This carnival ride fascinated Brother Mikhaël, and he often referred to the 'butter dish' when speaking of the need to maintain a close bond with God, the centre of all things: 'If we do not want to be defeated and thrown off balance by life's difficulties, we must stay close to God, whatever comes.'

In contrast to so many fashionable speakers, Brother Mikhaël always talked simply, using ordinary, everyday expressions, illuminating the meaning of life in a unique way, and suggesting practical methods of self-transformation that anyone might use. His unpretentious imagery evoked an immediate response in many of his listeners, but the very ordinariness of the language he used in speaking about elevated subjects often disconcerted those who were more intellectually sophisticated. A few were offended when he remarked that 'even a baby could understand' what he was saying, but if they persevered they gradually discovered the depth and complexity of the ideas that lay behind his words.

Once his talk was over, so many people crowded around him that it was sometimes an hour before he could reach the car waiting to take him home. But even after a long and tiring evening, he never tried to avoid them: on the contrary, he answered all their questions patiently.

From the beginning, many of the Bulgarian disciples of Peter Deunov who were living in Paris attended these evening gatherings regularly. Most of them, however, remained reserved in their attitude toward Mikhaël. In his homeland, he had never been in the public eye or lectured on the teaching like so many others. When the news reached Bulgaria that he was giving public talks in Paris, it was the signal for a period of great difficulty, not only for him, but also for the Bulgarian brotherhood, for many members believed that he had gone to France and proclaimed himself Peter Deunov's representative on his own initiative. Even when a number of Bulgarians returned from Paris and spoke of his work with admiration, the scepticism remained.

During this contentious period Peter Deunov's main concern seems to have been to keep the peace among his disciples. In 1937 he had given Mikhaël a letter which clearly stated his mission in Paris. Later, in private conversations with other disciples, he spoke approvingly of the spiritual work Mikhaël was doing in France. Never once, however, did he announce publicly that it was he who had commissioned that work. It was hardly surprising, therefore, that some of his disciples concluded that their Master disapproved of Brother Mikhaël's activity and that it was only out of charity that he remained silent. In lieu of any public endorsement, however, Peter Deunov did take the precaution of writing to Mikhaël personally to reiterate his approval: 'Work as God directs you. I am pleased with what you are doing. Do as you think best.' And in October 1938, his secretary, Brother Boëv, wrote:

'You can be sure that what you are doing has the Master's complete approval. Pay no attention to those who are being negative. All those I talk to here hold you in great affection.'

Brother Mikhaël was well aware of the criticisms aimed at him. One day he assured his audience that he was simply passing on what he had received in Bulgaria from Peter Deunov and that he always communed mentally with him before speaking. Moreover, he regularly began his talks by quoting a text by Peter Deunov, which he then elaborated upon at length. His deep love for Peter Deunov was evident, and for years he hoped to bring him to Paris to instruct the French brotherhood himself.

Meanwhile, presenting himself as 'a disciple of no importance,' he continued to strive for the virtue of humility. Humility, he used to say, is a point of view, a way of looking at things: if we compare ourselves with an ant, we are bound to think that we are very big and grand, but if we compare ourselves with a star, an archangel, or a divinity, we become conscious of our smallness. Humility, in his view, is the one attitude that can stimulate us to achieve greater heights, for, 'if we think we have reached the top, we have no incentive to climb higher. There is nowhere to go but down.'

As always, Brother Mikhaël was not afraid of appearing ignorant, and frequently this led people to underestimate his knowledge or intelligence. The long-term consequence of this habitual self-depreciation was that, when the time came for him to broaden the scope of Peter Deunov's teaching, many members of the brotherhood reproached him for it. Even in those early days, however, it was evident to many that he possessed a vast store of knowledge drawn from the *Akasha Chronica*, as well as an exceptional gift for communicating that knowledge. He could not behave as though the light that flooded his being did not exist, and yet for years he continued to extol the reputation of Peter Deunov and to minimize his own. He accepted criticism as an inevitable part of his mission and never allowed it to hinder his work on behalf of the invisible world.

*
*   *

In the spring following his first public talk, Brother Mikhaël encouraged his students to attend the sunrise as often as possible in order to draw strength and inspiration from the light, as was the custom among the disciples of Pythagoras and other high initiates of Antiquity. When some complained that they were too tired to get up early, he replied that the apparent fatigue caused by getting up early would counteract their chronic state of exhaustion:

> When you are present as the sun rises, its rays dissolve the harmful fluidic layers that surround you, and the seeds that God has planted in your soul begin to germinate.[28]

Several of his followers subsequently admitted that the regular practice of attending the sunrise left them feeling stronger and more energetic; their complexion cleared, and they became more emotionally stable. Brother Mikhaël often assured them that the day would come when everyone attended the sunrise, and lived longer and healthier lives as a result.

On Sundays, he liked to leave the city with those who formed the core of the French brotherhood and spend the day in the forest, where he continued to instruct them in initiatic science and introduced them to the spiritual and physical exercises practised in the Bulgarian brotherhood. In the peaceful setting of a natural clearing among the great trees Brother Mikhaël was in his element. In May 1939, inviting his regular students to accompany him to the forest of St-Nom-la-Bretèche for further practise in the gymnastic exercises taught by Peter Deunov, he told them that these exercises could greatly benefit their physical and psychic health as well as the will, mind, and emotions. The rhythm with which they were carried out was of the greatest consequence: 'It is important to be attuned to the rhythm of cosmic forces and to execute each movement slowly and with concentration.'

---

28. Unpublished talk, April 24th, 1945.

On the appointed day more than a hundred people turned up. Once they were assembled in the clearing, he explained how these seven daily exercises could nourish, reinforce, and harmonize certain centres of the nervous system. Then, while talking about their symbolism, he demonstrated each movement. While the participants were doing their best to follow his gestures, dark storm clouds gathered overhead, but Brother Mikhaël, seeing their disappointment, reassured them with a smile:

'Don't worry. The clouds will disappear as soon as we begin to sing.'

As the first notes of their song rang out, the sky began to clear dramatically, as though a great wind had suddenly arisen in the heavens.

After a picnic lunch, Brother Mikhaël spoke about the beauty of the forest and explained how to tap the forces of nature and draw energy from great trees or running water. For him the link between the two worlds of spirit and matter was an ever-present reality and a potent means of realization in the physical world. The universe is an immense living organism whose elements, from the smallest atom through the angelic hierarchies to the supernal God, are interlinked. The cycles of nature were a means of strengthening his ties with the divine world. He used the phases of the moon or the energies of fire, wind, streams, and waterfalls as a means of self-transformation. He used to say, for instance, 'As this water washes and purifies all in its path, so may I be made pure.'

While he was speaking that day, his gaze followed the movements of a salamander as it crossed the space between himself and the circle of participants and came straight to where he was sitting. When he stretched out his hand, it remained perfectly still as though waiting for him to pick it up, and then sat in his palm watching him with its beady little eyes. Brother Mikhaël looked at it pensively but without comment. The incident was an eloquent illustration of what he had just explained about the harmony and trust that was possible between human beings and the natural world.

In addition to the gymnastic exercises, Brother Mikhaël introduced his students to the Paneurythmy, the symbolic circle dance created by Peter Deunov. He also taught basic breathing exercises, recommending that they be practised regularly every morning after the sunrise.

Saying that the 'essence of air' – that which Hindus call prana – is life itself, he explained that deep, conscious breathing improves the circulation thus causing the organs of the body to function better: 'The brain thinks more clearly, the heart and stomach work more efficiently.' While insisting on the beneficial effects of these exercises, however, he was always careful to warn against techniques reputed to promote rapid psychic development. In the years that followed, he often explained that the simplest breathing exercises were the most effective, for they involved no risk, and were beneficial to both physical and psychic health.

*
* *

The brotherhood began to attract more members throughout France following a talk Brother Mikhaël gave in Lyon in June, 1938. The subject of that talk was 'spiritual galvanoplasty', an original concept to which he attached great importance.

Using the example of the technique of electroplating,[29] by which an object is coated with gold or other precious metal, he explained how a pregnant woman had the power to influence the child in her womb:

> If [...] a woman knows the laws of gold-plating and decides to apply them in bringing her child into the world, then, when a seed is implanted in her womb (cathode), she will put a sheet of gold into her mind (anode), the gold of pure, lofty thoughts. The current is switched on and the blood flowing through her body conveys the precious metal to the seed. The child grows, clothed in gold and turns out to be robust, healthy and beautiful, both in physique and in character, and capable of overcoming all difficulties and diseases, all evil influences. [...] Mothers have the potential ability to work miracles for the world: it is they who possess the key to the forces of

---

29. A process in which two electrodes are placed in a solution of metallic salts – gold, silver, or copper, for instance. The anode, which is connected to the positive pole of the battery, is made of the same metal as the metallic ion in the solution. The cathode, which is connected to the negative pole of the battery, is a mould in the shape of a medal, coin, or statuette. When the current is switched on, the metal of the anode is ionised, thus replenishing the supply of metal in the solution, which gradually coats the cathode and produces a gold- or silver-plated object.

creation. Women could transform the whole of humanity within fifty years, if only they applied the methods of spiritual galvanoplasty.[30]

Throughout his life, Brother Mikhaël often spoke of a dream he cherished. This was an unusual scheme which would enable pregnant women to benefit from ideal conditions during the period of gestation. The only problem was, as he said, that this scheme required a government with the wisdom to provide accommodation for expectant mothers in beautifully landscaped estates, with spacious parks, trees, flowers and fountains. There, the mothers-to-be would live surrounded by music and colour, and be taught how to bring exceptional children into the world.

Mikhael had been told by Peter Deunov that he was especially destined to give spiritual assistance to women, and this was one of his principal concerns, but he did not restrict the notion of galvanoplasty to the realm of physical gestation alone. Transposing it on to the spiritual plane, he explained how all human beings can put golden thoughts in their minds and a divine image in their hearts, and be constantly connected to the great central powerhouse from which flows the current of life. He often affirmed that each one of us possessed great innate powers of self-perfection, and that meditation was one of the most effective means of achieving self-mastery and inner harmony.

Within a year after the talk in Lyon, the name of Brother Mikhaël was becoming well known in Paris. His ideas were discussed wherever there was an interest in spirituality, and people were eager to meet him and hear him, for his words spoke to the highest aspirations of the human soul. Listening to him, many discovered a new life. Their whole outlook changed as they began to see that it was within their power, by consciously entertaining thoughts of love and kindness, to improve their health and transform even their features; that it was possible to acquire all the beauty, all the wealth of the spiritual life.

In France at this time, it was fashionable to take an interest in the occult sciences, hypnotism, and extra-sensory phenomena. Spiritual

---

30. June 9th, 1938 (*Spiritual Alchemy*, p. 209f).

groups of every variety abounded in Paris, and desiring to understand better the milieu in which he was called to work, Brother Mikhaël attended some of their meetings. He saw that many of the speakers, whether astrologers, cabbalists, or alchemists, were content to dazzle their audience with a show of sublime ideas while concerning themselves not at all with applying them in practice. Scanning their faces, he looked in vain for a subtle emanation of light, for some hint of radiance, but in spite of their vast erudition, he found no light; some, indeed, seemed to emanate darkness.

As for his own audience, he was well aware that they were as heterogeneous a group as any in Paris. There was a small nucleus of those who considered themselves members of the budding fraternity and who called each other 'brother' and 'sister'. But a much greater number drifted from one spiritual group to another in search of knowledge, with no intention of committing themselves to anything. At one point, more than forty spiritual movements were represented among the audience at Brother Mikhaël's talks. Many, who were interested only in the occult arts or in a particular discipline such as hypnotism and who were not ready to alter their way of life, soon stopped attending the meetings when they realized that his teaching required certain hard choices, certain sacrifices. Finally, among his audience were several women for whom the attraction was not so much the spirituality of Brother Mikhaël as his radiant personality. Stella, who was in a position to observe all this, saw that Brother Mikhaël gave the same love and consideration to all, without regard for age, intelligence, or social rank.

As his reputation grew, he was besieged by invitations to talk, and in the hope of spreading the teaching he often accepted. In this way he found himself in contact with an ever more varied public, but although he attended their receptions he was not taken in by their modes and manners. More than once, when his hosts tried to use him to impress their friends, he managed to thwart their plans in such a way as to open their minds to a higher view of life. His audience did not always understand his message, but it never occurred to him to protect his personal reputation. The truth had to be spoken, and he was not deterred by the possibility that it might offend someone. He knew in advance that he would be criticized, even hated, and more than once he suffered the consequences of his words.

One evening, in a gathering of occultists and writers, a well-known author buttonholed him, and almost incoherent with fury, began to abuse him. A hush fell on the gathering, and Brother Mikhaël, listening in stunned silence, wondered what he could possibly have said or done to merit such venom. All of a sudden he understood: the man had attended one of his talks accompanied by his mistress, who had left him not long after. The subject that evening had been death and immortality, and he had spoken of the true nature of love, the love that vivifies rather than exploiting the loved one. After his talk the young woman had asked several questions about love, and having understood the wrong her lover was doing her by obliging her to practise sexual magic with him, she had decided to break off the relationship. Faced with the wrath of his adversary, Brother Mikhaël responded with humour:

'Believe me, sir, I had no idea that that young lady belonged to you and that you had such rights over her. If I unintentionally freed her from your designs, how can you blame me? The sun has the right to shine and those who have no hats are in danger of sunstroke. You should have worn a hat!'

At this, everyone laughed and the incident was closed, but for years the writer bore a grudge against Brother Mikhaël. And then, one day, he went to see him and told him that life had taught him a lesson and that, in spite of himself, he had come to regret his behaviour toward women.

From time to time, people approached Brother Mikhaël and offered to help him in various ways. A young American diplomat, for instance, who had been struck by his spiritual influence, told him that if he agreed to live in the United States she would put her immense wealth at his disposal and do all she could to make his teaching known in her country. Although Brother Mikhaël sensed that to accept her proposal would be to put himself under an obligation to her, the prospect seemed to offer such advantages that he felt he could not decide without first consulting Peter Deunov. The negative reply he received confirmed his own feeling and he went quietly on with the work he had already begun, devoting himself to instructing those who gathered to hear him speak.

At about this time, he began to be confronted with difficulties similar to those experienced by Peter Deunov in Bulgaria when the religious authorities opposed his work and exiled him from Sofia. With the intention of destroying Brother Mikhaël's reputation, some Church leaders in France launched a campaign of slander against him. It seems that these churchmen feared that their own authority would be undermined, and were distrustful of any spiritual activity not within their jurisdiction. Also, a foreigner who talked publicly and without charge about such topics as reincarnation or man's subtle bodies must be considered suspect.

It was true that Brother Mikhaël never charged for his talks. He had come to France for reasons that were entirely altruistic: all that he did was done without payment. Within the first year, after he had been giving his weekly talks for eight months, he took an unequivocal stand in this respect: speaking to a group of regular listeners, he declared that he would always work without payment, for Peter Deunov had taught him for twenty years without asking a penny in return. 'Above all,' he added, 'God gives freely and we must do the same.' His audience, sensing the absence of all self-interest, respected him all the more.

His attitude in this regard was always firm and unambiguous. Throughout his life he refused to charge for his talks. There were people around him, of course, who contributed voluntarily and anonymously to his expenses, but Brother Mikhaël was always content with very little. Later, when he received offers of property – houses or land – he invariably refused, for he knew the laws of the invisible world; he knew that by accepting a gift from someone he would be binding himself to that person in the future, and this he could not do; he owed it to himself and to his mission to remain free of all such ties. Such strong convictions meant that he continued to be poor. It was only much later that his circumstances would be eased somewhat thanks to the royalties received for his published talks.

*
*　　*

Brother Mikhaël continued to speak of the glorious future that awaited those who persevered in their striving for perfection. He often used to tell them that the highest ideal of every human being was to resemble God, even though that seemed utterly impossible. 'That is what is so wonderful!' he exclaimed, and he gave them a prayer, which he called the formula of the high ideal:

To have a heart as pure as crystal,
A mind as luminous as the sun,
A soul as vast as the universe,
A spirit as powerful as God and one with God.

He knew, of course, that most people needed time before they could assimilate the truths he put before them. Sometimes, he realized, they were overwhelmed when he talked of purity and the beauty of a life given to the pursuit of perfection. As in his youth, he had thought that it would be enough to show them where truth and splendour lay but he was soon disillusioned: some of those whom he had encouraged and instructed found that he asked too much of them.

Brother Mikhaël never tried to pressure people or use his clairvoyance or other psychic gifts to attract or impress. When asked if he was clairvoyant, he denied it, saying that at best he could 'sometimes feel things a little.' He maintained with complete sincerity that he did not possess the gift of seeing prosaic, everyday things. In his view, the only kind of clairvoyance worth having was that which came as an expansion of consciousness, an awareness 'of things that one has never before noticed, things that one has been too fast asleep or too blind to see.' And the best way to obtain this discernment was to follow the path of purity and love of God.

He never encouraged people to consult clairvoyants, for the good reason that to do so was not the best way to transform oneself. He often cautioned against experimenting with the occult, for he had seen too many people who had become psychologically unbalanced by such experimentation. 'As far as I am concerned,' he sometimes said, 'I would like to be clairvoyant, but only so that I might see angels.' Involuntarily, however, he often gave proof of his capacity for seeing things on a very elevated plane. The destinies of those around him held no secrets for him.

His frequent out-of-body experiences had taught him that Plato's 'world of ideas' was a reality, a realm that contained all truth, all the best, purest, and most noble thoughts. He asserted that it was possible for all these ideas, each in its own way and according to its own nature, to materialize as colour, form, movement, scent, or sound. Many clairvoyants who consulted him realized that he could speak of these materializations because he could see them and hear their music. They themselves often had to ask him to explain the meaning of phenomena they had seen but not understood.

On the other hand, people often thanked him for having helped them: 'I was in great difficulty, and you helped me to extricate myself.' Or, 'I was very ill and you healed me.' On these occasions, Brother Mikhaël simply smiled and said that he had nothing to do with it; that he had many friends in the invisible world who sometimes assumed his form and features and did things in his name. Furthermore, according to him, these spirits did many good deeds on earth and were always glad to let someone else take the credit for them.

'It is they who should be thanked,' he added.

Physical illness, as he well knew, is often caused by obstructions on a subtler plane, and it was to those planes that he directed his mental work. One day he went to see a man who was paralysed and who had already consulted the most eminent specialists without success. After sitting by his bed for a long time, listening to him and observing his reactions, Brother Mikhaël told him that he could be cured if he wanted it enough. 'If you believe with all your might, you will be walking in a month or two.'

Then he prescribed certain breathing exercises, meditations, and prayers. The sick man's family heard all this with scepticism, but the invalid followed Brother Mikhaël's instructions to the letter. Gradually the paralysis was defeated and he was able to walk again. One day, referring to the case of this man – who was known to all present – Brother Mikhaël insisted on the importance of guarding against the accumulation of poisons in one's system, of impregnating one's cells with light by means of the fluidic energy of thought, of immersing oneself in the torrent of heavenly life through prayer, meditation, and purification.

For Brother Mikhaël, thought – which is so tremendously potent when it is concentrated – was a natural instrument that he had always used in the service of good. He knew that many difficulties could be avoided if one was in unison with the rhythms of nature, for he had learned to respect the ebb and flow of energy that manifest within all human beings, reflecting the ebb and flow of the great forces of the universe.

16

A Fraternal Community

Brother Mikhaël talked with such love about Master Peter Deunov, about life in the Bulgarian brotherhood, and the marvellous ambience of their camps by the Seven Lakes of Rila, that several of his students planned a visit to Bulgaria in the summer of 1939. He was tempted to accompany them, for the obligation to renew his residential permit every week was a severe constraint and he thought he might more easily obtain a visa from his own country. But Peter Deunov, consulted by letter, advised him not to leave France, warning that he might never be allowed to go back, and twenty-five people left for Bulgaria without him.

One of those who stayed in Paris, André Jahan, invited Brother Mikhaël to join him in a tour of Italy. This brother, who had been a champion automobile racer, had placed himself and his professional skills at Brother Mikhaël's service ever since his first public lecture in 1938. His invitation was tempting and certainly less risky than a return to Bulgaria, but even a brief absence from France involved complications, for Brother Mikhaël needed the authorization of several different departments in order to be guaranteed re-entry into the country. After several attempts, however, the necessary permissions were granted and he set out with Jahan – whom he always spoke of as 'Brother Jean' – and two others.

They visited the length and breadth of Italy, camping out each evening wherever they found themselves. Long before they had planned to leave, however, Brother Mikhaël announced that they would have to cut short their vacation and return to France as quickly as possible, for hostilities would soon break out. Although his companions had seen no sign of imminent danger, they knew better than to discount his warning. Driving as fast as possible, they crossed into France just before the frontier closed on September 3rd, the very day France and England declared war on Germany. Those who had spent three weeks in the mountains of Bulgaria had returned only three days before. World War II had begun.

From then on, life was very different for the people of France, and when the enemy occupied Paris a few months later, many members of the brotherhood moved to the country. During 1940, Brother Mikhaël gave only a few talks; he could do little more than keep in touch with the many small groups of his regular listeners who met to meditate together. It was only in the second year of the Occupation that a few fraternal activities began again in a very discreet manner. Strict precautions were necessary, for public gatherings were forbidden and meetings had to be held in the private homes of the members. Moreover, Brother Mikhaël's situation was precarious, for most foreigners were being sent back to their homelands. To avoid being expelled from the country, he had to be careful not to forget to renew his papers well in advance.

In 1942, the constraints of the Occupation became more and more burdensome. Food supplies were running low and meals were reduced to the barest essentials. Severe regulations restricted the movements of French citizens and it became dangerous to gather even in small groups. In view of this, some of the members of the brotherhood agreed to rent a house of their own in which they could come together without drawing undue attention to themselves.

A suitable villa was found in Sèvres, and several people moved in with Brother Mikhaël. A loft with large windows was converted into a meeting room in which they could meditate at sunrise without being disturbed. Brother Mikhaël chose a small room for himself, in which he arranged his few belongings with his customary attention to detail. He continued to take care of his own needs and, as Stella Bellemin wrote later:

> He never allowed himself to be served in any way, even though the group could well have relieved him of certain chores. He made his

own bed and tidied and cleaned his room. He also took great care of his own clothes.[31]

His visitors were often surprised to find, instead of the ascetic cell they had expected, a bright room decorated in beautiful colours and enlivened by several crystals that caught the light of the sun. As they often arrived fatigued from their journey on the crowded Métro, Brother Mikhaël urged them to sit and relax for a few minutes in silence. Some were ill at ease to rest in his presence, but afterwards they were grateful to him for his exquisite sense of hospitality, more concerned with their deep needs than with conventional etiquette. The personal attention he gave to each guest, and the frankness and sensitivity with which he responded to them soon established an authentic spiritual exchange. At the time, one of the brothers wrote:

> Within a few minutes of meeting him, I was weighed up, illuminated, encouraged, and invigorated to the depths of my being. I was completely transparent to him, […] and when, in a few words and with the utmost tact, he sketched a portrait of my character, he gave me exactly the nourishment and the medicine I needed.[32]

From that year on, Brother Mikhaël gave a short talk for the residents almost every day after the sunrise, in addition to his regular weekly talks in the evening.

*
*   *

Throughout his life Brother Mikhaël stressed the importance of musical vibrations and their subtle influence. He often said that it was not so much the intellectual understanding of music that was important but the sensations it generated: 'Do we understand the song of birds, or waterfalls, or the wind in the branches? No, but we are captivated and enchanted by them.'

Music accompanied all the activities of the brotherhood, and Peter Deunov's songs had a special place of honour. Brother Mikhaël insisted on the value of four-part choral singing, because of the

---

31. Svezda, *op. cit.*, p. 55 (Our translation).
32. A. Laumonier, preface to Michaël Ivanoff, *Les Sept Lacs de Rila.* (Our translation)

equilibrium created by a mixed choir, but more importantly, because the four voices represent the four elements: 'Everything in nature sings with its own voice.' Years later, speaking of those early days, one of the musicians in the group said:

> It was impossible to associate with him without feeling called upon to outdo oneself, to give the best of oneself. Things that had been ordinary and routine became a challenge, an occasion for reflection and self-transformation. Under his guidance, professional musicians were urged to put aside all their erudition, all the conventions they had learned. If they allowed themselves to be guided by him, it was not long before they realized that they had begun to attain to levels of perception previously undreamed of.

For Brother Mikhaël, music was intimately associated with light and the pure colours of the spectrum; each note had its colour and its symbolism, and light was a great river of energy in which dwelt the archangels. During the brotherhood meetings, the more sensitive among them often perceived colours, perfume, or music, and sensed the presence of the angelic beings attracted by the spiritual work. Such moments gave them a deeply beneficial sense of joy and tranquillity, a keener awareness of the reality of their spiritual family.

One of Brother Mikhaël's favourite themes, which often recurred in his talks, was that of brotherhood. He used to paint a glowing picture of a life of sharing and harmony in which all would open themselves to love. A fraternal centre, he said, should be a veritable focal point of light.

When he talked of brotherhood, he was not referring principally to a gathering of human beings on earth, but rather to the great family of those of all eras who seek the light, who have embraced a philosophy of love and justice, and who belong, consciously or not, to one great universal family. As time went on he often talked about the great Brotherhood that exists on a higher plane:

> The Universal White Brotherhood is a power which extends to the limits of the solar system and beyond. You must not make the mistake of judging it by the brotherhood that exists here, on earth: a handful of men and women who are not always very wise or

enlightened. The true Universal White Brotherhood on high is composed of all the most highly evolved beings that have ever existed, whereas we are no more than a reflection, a 'branch', if you like, which exists to carry out their plans and benefit from their light and support. But the brotherhood on earth must become, more and more, a faithful reflection of the one on high.[33]

In Brother Mikhaël's eyes, the name of his own brotherhood – Universal White Brotherhood – was a marvellous reminder of a higher reality that could be actualized by human beings on earth. The name – in which the word 'white' had no racial connotation – inspired him because it evoked the energy of the white light that illuminates the whole of creation.

Brother Mikhaël's enthusiastic temperament led him to make all kinds of plans for the future. Not all materialized, but he was an indefatigable sower of ideas and impossible dreams which stimulated and invigorated his students. Already during his second year in France, he talked of his dream of a piece of land where all those who wanted to live together in a fraternal spirit could have a small house of their own.

His idea of a true brotherhood respected the differences between people; he did not encourage them to live permanently together in one house. The community he envisaged was more in the nature of a village in which all the members would have their own house or apartment. Places would be set aside for the Paneurythmy, a library, and an educational institute; there would be concerts, dancing, films, and studios for artists and craftsmen.

With infectious enthusiasm he talked of the beauty of a spiritual family in which the members came together at certain times of the day but in which the individuals were free to go about their own business, to stay or leave as they wished.

Never, either then or later, did he ask them to pool their financial resources; never did he attempt to control their private lives. He used to say, rather, that in the ideal family no one lays down the law, because where love reigns all is harmony. Over the years he often affirmed his faith in the coming of the kingdom of God on earth,

---

33. December 25th, 1963 (*La pédagogie initiatique III*, p. 250). Our translation.

saying that it would be a world of love, joy, and song; a world in which all human beings loved and respected each other, in which none would need to molest others to satisfy their own cravings.

During the war, he had an inspiring experience which suggested an image of a truly fraternal world. Returning home late one evening, he missed the last train. The ticket offices were closed; everyone was at home behind closed and bolted shutters, and it was growing colder. Not knowing what else to do, he sat down on a bench and began to pray.

After a few minutes he heard the rhythmic tread of a German patrol, and hoping that he would not be arrested for being out after curfew, he stood up, walked briskly toward them and explained his predicament. To his surprise, they escorted him very courteously to a mansion in which there were a number of officers, and gave him a bed for the night. Lying in the dark, unable to sleep, he could hardly believe the strange adventure that had led him to be offered hospitality by the enemy. The next morning he was invited to breakfast with them. No one asked him what he was doing there, and when he was ready to leave, one of the officers walked with him to the station.

Speaking of this incident years later, he said:

Just think. If all men and women lived in brotherhood and love, you could move freely about the world and be welcomed with open arms in every country as members of the same family.[34]

In his view, the age of Aquarius would be an era in which fraternal communities thrived in the world, for Aquarius is synonymous with universality. But in order to adapt themselves and respond to the subtle vibrations of Aquarius, human beings will have to perfect and refine their intuition, become more spiritual, and make room in their hearts for the love of others.

He dreamed not only of a fraternal centre near Paris, but, in his desire to share with the members of the brotherhood in France the joys he had known at Rila, he spoke of spending several months in the mountains with the whole group. He often spoke of the

---

34. March 6th, 1966 (*A New Dawn: Society and Politics in the Light of Initiatic Science II, p. 116*)

mountains, of the wealth to be found in them, of the pure, luminous spirits that dwell in their heights and with whom it is possible to communicate. At the same time, he was well aware that most people were not ready to live in a spirit of true sharing. Even the few people who lived together in the villa, who had chosen an ideal of brotherhood and were fully supportive of Brother Mikhaël's ideas, found it difficult to adapt to each other without conflict. In April 1942, he told them frankly that they were not ready for a truly fraternal community.

'Many communities have sprung up in the West,' he added, 'but many have been unsuccessful, because they were founded on self-interest or commercial and financial gain, instead of being founded on love and wisdom. They did not live in a spirit of humility.'

It would be another five years before the members of the brotherhood finally achieved something more substantial, for Brother Mikhaël's enthusiasm for a fraternal community was accompanied by a strong sense of reality.

In the meantime, they rented this first villa until 1947 and the residents did their best to live as a family, taking all their meals in common. Brother Mikhaël had always continued to practise what he called Hrani-yoga (from the Bulgarian word meaning 'to eat'). For him, food was a love-letter from God. It is capable, he explained, of preserving life and restoring energies, for, in addition to its physical properties, food contains precious etheric properties and it is important to be aware of this when eating, for the mouth is a marvellous 'laboratory' which can assimilate even the subtlest elements. For this reason he asked the residents to take their meals in silence in order to facilitate this conscious work, adding that noise, discussion and arguments during meals are harmful to health.

He was asking them, in fact, to practise a discipline, a form of yoga: learning to avoid any noise while eating is an extraordinarily effective way of acquiring true self-mastery. Explaining that the control of small things is conducive to inner harmony and a first step toward the control of larger things, he asked them to refrain from even the slightest sound with the dishes or the cutlery. Such attentiveness was so different from their habitual behaviour that he had great difficulty in obtaining it. He had to keep insisting on the need for care and respect, reminding them repeatedly that true silence is both uplifting and nourishing: 'You must learn to remain completely silent, without moving or even rustling a piece of paper.'

During this time of war and daily atrocities, Brother Mikhaël continued to speak about the purity that is indispensable for all great achievements, about the sun and the beneficial influence of its rays, about the spiritual intuition of the human heart, about music, and about the birth of a new humanity. He spoke also of prayer, by which one is united with the great current that rises ceaselessly from the hearts of all believers. For him, true prayer was vibrant and alive, free from routine:

> If you always recite the same prayer you will put yourself to sleep and your prayer will be without effect. A formula can be helpful to someone who really does not know how to pray, but I much prefer a prayer that is unrehearsed, one that flows spontaneously. When you ask a favour of a friend, you speak simply and naturally, without affectation. This is how you should pray.[35]

*
*   *

Despite the war Brother Mikhaël did not talk about politics more than before. It was not his role to do so. He spoke, rather, about the love that alone was capable of resolving all conflicts, and explained how to transform one's own nature so as to contribute to the

---

35. Unpublished talk, June 7th, 1942.

metamorphosis of the world. In his view, if war was ravaging Europe, it was because it existed in the minds of men and women. People were killing each other because they did not realize that they were all members of the same divine family.

Sensing the anguish that gripped most of his brothers and sisters during the air raids, he gave them methods to help them to control their emotions. On several occasions he spoke about fear from the initiatic point of view, saying that it was the greatest enemy of every human being. When, after one of his talks, a woman told him that she was always paralysed by terror during the air raids, he told her what she could do to overcome her instinctive reactions: 'Breathe deeply and unite yourself to God; in this way you will be in command of your cells.'

He himself had always seen silence and immobility as a means to self-mastery in moments of difficulty. Speaking to the residents of the villa on April 19th, 1944, he related that he had often been walking home from the railway station when the anti-aircraft guns began firing. In spite of the danger, he always continued calmly walking. Then one day when the thunder of the guns seemed louder than usual he suddenly felt impelled to hurry and began to run, hoping to avoid the shrapnel falling all around him. The faster he ran, the more frightened he felt, until, thoroughly annoyed with himself, he stopped and with great effort, managed to compose himself. In conclusion, he noted:

'That experience taught me that by running I had triggered the fear that lies dormant in every human being. You must not think that those whom we call brave do not know fear. In the course of their evolution, all human beings have to experience fear, it is a 'spirit' that has to be defeated. The only solution is to grow in love of God and work with the will and with purity and justice; in this way fear will disappear. The first thing to do is establish this link with God. This has a calming effect. One's inner light and self-control grow stronger, and all within becomes marvellously luminous.'

Brother Mikhaël did not hesitate to tell adolescents as well as adults to face up to fear. On one occasion he was awoken by the telephone at three o'clock in the morning and heard the voice of a friend who sometimes sheltered people wanted by the German police:

'Brother Mikhaël,' she said; 'the Gestapo hammered on my door a few minutes ago and woke me up. When I opened the door they demanded that I give up a young Jewish boy who is hiding here. His whole family has been arrested. I managed to persuade them to wait outside, and I have told the boy not to try to flee. I promised that you would get him out of this predicament. Can you do something?'

Brother Mikhaël, deciding to call on the co-operation of the boy himself, sent him this message:

'Don't hide. Keep calm and speak politely to the officers and you will come to no harm.'

To everyone's amazement, the boy had the courage to obey these terrifying instructions and was not arrested. The Gestapo questioned him and then told him to go back to bed. It was as though they had suddenly forgotten the purpose of their visit – or perhaps the boy's confident attitude reassured them. Brother Mikhaël, for his part, offered no explanation. If people were astonished by his methods, it was because they did not realize that he was aware of certain factors that were imperceptible to others. Without regard for his own safety, he continued to give spiritual help to all those who appealed to him in danger.

The summer of 1944 saw the last months of the war in France. In Paris it was common knowledge that Hitler had ordered the commanding officer to destroy the city. Large areas could be blown up at any moment, for it had been systematically mined, and immense quantities of explosives were stored in the tunnels of the Métro. While gun battles erupted in the streets, snipers fired from the rooftops and the few pedestrians hurried about their business as fast as they could. In August, during the chaotic week before Paris was liberated, Brother Mikhaël left Sèvres without explanation and went into the city, where he stayed for several days. At one point he found himself on Lafayette Street, as bullets ricocheted off buildings. Several people were gunned down before his eyes, while he was struck by flying fragments of stone.

In spite of the danger, he remained in Paris, continuing the special work that had brought him there. In Sèvres, the members of the brotherhood could not help wondering what his strange behaviour signified. Experience had taught them that he never did anything of consequence without an indication from above. They knew also that he continually united himself mentally with all those who worked with the forces of light, joining his prayer to theirs to create a spiritual force of great potency. When Paris was liberated a few days later, they understood that Brother Mikhaël had thought it necessary to be at the centre of the city for this spiritual work. His prayer united to that of all believers throughout the world had certainly contributed to bringing about the end of hostilities. Often in the course of his life he did such things which seemed mysterious to those around him, but which were quite natural to him. In his single-minded desire to realize the kingdom of God on earth he worked untiringly with light, acting, as it were, as a prism which receives the light of the sun and refracts it in life-giving rays of colour.

Once the war was over, the rhythm of life gradually returned to normal and in the brotherhood, as in society as a whole, people began to breathe freely again. Toward the end of 1945 the French brotherhood was officially informed that Peter Deunov had died on December 27th, 1944. The news had not reached them earlier, owing to the difficult circumstances that had interrupted postal services between certain countries toward the end of hostilities.

When he received the news, Brother Mikhaël thought back to the previous December, remembering his premonitory dreams about Peter Deunov's death, which, at the time, he had not wanted to believe. Perhaps he had been unable to recognize the truth of these messages because Peter Deunov was too dear to him, for in spite of them, he had continued to make plans to bring him to France. This separation was a great personal distress for Mikhaël. It also marked the beginning of the anticipated period of tribulation.

17

The Conspiracy

Peter Deunov had not misread the signs when, in 1918, he had told
Mikhaël that the powers of darkness would put obstacles in his path
'in the twenty-sixth year.' The prophecy came true toward the end of
the war, when dark forces began to conspire against Brother Mikhaël
in an effort to destroy him and annihilate his work. In June 1944,
recognizing the imminent danger, he urged the members of the
brotherhood to be attentive to what was going on around them,
not to be swayed by the tactics of those who served the powers of
darkness, and to ally themselves constantly with all those who
worked with 'white forces', the forces of light. For Brother Mikhaël,
the four-year period from 1944 to 1948 was fraught with attacks,
temptations, and ordeals calculated to bring down even the greatest
spiritual master, saint, or prophet.

One such attack occurred in his native land after the death of
Peter Deunov. In an attempt to counteract any influence he might
still have, some members of the Bulgarian brotherhood held public
meetings in various towns and villages in a deliberate attempt to
discredit him. Even Boyan Boëv, Peter Deunov's secretary, weakened
by poor health, was drawn into this campaign and denied having
written to Mikhaël about his mission at the dictation of the Master.
A little later, however, he regretted this injustice, and admitted that
he had lied.

In spite of the slander, no one could erase the deep impression
Mikhaël had left on his friends, on the members of the brotherhood,
on his pupils and their parents. In 1945 and 1946, he received many
letters from compatriots, assuring him of their esteem. The letters

that touched him most profoundly were from those who had been with Peter Deunov shortly before his death. The Master had talked to them about 'the great white brotherhood on high,' which must be materialized on earth, and had added: 'It is Mikhaël who will realize it on earth.' He had also said: 'Mikhaël will experience great ordeals, but afterwards he will go further than I.'

Within the French brotherhood, a few of those who had stayed with the Bulgarian brothers and sisters at Rila in 1939 reproached Mikhaël for giving his own interpretation of the teaching. They did not know – or did not want to admit – that Peter Deunov himself had written to him to endorse the work he was doing in France.

But the most perfidious attacks came from some of the secret societies in Paris, which attempted to bribe him and gain control of his brotherhood, for it was now a factor to be reckoned with. Brother Mikhaël's stature and spiritual influence were such that more than one of the occult organizations in Paris sought to use him in order to enhance their own power. Their leaders' tactics were shrewd: they praised him publicly, declared that he was uniquely capable of assuming great responsibilities in the world, and offered him wealth and renown if he agreed to fuse his brotherhood with their own association.

Brother Mikhaël refused. Speaking about one of these groups later, he said that although they had retained certain aspects of ancient Egyptian initiation their goal today was domination, and that when he had 'had the misfortune to refuse to join them' he had brought terrible reprisals upon himself.

In addition to these powerful adversaries, there were those who, seeing him in the light of their own narrow interests, offered him expensive gifts or money to use magic for their personal benefit. At this period he also had to contend with frequent difficulties caused by women who fell in love with him. One of them, confident of success, announced that she was going to marry him. When she saw that this was not to be, she became one of his most implacable enemies, and even went to the immigration authorities to persuade them not to issue the identity card he was due to receive. Another admirer offered him her estates and her immense fortune in return for marriage. Brother Mikhaël brushed aside all these offers as unrealistic fantasies. He knew very well that any benefits he might gain from such associations with the rich of this world would cost him his freedom. As might have been expected, however, many of those whose offers were rejected turned against him and bore him a lasting grudge. Some of them were to play a key role in the ordeal that was being prepared for him.

As though all this were not enough, he was once again being harassed by police inspectors, who questioned him about his reasons for staying in France. Fortunately, the officers of the local precinct knew perfectly well what kind of work he was doing, for they had interviewed him regularly during the past eight years – each time he had applied for a renewal of his residential permit – and had great respect for him. During the war, however, the alliance between King Boris of Bulgaria and Hitler had often led to Bulgarian nationals in France being suspected of espionage. Most of them had been expelled from France immediately after the war, but Brother Mikhaël, having refused to return to his homeland, had acquired official status as a stateless person and could not legally be expelled. For a time he was under close surveillance by secret service agents who managed to infiltrate the brotherhood meetings. This surveillance ceased when they failed to find the slightest evidence to justify their suspicions.

*
* *

Nineteen forty-six saw an influx of new members into the brotherhood from the secret societies that had failed to win over Brother Mikhaël. Their goal was to infiltrate and undermine the brotherhood from within. In particular, they hoped to detect something in his behaviour toward women that could be used against him. Their efforts were in vain, for his conduct toward women was so transparent and impartial that they could find no hint of impropriety. Beauty and purity were an inspiration to him, and his attitude had not changed since his youth. For want of anything more substantial, these people spread increasingly insidious and corrosive innuendoes impugning his moral integrity, and the climate of suspicion and conflict in the fraternity made it difficult to see exactly what was going on.

Brother Mikhaël knew that he could not avoid the ordeals that were coming closer, and recalled one in particular that had been foretold by Peter Deunov: 'Brother Mikhaël will know great misfortunes, particularly through women.' He was not blind to the prevailing rumours and deceitful manoeuvres, but he did not allow them to distract him. He welcomed all who came and did his best to enlighten them, for he always hoped to leave in their souls some trace of beauty and harmony. In fact, throughout this trying period, he continued his teaching, excluding no one and taking little heed of any possible repercussions. At the same time, although his tendency was to 'invite the whole world to dine at the table of the brotherhood,' he still warned his regular students not to bring to his talks people who had no notion of spirituality or who were looking for miracles or ready-made solutions to their problems.

He remained present to each person and as attentive as ever to their needs. He seemed to be suffused with light and inspiration as never before. Hoping to kindle enthusiasm in the heart of each member of his audience, he spoke of the energy of the sun, of sacred fire, of the music that awakens the chakras, of true and universal brotherhood.

In April 1946, however, seeing that the climate was unchanged, he took a very serious decision. Speaking in a tone that revealed deep sadness, he began by reminding them that it was in response to their own insistence and in the desire to be useful to them that he had attempted to be their instructor. And he added:

'My failure to convince you to put this teaching into practice shows me that it was very presumptuous of me to undertake the task. Henceforth I abandon my role as your guide.'

He said no more, and the members of the brotherhood were aghast. They had recognized long since that Brother Mikhaël was a true spiritual master and they had no desire to lose him. A ripple went through the group, as one after the other stood up and assured him that they sincerely wanted to live in harmony. Several asked him explicitly in the name of the group to be their spiritual master. Even those who later betrayed him and bore false witness against him joined in the general consensus. Stella, who knew who they were, heard them asserting:

'Brother Mikhaël, you are truly a Master! We shall always be faithful to you whatever comes.'

At that moment, there was a keen awareness in the group of the gravity of a spiritual commitment and the demands it made on them. But Brother Mikhaël, although deeply moved, refused to take advantage of the general emotion. Yes, he would remain their teacher, but on condition that he continued to be simply their 'Brother Mikhaël'.

In spite of his insistence, from that day on those whom he called his brothers and sisters considered themselves his disciples. The evidence of their eyes was convincing: his purity and magnanimity, the integrity and fortitude with which he faced his ordeals, and the clarity with which he taught only served to confirm their high opinion of him. Stella in particular defended him faithfully and continued to believe in him in the face of all opposition. She could never forget that he had been for her 'the occasion of a prodigious expansion of consciousness.' Several years later she would write that he had guided her 'as a sighted person guides one who is blind, to help her to awaken her higher sense of sight.'

That episode marked an important phase in the life of the brotherhood. Something powerful had taken shape: a subtle force, a collective entity now surrounded and protected the members, but this entity needed to be nurtured and reinforced. Brother Mikhaël's attitude did not change; he continued to speak to them with the same simplicity. Despite the agitation surrounding his person and the sadness he sometimes felt, his visitors always found him serene. He continued to insist that they should always verify what he put before them. On April 25th, he told them:

'Do not bother your heads about whether I am an initiate or not; try simply to check the authenticity of what I give you. Before eating, make sure that this 'food' is pure, unadulterated, and true.'

In the weeks that followed several people wrote to him to express their admiration and respect. But he, as always, kept his sights fixed on a higher world so as not to forget his own lowliness and succumb to the temptation of pride. Referring to these letters one day in June, he made it quite clear that he had no desire to be praised, that he was content to be an insignificant servant. He added: 'Focus all your attention on the teaching. It is the teaching that has every virtue.'

*
* *

Mikhaël's tenth year in France was to be one of the most difficult in the history of the brotherhood. Nineteen forty-seven would see both the realization of their dream of a fraternal community and the tornado that would sweep Brother Mikhaël toward one of the most painful ordeals of his life. For his part, although he sensed the approaching storm, he did nothing to forestall its fury. In his New Year message to the brotherhood, he wrote:

'Nineteen forty-seven is poised before us, as mysterious, dark, and impenetrable as the sphinx of ancient Egypt which waited to be conquered by the response of wise and enlightened disciples before opening its treasure-house and dispensing its blessings.'

That year, he faced two opposing tendencies in the way he was perceived by others; the one glorified him, the other did everything possible to defile him. The first manifested itself when a film producer, wishing to make a documentary about the brotherhood, was given permission to film everyday life at the villa. The shooting took place in an atmosphere of great cordiality. Some time later, the film was shown in the cinemas of Paris following the newsreels, and Brother Mikhaël went with a few friends to watch it. The photography was superb and the editing was done with great subtlety. The film ended on a powerful note: it showed Brother Mikhaël as an immense figure rising with the sun above the terrestrial globe. Paradoxically, just before being publicly debased and humiliated, he was being glorified in the most extraordinary way. This film led to a radio interview during which he spoke about Peter Deunov, Bulgaria, and the fraternal camps at Rila.

The contrary tendency was expressed in a fierce attack published in a major newspaper. Some journalists who had been allowed to visit the villa wrote an article which attempted to discredit him and ridicule the brotherhood. On April 24th, 1947, aware of the distress and indignation of the members, Brother Mikhaël told them that instead of being angry, they should be joyful about all they had received; above all, that they must be prepared for the difficulties to come. He added: 'Public opinion will be divided about us.'

During the following months he took advantage of several occasions to instil greater energy and ardour into his followers. On May 1st, he spoke to them about the approaching feast of Wesak. He explained that each year on the day of the full moon of May, great numbers of initiates gather in the Himalayas, some physically, others in their astral bodies, to commemorate the birth of the Buddha and work together with the forces of white light.

'In the course of this ceremony, which falls on Monday, May 5th, these 'white brothers', linking themselves by means of potent invocations to the celestial hierarchies, will work to bring cosmic forces to earth and send waves and vibrations of the highest spirituality throughout space for the benefit of humanity.'

He urged them to forgive their enemies and to take special care, during these days of preparation, to avoid all negative thoughts. Knowing that many of them were afraid of the intrigues going on in the background, he added:

'If you do not light your lamps no one will see you. We are all afloat on the ocean of life, and our ship is often in danger of sinking in the terrible storms that threaten it. If we want to be saved we must be capable of sending luminous signals heavenward. Then someone will come and rescue us.'

All those who were able to do so prepared themselves by meditation for the celebration of Wesak. Four days later, Brother Mikhaël spoke to them about inner peace and described how a dove had come to him while he was meditating, settling on his left hand. 'It is because of that dove,' he added, 'that I tell you now not to grovel, but to become like birds.'

In the spring of 1947, in the midst of all the difficulties the brotherhood was experiencing, the members realized a cherished dream. After much searching, they at last found a house on the outskirts of Paris which seemed to suit their needs, and they decided to buy it, rather than continuing to rent their present house. The new house was at the top of the rue du Belvédère de la Ronce above Sèvres, on a hectare of land bordering the forest. Around it was the countryside dotted with occasional houses and clusters of trees. In the distance, the dim forms of the Paris skyline could just be seen.

The brotherhood took possession of the new property that spring, but a tremendous effort of co-operation was needed to make it habitable. The house had not been lived in for eighteen years and was in a state of extreme disrepair. Several weeks of back-breaking labour were needed to bring order out of chaos, but the brothers and sisters of this great family toiled together in a spirit of joy which often expressed itself in a burst of song.

Brother Mikhaël, in gray overalls and a beret, was everywhere at once, helping with all the different tasks. He had lost none of his practical common sense and had not forgotten the lessons learned in Bulgaria when he had worked as carpenter, brick-layer, and house-painter. When he took a paintbrush from someone's hand to demonstrate a better way to use it, it was because he knew not only how each tool should be handled, but also its hidden symbolism.

By June, the greater part of the work was done: the grounds had been cleared and levelled and the house was ready for occupation. The ground floor was arranged as one large meeting room. In one corner of the top floor under the mansard roof, Brother Mikhaël chose a tiny bedroom with a window looking out to the east, and a sitting-room next to it. On one wall of this room he hung a magnificent portrait of Peter Deunov, and it was here that he received his visitors.

At last, the dream of a good number of people who had longed to share a home in which they could live together in harmony was to be realized, and their mood was euphoric. In spite of the numerous difficulties they were full of hope. The shared work of renovation had given them the feeling that they were building a better future together. Even the threatened storm seemed to be receding.

Once the work was completed, Brother Mikhaël consecrated the property and gave it the name that Peter Deunov had chosen for the brotherhood centre in Bulgaria: Izgrev. All the members were invited to come for the sunrise whenever they were free, and on Sundays they gathered to hear Brother Mikhaël speak, perform the gymnastic exercises and dance the Paneurythmy to the accompaniment of flute and violin.

*
*   *

This harmonious interlude was short-lived, for Brother Mikhaël's enemies, who had tried in vain to find something blameworthy in his attitude toward women, multiplied the rumours and innuendoes. Those who considered themselves his disciples felt as though they were being torn apart by the conflicts and slanderous rumours; they could not help but be influenced by the climate of anxiety. In June, Brother Mikhaël told them:

'I am not asking you to believe me or follow me blindly. No. Open your eyes and you will see the difference between us and the others. Trust your intuition. Set it free; allow it to function; release it from impurities and from its old habits.'

At all times there was this constant preoccupation to liberate people so that they might attain their true stature. His knowledge of human nature told him that an ideal of perfection could never be imposed on anybody. He had never attempted to attract the masses; on the contrary, he excelled at screening his audience. In his talks, he sometimes began by discussing a seemingly random variety of subjects, knowing that those who were only superficially interested would not have the patience to stay to the end. Then, once they had left the room, he gathered up the threads of these different subjects and wove them into a coherent whole, a complete and well-balanced picture.

One day, noting the arrogant attitude of four individuals who had just come into the room, he introduced one subject after another, skimming superficially over each one, until at last the four men stood up and went out, remarking audibly on the insignificance of the speaker. They had discovered that Brother Mikhaël 'was not dangerous.' As soon as they had left, however, bringing all the apparently irrelevant elements together, he drew a masterly conclusion.

In July, most of his regular students left Paris and went their separate ways for the vacations. There would be no more talks from Brother Mikhaël for three months, and when the brotherhood gathered again at the end of September the climate would be very different. Brother Mikhaël, who spent part of his nights in prayer, defending himself against the various attacks aimed at him – which even included black magic – decided to go away for a rest. He left for the Alps with one of the brothers.

In the mountains one day, he stretched out on the ground to rest and in a half-sleep had the first of four visions that would come to him within the year, symbolic visions of trial by way of the four elements. He saw himself standing on a mountain that was crumbling beneath his feet. Although the ground was disappearing at dizzying speed, he sensed that he would not fall, and began to leap lightly from rock to rock. Afterwards, he understood that the time of his great tests had begun; this vision heralded the ordeal of earth, designed to test steadfastness of will.

In the meantime, having readied themselves for the attack, his enemies set out to break him. The man who served as catalyst to the alliance of destructive forces ranged against him was a mysterious individual who had been living in Paris for some time, but who professed to hail from Tibet. The names he claimed as his own were those of the most prestigious of high initiates: Sherenzi Lind, Kut Humi, and many more. His followers called him King of the World. It was learned later that he was an international spy who had come from Cuba, but for a long time he succeeded in hoodwinking many people by means of his considerable occult powers. As far as is known, neither 'the Cuban's' true nationality nor his name were ever divulged.

This unscrupulous individual was a formidable hypnotist who used his powers to influence many people and force them to do his will. His aim – which came to light only later – was to gain ascendancy over the different spiritual movements and use them as a cover for his clandestine activities. Being determined to take over the brotherhood, he used every means in his power to subjugate Brother Mikhaël and make him serve him. His first step was to attempt to win the trust of the members of the brotherhood by speaking of their spiritual guide in highly flattering terms.

As long as he had not met the man, Brother Mikhaël avoided speaking about him. As soon as he met him in the flesh, however, he recognized him for what he was, and in the weeks that followed realized that he had acquired a dangerous enemy. But even then, faithful to his method of leaving people to verify a situation for themselves before forming an opinion, he spoke of him several times in terms which left his listeners free to make up their own minds.

Those who sensed the falsity of the Cuban's claims found this magnanimous attitude unwise. For a long time, some even believed that he had managed to deceive Brother Mikhaël. One day however, Brother Mikhaël took three members of the brotherhood into his confidence and disclosed his true perception of the self-styled 'King of the World.' Did he do this deliberately, acting on the intuition that his destiny would be accomplished through this man? However that may be, one of the three betrayed his confidence.

When his enemy learned that he had been unmasked, he launched his attack – although he still endeavoured to remain in Brother Mikhaël's good graces. His first step was to win over a Bulgarian who nursed a long-standing grievance against Brother Mikhaël, and to invite to his home some of the women who had a grudge against him. Fascinated by his flamboyant personality and rough-hewn, dominating visage, most of those who accepted his invitations were easily persuaded to let him hypnotize them, and several of them became his docile instruments, ready to do whatever he asked.

*
* *

In September the storm clouds broke. Witnesses in the pay of his enemies falsely accused Brother Mikhaël of raping forty women. The major newspapers published these allegations in front-page headlines, depicting him as the most debauched satyr of all times and accusing him of conducting orgies in the forest with his disciples. No words were too abusive to be applied to him. Immediately, Izgrev was besieged by journalists, many of whom, armed with cameras, climbed the trees outside the walls, trying to spy on Brother Mikhaël's every movement. Complete strangers threatened and insulted him.

On September 28th, 1947, Brother Mikhaël spoke to a hushed gathering. His usual audience was there in force, a heterogeneous group which included members of the brotherhood, occasional visitors, members of other movements who were still drawn by his radiance, and the enemies who had already secretly betrayed him. After a brief meditation he spoke of the attacks a man in his position might be subject to: the poisoned arrows, the destructive vibrations, the tornadoes that could eventually bring him down. Besieged by so many negative forces, he was obliged to strive like a tightrope-walker to keep his balance. 'There are very few to help me,' he said, adding that he knew the identity of those who had joined the brotherhood with the intention of causing his downfall. After alluding to the improbable accusations made against him, he added that he was willing to continue his work:

'If you want me to go on talking to you, to go on encouraging you and giving you joys of a higher kind, I will stay with you. But you may be sure of one thing: wherever I may be, in prison or elsewhere, I shall always be ready to praise God.'

Then, reminding them that it was Peter Deunov who had sent him to France, he invited those whom he knew to be his enemies to speak out openly in front of the group. Seeing that they were too ill at ease to speak, he said:

'You say nothing. You accept that I should remain with you... I ask you then to help me by praying for me tonight. You need the support of others to evolve. So do I.'

At this, trying not to draw attention to themselves, those who had betrayed him slipped from the room. By then, however, everyone knew who they were, and they would never come back. After a brief pause, Brother Mikhaël concluded the meeting by saying that they were all free to leave him, but that it was in the teaching that they would find all spiritual riches.

At Izgrev and in the other groups, most of the members passed the night in prayer. Knowing Brother Mikhaël's purity and integrity, they realized that the accusations levelled against him must cause him the greatest possible moral torture.

During the next months Brother Mikhaël gave few talks. He was often burdened by a great sadness caused not so much by what he was going through as by the fact that so few human beings are capable of committing themselves to a high ideal. This sadness was palpable in the two or three talks he gave in October. At the same time, seeking to prepare his disciples for the trials to come, he repeated that they would winnow out some of their number, and urged them to cultivate discernment, and work with diligence to purify themselves.

That autumn was a waking nightmare for the brotherhood. The Cuban continued his work in concert with Brother Mikhaël's other enemies who had assembled the false proofs they needed to get him arrested. Since Brother Mikhaël had proved to be incorruptible, it did not really matter what pretext was invoked; what mattered was to get rid of him and take over his movement. From several women, who had been transformed through repeated hypnosis into their docile tools, they obtained signed declarations charging that Brother Mikhaël had seduced them. Some of these women seem to have been infected by a current of hysteria, and sincerely believed that the Cuban spy was the Master of the world. Others had never forgiven Brother Mikhaël for resisting their charms. Still others, who had succumbed to the offer of money or had been set up in business, signed because they were in no position to refuse. It must be said, however, that most of the women in the brotherhood took no part in these machinations.

One day, Brother Mikhaël was given another warning, even more important and significant than his initial vision. While meditating in his room he had the second symbolic vision of ordeal by the four elements. He saw himself suspended over a pool of dark water swarming with crocodiles which were trying to seize and devour him. The waters rose, the earth disappeared under terrible floods, and he saw many of his brothers and sisters drowning.

After this vision he understood that the dark water symbolized hatred and evil, and he knew that his enemies were determined to crush him. As he would say later, it is when one is subjected to ordeal by water that one finds out 'if one is capable of withstanding feelings of hatred.'

There was no hatred in Brother Mikhaël's heart. He continued to work mentally for his enemies, picturing them bathed in light. One day, he confided to his disciples that his dearest wish was to win the heart of his most bitter enemy so that he could help him, even at the risk of incurring the condemnation of the world. He raised no objection, therefore, when the Cuban, seeking to benefit from Brother Mikhaël's reputation, spoke of him as one of his closest associates.

Later that autumn he agreed to participate with the brotherhood in a three-day convention to which all the major spiritual movements were invited. He prepared for the event by fasting. At the convention, the Cuban, in a long saffron robe, spoke at length. When his turn came, Brother Mikhaël, in a light-coloured suit, walked up the steps and seated himself in the lotus position at the front of the stage, as close as possible to the audience. His expression was serene, his gaze direct and full of warmth, and with his first words the atmosphere in the auditorium was transformed. Using simple, everyday terms, in strong contrast to the solemn orations of the other speakers, he spoke to the people in front of him as to friends. That evening, he revealed himself in public as never before.

The convention was followed by a lull before the opening of a new round of hostilities. Although Brother Mikhaël gave no more talks until the New Year he remained readily accessible to those around him. He wanted only to help them to make their own choices in complete freedom and without undue influence from him, and was ready to put himself at risk to help them to develop their discernment. It was with this in mind that he invited the Cuban to Izgrev to address the members of the brotherhood, their friends, and families.

For most of those present the occasion was a turning point. His regular students were accustomed to clear language and highly spiritual ideas and they soon realized that the guest speaker, in spite of his undeniable and rather disturbing power of fascination, was an impostor. Many of them, not understanding Brother Mikhaël's purpose, had looked forward to this meeting with trepidation and were deeply impressed by the outcome, for it gave them a glimpse – not for the first time – of the extraordinary inner liberty which allowed him to take such unprecedented action. In spite of what he knew of the influence and power of his enemy, he had given the members of his group the opportunity to make their own choice. In fact, he would go even further: until the end he would endeavour to help each one of his enemies, surrounding them mentally with light. Many years later, he would say that he had since had several opportunities to use his psychic powers to avenge himself on them, but that he had never done so.

Nineteen forty-seven drew to a close. The journalists had not abandoned their quarry, and many scurrilous and libellous articles continued to appear in the press. In spite of this, Brother Mikhaël declared in his New Year message that the year just ending had been one of the best in the life of the brotherhood. It was an astonishing statement. Referring to the ordeals they had experienced, he said that each member had been tried and tempted in every dimension: heart, intelligence, and will. Then, referring to his enemies, he added that his only concern was to assist them spiritually.

The magnanimity he showed to those enemies was not always understood. He spoke repeatedly of illuminating their minds and winning their hearts through love. The prediction with which he closed that New Year message was remembered in the brotherhood for a long time: the coming year, he wrote, would be a year of tribulation, marked by the separation of the sheep from the goats. 'The children of light will seek each other out. They will come together and gain strength from each other.'

During the month of January Brother Mikhaël took no part in public activities. At home one night, he had a phone call from a brother who had learned what his enemies were planning and urged him to escape, saying: 'You must leave the country. They are plotting to have you put in prison.'

But Brother Mikhaël had no intention of running away, and refused to abandon his brotherhood and his work. He had consented long since to the suffering and trials that would be part of the life he had chosen, and that night, more conscious than ever of the viciousness of his enemies, he agreed to go through fire. The moment was, perhaps, a turning point in his mission: on one side of the balance were the terrible ordeals that threatened to undermine his work; on the other, was the possibility of escape and a new beginning elsewhere. In one sense he was free to refuse the bitter cup offered to him, but he knew that if he wanted to emerge into the light, he would first have to descend into the most terrible darkness. Not long before this, speaking about the trials that he and his disciples were undergoing, he had said that there came a point when all human beings had to go through hell:

Jesus descended into hell because the road to heaven goes that way. Everyone has to go through hell to reach paradise. In other words, when you begin to work at overcoming your faults, a kind of hell opens before you, and for a time you have to make your way through that hell. When you emerge victorious, another external struggle awaits you, and if you are once more victorious, all will fall silent, no voice will ever be raised against you again. But until that last moment you have to be heroes.[36]

*
*   *

On Wednesday, January 21st, 1948, Brother Mikhaël was arrested without warning and booked on a trumped-up charge at the local police station. Later, on the strength of false testimony sworn to by several women, he was transferred to a cell in the Santé prison in Paris. Jean, who had been with him when the police arrived, was also taken into custody but was released the next day.

The members of the brotherhood, paralysed by shock, were completely at a loss. They did not believe Brother Mikhaël to be guilty, but some were intimidated by the climate of hostility, or embarrassed to acknowledge that they were his disciples. Only a

---

36. Unpublished talk, October 12th, 1947.

small nucleus remained absolutely loyal, and these, with heavy hearts and in constant anguish, tried to decide how to defend him. Articles continued to appear in the press, and the brotherhood was surrounded by an ambience of threats, hostility, and derision. Stella, who had taken it on herself to preserve the existence of the brotherhood at all costs, devoted herself heart and soul to this cause. With the help of the president of the association – also called Jean – she did her best to keep everyone calm and bolster their courage.

Only the deeply troubled climate of post-war society can explain certain aspects of Brother Mikhaël's arrest and long detention before being brought to trial, or the trial itself which contravened several specific requirements of the justice system. Twenty years later Stella was to write that the ambience of those times had allowed what would have been impossible later: five months after his arrest he was still detained at the Santé prison without having been brought to trial.

Brother Mikhaël would speak little about those long months of detention in the harrowing conditions of that prison, and about the terrible treatment to which he was subjected. Years later, however, referring briefly to his state of mind at the time, he spoke of the inner voices that attempt to lead human beings to despair:

> When I was falsely accused, I, too, heard the voices that cause one to doubt. No one is beyond their reach. In 1948 and 1949 they tempted me, tried to make me doubt myself and my ability to accomplish my mission. But I clung to the memory of the luminous experiences I had had, and my doubts vanished.[37]

Omraam Mikhaël Aïvanhov's teaching makes it clear that good and evil are both necessary to life. Just as fire can be used to warm or to destroy, just as poisonous plants can be used to kill or to heal, good and evil have a twofold task. What is important is to know how to use evil and transform it into good. As a mountaineer uses the irregularities on a rock-face as toe-holds on his climb to the summit, or as nature transforms refuse into nourishment for trees and flowers, so can we use trials, illness, and suffering as a means of rising to higher

---

37. Unpublished talk, July 14th, 1956.

things. In this sense, what appears as evil to those who suffer is often a hidden form of good. Many years later, he would say:

> All that had happened to me – to have the press present me before the world as a satyr, a monster – was it not the worst that could happen? I tell you frankly, all those unfounded accusations, all that derision, were very hard to bear. There are times when one would rather die than be dishonoured to such an extent. Many people have committed suicide for one hundredth of what I endured. Calumny works in one like a deadly poison. But initiatic science was there to show me that it was perhaps the greatest good that could have happened to me, for it obliged me to tread a path that was yet unknown, to find undreamed-of weapons and resources, untapped inner energies that I would never have known otherwise.[38]

During the five months following Brother Mikhaël's arrest Stella and several others devoted days and nights to the preparation of his defence. They had engaged a team of lawyers, but to their despair the most competent of them died just before the trial, which had been set for June 26th, 1948. They were obliged to fall back on others who were unknown to them, and the results were decidedly inferior.

On Saturday, June 26th, a dozen faithful followers were present at the Palais de Justice when Brother Mikhaël was brought into the courtroom, but there was to be no trial that day: he had been brought to court only to be told that the hearing had been postponed. As he was led out, his followers were allowed to shake his hand.

In spite of this delay, his defence team was feeling quite hopeful, for that day one of his accusers had signed an official retraction. It turned out to be the first of a series. Also, an unexpected ally had just come forward: a woman who had been the Cuban's representative in France had realized, not long before, that she had been taken in by him. On entering his office unexpectedly, she had surprised him in the act of dictating a letter to one of Brother Mikhaël's most virulent adversaries, in which she accused him of seducing her. Realizing what was going on, this witness had written to the judge to describe what she had seen, concluding her letter by

---

38. July 29th, 1963 (*La pédagogie initiatique II*, p. 149). Our translation.

asserting that the accusations against 'Monsieur Ivanoff' were totally unfounded.

The following Saturday, Brother Mikhaël was again taken to the courthouse, only to learn that his trial would take place two weeks later, on July 17th. But this time no one was allowed to approach him before he was hurried off to prison again.

It was at this point that a voice was raised in the media in his defence. Acting on information that would come to the ears of the competent authorities only several months later, a reputable journalist published an article in *Le Populaire*, in which he revealed that the stranger who had come to Paris claiming to be a Tibetan initiate was in fact a spy in the pay of the Soviet Union.

Brother Mikhaël's trial began at one o'clock in the afternoon of July 17th and was over the same day. Those who were present as witnesses for the defence described it as a travesty of justice. The proceedings were supposed to take place behind closed doors, but several legal stipulations were flagrantly ignored. A number of reporters and photographers were admitted. Also, an influential member of the government, the Garde des Sceaux, was present throughout the trial. This was a gross breach of the law, but he was determined to see the accused convicted and deported from France. The witnesses for the defence, in an atmosphere of hostility that was almost palpable, sensed their powerlessness. When called on to speak, they could barely be heard above the jeers.

Brother Mikhaël was sentenced to four years in prison.

At seven o'clock the next morning, Sunday, a small group of his followers gathered at Izgrev to pray together. Their hearts were heavy, their minds in turmoil, and their courage at a low ebb. Two hours later, some of those who had plotted the destruction of Brother Mikhaël's reputation arrived in a body. Claiming recognition as 'members in good standing' of the brotherhood, they had come to carry out the second phase of their plan: to shut down the centre preliminary to taking it over for themselves. Mustering all their powers of persuasion, they did their utmost to demoralise those present and split their ranks. But all their arguments met with immovable resistance, and they were forced to withdraw in defeat.

In the days that followed, the women who had falsely accused Brother Mikhaël began, one by one, to sign official retractions. Fear, blackmail, hypnotism, or bribery had been used to obtain their testimony, and on the day of the trial several of them had been close to panic when they began to understand the horrifying consequences of what they had done, and found themselves obliged to go through with it and perjure themselves in court. It was only when they could look back on events with some objectivity that most of them realized clearly what had happened to them. Even then there were some who, for the sake of their families who had received large sums of money or in an attempt to protect their own reputations, never publicly acknowledged that they had lied.

The trial, as might be expected, was the occasion of a further winnowing among the members of the brotherhood. Revolted by the injustice and iniquity of the proceedings they had witnessed, they felt like grains of sand being filtered through an ever finer mesh. Meanwhile they continued the struggle and filed an appeal against the judgement. They could not allow themselves to give up hope, for Brother Mikhaël had prepared them specifically for this ordeal. Remembering what he had said about the divisions and the winnowing to come, they could only try to understand the meaning of all this suffering for the brotherhood. Reading the offensive articles that continued to appear in the papers, on the one hand, and the letters from those who admired Brother Mikhaël's work and declared that he was a saint, on the other, they felt like steel that is being tempered, passing alternately from heat to cold, from profound discouragement to extravagant hope.

On July 22nd, Brother Mikhaël was transferred from the Santé prison to the huge prison camp at Celle St-Cloud known as the Châtaigneraie, where conditions were slightly more humane and the rules less stringent. Stella and Jean, the only ones to be granted a thirty-minute visit, found him serene, his face radiating a subtle inner light. He inquired affectionately after each member of the brotherhood before giving his visitors encouraging advice and assuring them of his faith in the victory of light and truth. In prison, he added, he felt truly free.

18

Prison

At the Châtaigneraie the prisoners lived in huge barracks. Well aware of the accusation against the new arrival, the other prisoners were free with their jeers and insults, calling him derisively 'the Magus', a title that many of the newspapers had used. To test him they played all sorts of tricks on him and charged their tobacco or other items from the prison shop to his account. But before long the serene kindness of his regard disarmed even the most relentless. None of his fellow prisoners was completely indifferent to his presence. Some, too deeply disillusioned or discouraged to trust another human being, simply observed their strange comrade in silence.

One of these men later wrote that he used to watch him meditating for hours, seated in the lotus position on his bunk, always clean and neat in spite of the difficult conditions, his abundant silver hair carefully combed beneath his Basque beret. This fellow-prisoner gave a vivid description of the violent disputes of the card-players at one end of the shed, the deafening noise, the constant coming and going of the various cliques: the swindlers, the pimps, the vagrants with criminal records, felons of every kind, rotted by vice:

> And there, far above and detached from all this slime, lives, ponders, works, and meditates our living example, one who radiates peace and whose presence alone, like a ray of sunlight, illuminates and purifies the oppressive atmosphere of that accursed shed – one of the best, apparently, in this enormous camp of the Châtaigneraie. [...] To be frank, I have to admit that I hung back for a long time. I wanted to study the man and get to know him before I could consider him not

just as a comrade, but as a friend and confidant. It was the sight of the way he lived, of his attitude toward everyone that imperceptibly won me over. I was gradually drawn to him, attracted by what he had to say. His love of nature made me understand that a man who was capable of standing for long periods of time behind the bars admiring the dawn at sunrise, as nature awoke to the song of the nightingale, was not, could not be, the man described by some of the newspapers. [...] One only had to live with him and observe him to be convinced of his innocence.[39]

From the beginning, Brother Mikhaël took careful stock of the milieu in which he would have to live for an undetermined length of time. Exerting every ounce of his mental strength, he surrounded himself with light to ward off the noxious emanations that he sensed all around him, on both the physical and the subtler planes. Later, he would say that he had worked to reinforce his aura to prevent all that from reaching him and 'weakening his faith and love.' If he was to do any good in his present situation, he needed to conserve his strength.

The two winters he spent in prison were particularly cold. For reasons of hygiene and to dissipate the nauseating stench in the shed, prison regulations required that the windows be kept open day and night. With so many prisoners crowded into one place, the air was thick with the smoke of their cigarettes, and the open windows at least assured that there was a minimum supply of oxygen. Stiff with cold, the men paced up and down the shed for hours on end, stamping their feet in an effort to keep warm, but Brother Mikhaël, sensitive though he was to the cold, spent long hours meditating on his bed under the open window.

Most of his fellow-prisoners suffered from nightmares, and his nights were often disturbed by their cries and groans. Every morning he awoke to the four walls that shut out the sun. Every meal brought the same mouldy bread, rancid oil, and rotten, unpeeled potatoes swimming in water.

Far from condemning the conduct of the prisoners, many of whom behaved with the frenzy of rampaging beasts, Brother

---

39. Quoted in Svezda, *op. cit.*, p. 93. (Our translation).

Mikhaël could not help seeing them 'as children, full of a wild, unbridled energy, who had never learned how to behave.' But he also said that he had never envied hermits so much as during his imprisonment. He prayed ceaselessly, asking always for light and more light, because 'light always goes hand in hand with gratitude, not with a spirit of revenge.'

One young boy, member of a gang that had committed certain crimes during the Occupation, observed him from a distance. On the brink of despair, he was only waiting for the right moment to carry out the suicide pact he had made with his comrades. The wretchedness of his life in prison and the thought of what awaited him afterwards was more than he could bear. But he could not help being touched by this prisoner who was so different from the others, whose attitude was that of a free man, who talked courteously to each one, and who gave to the least privileged the gifts he received from his visitors. Finally, he decided to confide in him about his plans for suicide. To his astonishment, Brother Mikhaël scolded him vigorously and talked to him about the meaning of life and its difficulties, before explaining with great kindness and compassion how he could transform his own existence if he had the will to do so. Every day after that, the boy returned with more questions, reflected on what Brother Mikhaël told him, and gradually achieved a certain serenity. His desire to end his life faded and was replaced by the will to transform it.

Imperceptibly, other prisoners were surprised to find that they too were beginning to trust the newcomer. Something strange was going on in this barrack: here was a spiritual master who was a prisoner and yet manifestly free, who listened to them, who counselled and instructed them. Capable of abstracting himself from the filth, the crude language, the cruel and amoral behaviour, he was gradually restoring the hope and courage of those who were willing to listen to him.

*
* *

After a time, Brother Mikhaël noticed that at the end of their compulsory outdoor exercise the prisoners were always exhausted. Their environment was unhealthy: they were not getting enough

food, and they took no exercise other than the daily walk round the prison yard – which resembled nothing so much as a funeral cortege. One day, disregarding the suspicious frowns of the guards, he detached himself from the procession and began to step briskly round the yard with another man, explaining to him how to walk without becoming tired.

Encouraged by his example, someone else took the initiative of forming a group of runners. But when the runners returned to the shed they were more exhausted than ever. Little by little, Brother Mikhaël's group of walkers became more numerous and more receptive to his ideas, and he began to instruct them in the value of their movements, the rhythm most beneficial to the human organism, and the importance of synchronizing their breathing with this rhythm.

He also took advantage of these occasions to respond to some of the inmates who questioned him about the eternal problem of evil in the world. Why did God allow evil to exist? Why was there so much injustice? To help them he talked about the innate ability they all possessed to transform their lives, and he was not afraid to offend by talking openly of their present situation and the reasons that had brought them to it.

He spoke as their friend, meeting them on their own ground in order to help them to rise above the conditions they had resigned themselves to. Listening to their conversations, he realized that money was the god through which they proposed to avenge themselves on society. One day he undertook to persuade them that another God existed, and began a discussion with a small group. It was not long before others joined in, many of them insisting that they had no intention of allowing themselves to be convinced.

'What is God?' asked Brother Mikhaël. 'What is the deity? In a moment you too will be able to prove that God exists. Listen: do you believe that there are any just people on earth?'

A chorus of denial greeted this, but when Brother Mikhaël insisted: 'Not even you?' several admitted that they considered themselves just. It was society that was at fault for failing to understand or help them.

'And are there intelligent people on earth? Are there people who are beautiful?'

All agreed that intelligence existed and that beauty existed, particularly in women and children.

'In other words,' said Brother Mikhaël, 'you admit that intelligence, justice, and beauty exist. What about strength? Do you know anyone who is strong?'

Yes, they all agreed, and Brother Mikhaël continued:

'So you agree that there is such a thing as strength. And surely you must admit that there are other virtues as well? Now, imagine that all the qualities and virtues whose existence you acknowledge are multiplied, amplified, and intensified to an infinite degree. The deity is precisely that: the sum of all virtues and qualities carried to an infinite, unlimited dimension. We cannot deny this reality because we all possess some fragments of it. If the deity does not exist, where do the particles of virtue we possess come from? What is their source? It is very difficult to deny this truth. You can certainly refuse the notion of God as an old man with a beard and a notebook and pencil, who spends his time recording the sins of human beings, but the virtues, these you cannot deny or ignore.'

His audience stared at him in silence, and he went on:

'I can even prove to you that although you don't realize it, you are all seeking God.'

'Oh no! Impossible!' exclaimed one of the men.

'Yes. You are always thinking of God, always looking for him,' insisted Brother Mikhaël.

Turning to one of the men, he asked why he was in prison.

'Because of a woman,' replied the man.

'That means that you are drawn to beauty, that you look for it. Why?'

'Because it makes me happy.'

'Well, this simply means that you are looking for God, but in a limited form.'

Turning to the men around him, one after the other, he continued:

'And you, who fight because you like strength, can't you see that strength, even wrongly understood, is God in another form? And you, you steal from shops because you love wealth; but wealth is God. Wealth belongs to God and comes from God, and henceforth you must look for it elsewhere and in other ways. There are those who desire knowledge or power, and these too are attributes of God. And aren't those who are looking for tenderness looking for God? Yes, we are all looking for God; we are all in pursuit of the deity in one form or another. It is the means and methods we use to reach and lay hold of our goal that are too ineffectual, false, twisted, inappropriate, and base. But in reality we are all drawn to great things, to the one thing that is great, limitless, infinite.'

*
* *

The relationship between Brother Mikhaël and many of his companions in misfortune was established only progressively, and the same was true of his relationship with the personnel. For the first few months, they made life extremely difficult for him. The Governor and overseers even forbade visits from his lawyers. The guards on duty in his barrack were changed frequently and ordered not to talk to him. They were warned, on the strength of some newspaper reports, that this prisoner was capable of hypnotizing them in order to escape. At one point, Brother Mikhaël discovered that one of the new inmates in the shed was in reality a detective inspector who hoped to trick him into incriminating himself.

One day, a guard approached him and without a word struck the Bible he was holding, knocking it to the other end of the room. When Brother Mikhaël protested and reproached him for his brutality, the man had the pretext he needed to accuse him of insolence. Surrounded by a detachment of guards, he was taken before the prison tribunal. His companions, watching him go, were convinced that he would be condemned to that terrible, dark cell from which he would return, like so many others, with his health broken.

But the outcome of his appearance before the tribunal was not what they had expected. When he explained what had happened, the judges simply smiled and sentenced him to three months without the meagre ration of cigarettes and wine that prisoners were entitled to. Brother Mikhaël, who had never smoked in his life and who did not drink wine, was greatly amused. 'But the other prisoners were unhappy to be deprived of the rations I used to distribute to them,' he said later.

Gradually the guards became less suspicious of him. The harshness of their attitude gave way to a certain curiosity and, finally, to friendliness, for they could not help but notice that most of the inmates talked to him and confided their problems to him. It was obvious that Brother Mikhaël was a pacifying influence in the shed. Eventually, the guards themselves began to seek him out and ask his advice. Pretending that an officer wanted to see him, one of the overseers sometimes came and took him discreetly to an office where they could talk without being disturbed. Even the prison Governor, who had developed a feeling of genuine friendship and respect for this unusual prisoner, had long conversations with him. Brother Mikhaël's inner freedom was such that he could say many years later:

> I found that in the midst of the greatest difficulties there was always someone singing within me. In each one of us is this being who watches and sees everything, who sings and laughs at what goes on.[40]

During his days in prison Brother Mikhaël continued to listen to his companions, to console and instruct them, but it was at night that he felt truly free. In spirit he could slip through the bars, send his thoughts out to the world, and work mentally with light. He lived as much in his soul and spirit as in his physical body.

*
* *

In his New Year message for 1949, Brother Mikhaël wrote to his 'dear brothers and sisters,' begging them not to panic, not to see enemies lurking in every corner, but to remain united and understand that God, who dwells in every visible form, manifests through even the most terrifying events. He encouraged them to treat everyone with love, above all, those who criticized or slandered them. 'This is what I have always done, even with my worst enemies,' he told them; 'They may have caused my downfall, but who knows: I may yet touch the depths of their hearts and souls.'

While still in prison he had two visions symbolizing trials by air and fire. In the first, he found himself surrounded by the wild shrieking of a tornado. Sinister faces peered at him, while objects

---

40. Unpublished talk, June 4th, 1958.

hurled by the wind were falling all around. Taking shelter behind a large rock he could only wait for the storm to abate. The vision of the trial by fire came a little later. He saw fires ravaging the earth and found himself in the middle of a blazing furnace with thick clouds of smoke swirling overhead. Again, he succeeded in passing through the ordeal and emerging unscathed from the fire.

In his first talk after his release from prison, he described the four visions he had been given before and during his incarceration and explained their meaning. The trial by earth is necessary to test one's strength of will, one's steadfastness. The trial by water is designed to test the reactions of the heart, of the emotions. The trial by air reveals the equilibrium of the intellect, and the last and most painful, the trial by fire, is necessary to burn away all the wastes that prevent the soul from uniting with the forces of the cosmos. These are, in fact, the four indispensable ordeals imposed on initiates in the temples of ancient Egypt and India.

Endeavouring to understand the full import of the ordeal he was undergoing in prison, Brother Mikhaël methodically reviewed his life up to that moment, and it was then that Peter Deunov's words came back to him: 'A time will come when the forces of darkness will put obstacles in your way and try to prevent you from advancing.' At the age of seventeen, he had not known exactly what those 'forces of darkness' represented. Also, although Peter Deunov had foretold great trials, he had not been at liberty to mention the prison, and it was only when Brother Mikhaël was deprived of his physical freedom that he remembered the allegory of the young man charged with carrying a precious stone through a forest.

He understood then what he had not understood fifteen years earlier: the precious stone, symbol of the teaching he had brought to France, had been horribly defiled and trampled underfoot. And he too, the bearer of this stone, had been vilely dishonoured and slandered, dragged through filth by those who wanted to destroy him. Just as Peter Deunov had foretold, he was making his way through a forest infested with bandits and wild beasts.

When he had recounted this parable, Peter Deunov had said that after his ordeal, the bearer of the precious stone would be cleansed of all the impurities cast upon him; that he would be given all he needed, and that the gem would shine in all its splendour. Brother Mikhaël was to say later that there had been a moment in prison when he had sensed the presence of Peter Deunov. He had seen an indication of this presence in the changed attitude of the Governor and guards who, having once treated him with inhumanity, began to protect him.

*
* *

Two years were to pass, however, before he was released. Certain charges against him had fallen under the weight of their own absurdity, and others had been withdrawn. Several prominent people who had been taken in by the Cuban spy and had used their influence to get Brother Mikhaël condemned now did everything in their power to make amends. Years later the Garde des Sceaux who had been present illegally at his trial, was to write and ask his forgiveness for having influenced the judge. He explained that at the time, he had been convinced of Brother Mikhaël's guilt; only later had he found out that the whole affair had been a conspiracy.

At Brother Mikhaël's request, the date of his liberation was kept secret from all but Stella and Jean, who went without a word to anyone to meet him at the gates of the Châtaigneraie. In view of the complex web of influences involved in the conspiracy against him, he was released with the proviso that he would not live in Paris for the next five years. It was only in the spring of 1955 that he was authorised to live at Izgrev. In the meantime he stayed with friends in the south of France.

The brotherhood in France had grown and become stronger in the midst of adversity and was ready for the reunion with its spiritual master. On March 19th, 1950, Brother Mikhaël visited Izgrev briefly and gave a talk to a small group of disciples. His face was emaciated and deeply etched, but a flame burned in his eyes and his expression radiated serenity.

He began this first meeting, as always, by reading a text by Peter Deunov. Afterwards, with the utmost simplicity, he spoke of his time in prison and his relationship with his fellow-prisoners. He touched lightly on his feelings when he had been slandered and vilified. 'The hardest thing of all,' he said, 'is to be dishonoured.' But knowing how much his brothers and sisters had suffered all this time, and in order to help them to forget past hardships and concentrate on their spiritual work, he added:

'Perhaps you think that I should have endured these trials alone. Yes, but if I had, the victory would have been mine alone. You had to win with me. [...] May all the dark clouds, all thoughts and feelings of hatred disappear, may the springs of love flow freely again, and may we truly feel ourselves to be children of God.'

The majority of those present wept for joy. Throughout his life Brother Mikhaël had accepted the trials that are the lot of all human beings. He had 'worked', as he put it, on different kinds of problems, on different kinds of suffering and limitations, in order to open a new path. It was this constancy that was the measure of his love, of his capacity for sacrifice. Some years later, a brother asked him why the life of initiates was always marked by tragedy; his answer undoubtedly applies to himself:

You will remember that Greek mythology speaks of Prometheus who was punished for giving heavenly fire to mankind. Every saviour of humanity shares the fate of Prometheus. Tradition reveals that through original sin the first beings created monstrous entities that peopled the earth. More than once since then, the phenomenon has been repeated because of the transgressions of humanity, and it is this propagation of monsters that is the cause of all our misfortunes. In sacrificing their lives, the saints, prophets, and martyrs wiped out a great part of the debt owed by humanity. In other words they liberated part of the road that humanity must travel. The blood of Jesus Christ cleansed a great expanse of this road. The sacrifices of all highly evolved beings are very precious, because they cancel out all the darkness that, on the astral plane, still weighs on humanity.[41]

It would be ten years before Brother Mikhaël's reputation was completely cleared. On September 28th, 1960, he was with the brotherhood in the south of France when he received a summons to the Court of Appeal in Aix-en-Provence. That morning, as on many other occasions in his life, his winged friends were present: hundreds

---

41. Unpublished talk, August 13th, 1956.

of swallows suddenly appeared, flying low over his car and accompanying it a great part of the way. When he returned home later that afternoon, he was able to announce that the Court had pronounced his rehabilitation.

*
*   *

After that first visit to Paris in 1950, Brother Mikhaël returned to Pau. There, living in a house surrounded by trees, he followed a rhythm of life that helped him gradually to rebuild his strength, devoting the mornings to his spiritual life, in communion with the generous sun of these southern climes, and his afternoons to 'giving what he had received.'

Resting on a bench one day after a long walk in one of the city parks, he noticed that a woman sitting nearby was glancing at him. He realized that she must have recognized him, for his photograph had appeared in all the French papers two years earlier. Turning to her, he asked quietly:

'Do you believe what they said about me?'

At that, she dared to look him in the face, and her answer was spontaneous:

'No, I don't believe it. It's impossible. You have the face of a prophet.'

After a moment's hesitation, she added:

'What you went through was terrible.'

'You know,' he said gently; 'the surest way of losing all strength and courage is to consider evil as an enemy. If you see it as a factor that can help you to evolve, you transform it into good. We must not forget that it is our trials that allow us to find unknown resources within ourselves. This is why evil is often a blessing in disguise.'

His new acquaintance was profoundly receptive to what he was saying, and not long after this first encounter she was one of a number of people who visited him regularly.

Beginning in June 1950, Brother Mikhaël made the round trip from Pau to Sèvres almost every Sunday. As before, he gave much of his time to those who asked for a personal conversation. On these occasions, many people told him that they had seen him physically before them while he was still in prison, and thanked him for what he had done for them. But although he never hesitated to help those in need, he always refused to be seen as a miracle-worker with powers of bilocation. When someone claimed to have seen him in a dream or to have been helped by his intervention, he alluded to the many spirits who supported him in his work, saying: 'I do not know which one of them brought you peace or helped you to solve your problem.'

His talks that year were often very long, and his disciples spent many hours at a time with him. They were regaining strength and drinking their fill of light after the long months of darkness. They sang, shared a meal, and listened to Brother Mikhaël as he talked about forgiveness and inner light, about prayer and meditation, about purity and the subtle bodies, and about the role of music in achieving harmony. He was so inspired that they never tired of listening to him. The atmosphere at these meetings was unique: the very air seemed to be suffused with joy. Now and then a spontaneous burst of laughter or song arose; the musicians played selections of classical music, and it was with reluctance that the group dispersed at the end of the day.

Brother Mikhaël's radiance attracted people from every level of society. He was extremely active, giving talks in many different locations, and it was obvious to those around him that he was constantly accompanied by intangible beings whose task it was to aid him in his work and replenish his reserves of strength. Judging from the themes of his talks, this was also a period of intense mystical experiences. It is clear that since his ecstasy at the age of fifteen, he had had many others, but a talk he gave on January 28th, 1951, is so vibrant that it seems to be the echo of a recent experience. Before his talk that day, he had opened a small book of meditations by Peter Deunov, asking the invisible world to show him what he should talk about. His gaze had fallen upon a text about ecstasy, which he proceeded to comment with particular intensity:

'Ecstasy is a marvellous, indescribable state. One has to experience it to understand. One's whole being is pervaded by sentiments of self-abnegation, altruism, and nobility. One loves with a love that embraces all creatures and renounces all trivial, material pleasures. The heart is filled with impersonal, selfless, generous feelings. This gives you some slight idea of ecstasy. It is something that can be experienced only when one has admired, adored, and contemplated the deity for a very long time.'

In spite of their joy at having their spiritual guide with them once again, things were still not easy for the members of the brotherhood in those years. The troubled atmosphere of the past was not wholly dissipated and hostile articles continued to appear in the press. In March, Brother Mikhaël told those assembled at Izgrev that he was the happiest of men and was determined not to follow the advice of all those who said he should speak out in his own defence. He had no wish to threaten anyone or to appeal to the courts. In his view, either there was nothing to defend, or what existed was good, and in this case, nothing could destroy it. A few months later, after the sunrise on April 9th, 1951, he spoke of the darkness in which seeds must lie before they can germinate, and threw a ray of light on a profound initiatic truth:

'For two years I was immersed in darkness, and it was with joy that I amassed that darkness. It was very, very dark, completely black. This darkness is a mystery. Things are formed in darkness. White is manifestation; black is formation. A child is formed in darkness. Darkness is a twofold symbol: for ordinary human beings, it is equated with evil, egoism, and hell. For an initiate, it is a mystery that has not yet been illuminated or explained.'

In the autumn of the following year, he at last felt free to make an excursion into the mountains, as in the days of his youth in Bulgaria. Early one bright Sunday morning in October, he and several brothers set out for the Midi d'Ossau, a peak that rises to more than 9,000 feet in the Pyrenees. Once they had reached the heights, Brother Mikhaël went off alone for a long meditation before giving a brief talk to his companions. As they were about to start on the return journey, the whole area was suddenly wrapped in fog and they could see barely a yard before them. It was then that an unusual phenomenon occurred: in front of them, reflected on the thick white mist, they saw their individual silhouettes, each surrounded by concentric circles of rainbow-hued light. Compared to theirs, Brother Mikhaël's aura was immense. 'It was a marvellous, overwhelming, unforgettable experience,' wrote one of those present that day.

Turning to his companions, Brother Mikhaël said that the invisible world had allowed them to see their auras reflected in the mist as in a mirror, so that they might be more conscious of the subtle dimensions of life. Then he set off ahead of them, almost running down the mountain side, and the brothers watched in astonishment as, with sweeping gestures, he cut a path through the mist which folded away on either side. He seemed to be blazing a path of light.

*'I would rather live in a tiny cabin, with all humanity in my heart,
than in a spacious comfortable mansion.'*

19

The Bonfin

In the hinterland of the French Riviera, near the town of Fréjus, brother Jean owned a piece of land known as the Bonfin. It consisted of a few acres of barren, slaty ground on which grew one ancient evergreen oak, a few meagre pines and fig trees, and some old vines. In the centre, surrounded by thorn and scrub, stood the ruins of an old farmhouse. Jean hoped that one day his land would be a home for the brotherhood, and while Brother Mikhaël was absent, he had recruited a few friends to help him to prepare it for occupation. When Brother Mikhaël visited it in 1947, he had been particularly attracted by a steep hill to the east of the land with a splendid view of the rising sun, which came to be known as 'the Rock of Prayer.'

Three years later, ownership of the Bonfin was transferred to the fraternity, and Brother Mikhaël approved its use as a convention centre. From then on, a great work of landscaping and construction was carried out, but for years the land remained barren. It took tremendous effort with pick and shovel to build even the most rudimentary structures on the unforgiving ground. In this country regularly swept by the *mistral*, tents and temporary shelters had to be firmly anchored to the land, and even then they were sometimes carried off with all their contents by violent gusts of wind. Brother Mikhaël occupied a minuscule caravan which Jean had built for him out of used materials collected over the years. When the *mistral* blew, this precarious dwelling rocked and swayed and threatened to fly away.

Most of the sleeping and living quarters were makeshift constructions of *canisses*, the tall reeds which grew in abundance in the surrounding countryside and served to make fences, as well as walls and roofs for kitchens, dormitories, and washrooms. The campers laboured long hours under a broiling sun, clearing the scrub, digging up dead vines, laying out paths. When they needed to cool off they tied a wet handkerchief on their head. There were two wells on the property, but they provided almost no water and frequently had to be cleaned and disinfected. Jean assumed the task of providing the camp with drinking water; every evening, accompanied by one or two brothers, he rode down to the river Reyran on his motor cycle and filled barrels of water to take back to the Bonfin in his side-car.

In the summer of 1953, the minimum equipment was in place for a first convention of two weeks. Gradually over the years, the duration of the summer convention would be extended from two weeks to three months. Members of the brotherhood arrived from every corner of France and Switzerland for stays of various lengths, and the coming and going was constant. They gathered at the Bonfin, eager to live together and share the difficult conditions in a spirit of brotherhood.

For most of them the change of scenery was radical. In the still-untamed nature of the Mediterranean hinterland, they felt as though they were living in biblical times. They could walk for hours without meeting another human being, with only the immensity of the blue sky overhead, the twisted pine trees and parched scrub all around, the little black pebbles rolling underfoot. In the distance rose the mountain known as *le Gisant*, because its silhouette resembled the recumbent statue of a knight on a mediaeval tomb. When the campers wanted a bath, it meant a half-hour walk to the Reyran: there, after bathing and washing their clothes, they donned their wet garments and let the sun dry them as they walked back to the Bonfin.

As always, Brother Mikhaël was content with very little. For several years, he occupied the small caravan built by brother Jean, before moving into a tiny cabin which measured six feet by nine. It was only several years later that the brothers could afford to provide him with one of three rudimentary wooden cottages built with cheap materials from a demolition site. When he talked of the spiritual work one could do in a restricted living space, he was speaking from experience. Since his youth he had had years of training in this, and, as he had said several years earlier:

Even when you are ill, alone, in prison, or in exile, you can work within yourself. Difficult external conditions often make it easier to improve one's inner state. It is then that one is stronger, because no help can be had from outside. When you meet obstacles and difficulties on all sides, one direction is always wide open: the upward direction. Thus, when you find yourself in the worst possible external conditions, when you can move neither forwards, nor backwards, nor downwards, you must not hesitate: move upwards. Rise to a higher plane. When we are overwhelmed by every kind of difficulty, we can always enter the world of the spirit and turn to God. In that direction, nobody can put barriers in our way.[42]

'Food is rich in forces and particles that come not only from the earth but from the whole cosmos, and it is elements from the cosmos that materialize on earth in the form of flowers, vegetables and fruits.'

The work of developing and improving the Bonfin continued for several years. Great quantities of top-soil had to be imported before it was possible to plant a few vines and grow the minimal crops of vegetables required to feed the campers. Brother Mikhaël made regular rounds of the teams at work, lending a hand wherever it was needed. Nothing escaped his vigilance, no task was beneath him. But the evenings were a time of relaxation when he strolled

42. Unpublished talk, December 3rd, 1950.

among the tents and talked to the campers. And always, in spite of the arduous nature of the work, he asked each one to have a care for the beauty of the environment: 'The beauty we create around us,' he said, 'is reflected in our soul.'

In general, however, while he noticed the smallest details and could wield a mason's trowel or a paintbrush to good effect, he left to the campers the responsibility of the physical organization. His role, he explained, was to keep water flowing in abundance – water being the symbol of life and love – for 'as long as there is water, things organize themselves.'

His role toward his disciples lay on different levels: he spoke to their intelligence, their heart, and their will; he appealed to their desire for perfection but also to their generosity or their aesthetic sense. He was not blind to the difficulties of a life-style based on collaboration, to the problems that arose between people of different temperaments, to the demands of a truly brotherly spirit. As he often said, however, all this constituted a school, a learning process. A spontaneous sympathy or antipathy between individuals, for example, was often rooted in a distant past, in a previous incarnation, and one must learn to put these manifestations of the personality at the service of the individuality.

To explain the respective roles of these two natures in human beings, he used the example of a tree. The personality, like the roots of a tree, can draw on great reserves of 'subterranean' riches, the raw materials that are the instincts, passions and desires. The personality is very powerful, but it has one defect: it tends to use everything for the benefit of the inferior self. The individuality, on the other hand, has received the most beautiful and most radiant attributes: the power to produce flowers and fruit. 'All that is truly spiritual is inspired by the individuality,' he used to say.

Using this example of the tree, he explained that the personality is as ever-present and as necessary to a human being as the roots, trunk, and branches. Whereas the individuality, like the fruit and flowers of a tree, is not always present, and it is important that we learn to recognize where our impulses are coming from: the personality or the individuality. The personality is capable of becoming the best of servants, and we must not attempt to destroy it as did certain ascetics of the past. As for our individuality, if we give it first place and allow it to govern and dominate the personality completely, our physical body can become a focus for the manifestation of the Lord.

The Bonfin was a school; his school. He asked those who came there to behave as exceptional human beings, to be pure in thought, word, and deed. He gave them methods they could use to harmonize themselves with the cosmos, to model themselves on the infinite world, to live in union with the source of all life, the universal soul, God himself. 'It is in this communion with universal life that you will find the meaning of life,' he told them.

A stay at the Bonfin was an apprenticeship in what he called 'the real work', that which is capable of balancing all other activities. 'Never neglect the practice of concentration and meditation,' he used to say. And as he often referred to progress in the spiritual life as 'a work' to be accomplished, he was asked more than once to explain what he meant.

> This work takes place where you would least suspect it. It is possible to remain completely motionless and silent and yet take an active part in God's work. How? By rising to the level of the universal soul. Once there, you unite yourself to it and participate in its work. Nobody knows what you are doing; not even you. You can be in several different places in the universe at the same time.[43]

The implication is clear: perseverance is an essential ingredient of the spiritual quest, and it was in this sense that he liked to use the popular expression, '*Bonne continuation!* – Keep up the good work! – thereby stimulating in his disciples the forces necessary for the continuation and completion of the work undertaken. He knew that the greatest strength of human beings lay in perseverance in the face of all that might conspire to hinder their work of self-transformation. In fact, the transformation he refers to is an alchemical process, which he likens to the change in colour of a litmus die when the last crucial drop of acid or alkali is added. 'One more drop! Just one more! Keep up the good work, until the red

---

43. Unpublished talk, January 4th, 1959.

turns to blue.' What matters is to continue, to continue one's efforts until the ultimate transmutation is achieved.

*
* *

As the years passed, the Bonfin was transformed. Flowers, shrubs and trees were planted, oleander, mimosa, and eucalyptus, and a level area was laid out next to the old oak tree for the morning exercises. The scene that unfolded every day at dawn must have reminded Brother Mikhaël of his days at Rila: the stars were still bright in the sky when the first campers emerged from their tents. After summary ablutions because of the scarcity of water, they dressed warmly, took up a blanket as a protection against the chilly morning air, and set off in silence for the Rock. A brief climb up some steep boulders led to a slope of sandy soil scattered with pine trees which brought them to the summit where they settled down for their meditation.

The site is beautiful. Against the gradually lightening sky to the east, the outlines of distant mountains stand out in a graceful succession of dark blue curves, and in clear weather the Mediterranean can be glimpsed through a cleft in the hills to the south. An hour or so after the sun had risen, Brother Mikhaël turned to the group for a short talk. Then came the descent to the camp, the exercises, and breakfast which was set out on three tables under an awning of reeds.

At noon the meetings sometimes took place in a room in the old farmhouse, but usually the campers remained sitting around the tables out of doors. And when the *mistral* blew and a fine layer of dust settled on the soup, everyone was too happy to care.

But the time had come for renewed efforts. During the first convention in 1953, Brother Mikhaël encouraged the participants to spend a little more time in front of the sun in the morning, simply to contemplate it, like children. Five years later, he suggested longer meditations and emphasised the importance of the conditions conducive to real concentration.

Brother Mikhaël's love of the sun was contagious. It was impossible to listen to him without wishing to be as radiant as he who had contemplated the sun since his childhood, who had accepted the most terrible ordeals without losing his inner light. He had passed through the 'narrow gate' foretold by Peter Deunov and had emerged luminous as a sun. He communicated warmth, light, and life to all.

During the 1958 convention, he declared that an immense work was going on in the subtler dimensions of earth and of the cosmos, and that entirely new elements were beginning to appear in the world. He prophesied the impending dawn of a new era that would endure for many centuries, during which humanity would be free from war, disease, and crime. He often said that this new era would dawn first in the souls of a handful of men and women toward the end of the 20th century, and that a Golden Age would manifest as love in the hearts of human beings.

All his labours to bring about the kingdom of God on earth bore the mark of his close relationship with the angels of the four elements. He did everything he could to create an elevated spiritual ambience for his disciples, to help them to be more aware of certain aspects of nature and their own links with her. On August 6th, 1958, when running water was at last installed at the Bonfin, he made it an occasion to thank the Angel of Water for this gift, and to explain:

'Water represents the fluidic dimension of nature. It is the earth's blood [...] and this water is transformed into blood in human beings. This is the true blood that nourishes all the creatures of nature. You must meditate on water, for it is a very profound symbol. When you drink it with love, respect, and gratitude it is transformed into life, for it is the bearer of life. No chemical process can exist without water; even precious stones cannot exist without some particles of water, crystals cannot form without water. It is thanks to a minute quantity of water that a precious stone is hard and transparent and capable of reflecting the sun's rays. [...] Ask water to communicate its transparency to you.'

Sometimes at sunrise he asked those present to join in his spiritual work by praying with him to the Angel of Air or the Angel of the Sun; and in the evenings around the fire, he spoke of the importance of burning all that is old and obsolete within oneself in order to enhance life. He often spoke of fire and water, the two elements that are indispensable to life. It was his understanding of these two principles that led him, on August 29th, 1958, to speak of the respective roles of man and woman:

'Man possesses immense energies, but if it were not for woman, those energies would simply return to the great cosmic reservoir. Woman has the tremendously important role of capturing the spirit, the energies of the spirit, and creating forms that allow the spirit to act. It is thanks to the union of these two principles that the earth and the forms that people it exist. The spirit is so subtle that without woman it could not survive on earth.'

Toward the middle of September he announced that he would leave shortly for a visit to India. The summer convention of that year had been the last in a particular phase of his own life as well as that of his brotherhood. He would remain in India for a year, and when he returned a new phase would begin.

On September 29th, he talked at length about the meaning of the feast of the Archangel Mikhaël which falls in the autumn, at the beginning of a cycle of disengagement and liberation. At this time, the whole of nature takes part in the celebration; the divine Mother, angels, archangels, and all the forces of nature are present.

During the three months before his departure for India, several events made a great impression on the brotherhood. One day, on developing a photograph taken during the meditation after lunch, a form could be distinguished over Brother Mikhaël's head: it was the cabbalistic symbol of the Shin, whose vertical and horizontal lines represent the masculine and feminine principles respectively. The same form appeared on a photograph on three different occasions. The phenomenon, which could have been attributed to unusual reflections of light, was remarkable because the sacred symbol was so perfectly formed. In the brotherhood it was seen as an expression of the equilibrium that reigns in a human being who has developed the two principles within himself.

On January 1st, 1959, Brother Mikhaël told those gathered at Izgrev that his absence would benefit them; that it would perhaps allow them to find their true strength within themselves. He had been with them for twenty-one years, and it was now time for him to go in search of certain sacred things that had been conserved in an

oriental country deeply imbued with the mysticism of the great spiritual Masters. He told them:

'You are under the protection of one who is all-powerful. It is he, this great being from on high, who told me: "I have taken them under my protection." All powers are his. For a long time now he has taken care of me. Several times in the past forty years I have sensed his presence, but I have never been able to speak to him. Now, by the grace of heaven, he has spoken directly to me. I believe what he says. I know he will take good care of you. I have been instructed to make this voyage, and I obey heaven's commands.'

Brother Mikhaël was entering his sixtieth year. This allusion to a mysterious being who had been by his side for forty years seems to relate to the 'extraordinary event' that had occurred in 1920 and which he had mentioned briefly a few years earlier. All indications are that he was speaking of the beginning of his relationship, at the age of twenty, with the one he called his 'true Master'.

The date of his departure for India was set for February 11th, 1959. He left alone. But more than two hundred people were at Orly to bid him goodbye and to watch as his plane carried him toward the Orient.

Part Four:
The Master

Great Masters are very highly evolved individuals who have already experienced at least once every possible aspect of human destiny.

Rudolf Steiner

20

The Land of the Devas

In India, Brother Mikhaël received the new name that seems always to have been destined for him. He never revealed the exact circumstances of the event, but in private he sometimes alluded to three Masters whom he met during a two-week retreat in a Himalayan temple. One of these three, by virtue of the supernatural power invested in him, gave him the name of Omraam.

After returning to Paris, he would tell his disciples: 'My new name is Omraam Mikhaël.' And a few days later, speaking of the one who had given him this name, he would simply say, 'It was someone who was greater than Babaji.'

Little is known of the essence of his stay in India. He himself referred to it with great discretion, but several of his later talks and occasional comments about that period of his life throw an interesting light on both his personal itinerary and his mission in India. Although those comments, often brief, do not constitute a chronological account of his travels they indicate that he spent the first few months of his stay in the mountains.

I was in the Himalayas, beyond Almora. The air was very pure and there were few people about. I talked very little and spent my time meditating. I spent several months there and meditated day and night.[44]

This was in Kashmir. He loved this country sheltered by the Himalayan foothills, its magnificent valleys studded with gentians, primroses, and edelweiss, and its torrents pouring from the glaciers above into the lakes and rivers below. Not far from Gulmarg he rented a small cottage where, in spite of the rudimentary physical conditions, he remained for several months. From Srinagar, the ancient lakeside city known as the 'Venice of the East', he set out, as so often in his youth, for a long hike into the mountains and reached a lake at an altitude of 16,000 feet. Lacking mountaineering equipment he could go no higher.

It was here that he had a rare experience. He knew of the technique that enabled certain initiates of India and Tibet to travel from one place to another in a state of weightlessness, but he also knew that they achieved this only after long years of practice. He was astonished, therefore, to be given the experience without having sought it. One day, while walking in the mountains and contemplating the summit of Nanga Parbat, he suddenly had a sensation of weightlessness. He began to run with such lightness that his feet barely touched the ground. Effortlessly he ran, uphill and down, as though flying over the slopes. 'It was an unforgettable experience,' he said later.

On the heights above Almora he met two exceptional beings, Anagarika Govinda and his wife, who became his friends. At last, in June, he met the great Babaji, one of the most mysterious beings in all India, whose role is believed to be to help prophets and spiritual Masters in the accomplishment of their particular mission.

It was said of Babaji that he always seemed to be the same age, that he had lived in the Himalayas for two hundred and fifty or three hundred years, and that he appeared and disappeared at will. His disciples were all highly evolved human beings toward whom he

---

44. Unpublished talk, April 13th, 1960.

could be extremely demanding. He had never been known to represent himself as a great lord; on the contrary, he always behaved with the utmost simplicity. It was said that he had foretold events which always came true, that he could see and hear people at a distance, and that among other powers, he had the ability to be present in several different places at once. Countless people told of being saved from danger or illuminated by the great Babaji, without ever having seen him.

Omraam Mikhaël ardently wished to see him, and in June, not knowing where to reach him he decided to communicate by telepathy. Babaji responded immediately by going to meet him in Almora. As soon as he arrived, he asked the disciples who had accompanied him to leave him alone with this Master from another land.

After their first encounter, they met a number of times and spent many hours together. Sri Babaji often sent one of his disciples to invite his new friend to join him wherever he happened to be. They went for long walks together in the mountains, and Babaji arranged for him to meet many interesting people, to whom he introduced him as 'the French saddhu, a yogi and great saint.' The people greeted Babaji's friend with respect, bowing down to his feet.

A communion existed between the two men that needed no words. Omraam Mikhaël recounted how, when they were in a car together one day, he put his hand on Babaji's knee in a gesture of respect and affection, whereupon Babaji turned to him with a smile: 'He began to sing in a mysterious language, and we exchanged a look such as I have never exchanged with anyone.'

At their last meeting, Babaji invited Omraam Mikhaël to stay in his ashram near Nainital. He himself would not be there, because he lived in another part of the Himalayas and visited Nainital only occasionally and unexpectedly. The ashram, set in a magnificent site high in the mountains, was directed by one of Babaji's disciples, Hanuman Baba, who welcomed his guest with every sign of respect and showed him, in silence, to his Master's room. Sri Babaji never lent his room to anyone, but he had told Hanuman Baba to put it at the disposition of his guest. Here in this room, looking out on the splendid scenery, Omraam Mikhaël spent two weeks in contemplation.

He used the evenings to learn more about Hinduism from Hanuman Baba, who, having taken a vow of silence, replied to his questions by writing on a slate. This disciple's only nourishment was a pint of milk a day; at night he slept only two or three hours in a hole dug in the ground. Thanks to this centuries-old technique he deprived the five senses of their nourishment thus achieving a certain numbness in his physical body:

> [...] once the senses cease their activity, they no longer absorb the psychic energy intended for the subtle force-centres, so these centres can be awakened and the yogi begins to see, hear, smell and touch the fluidic elements of the higher realms of reality. [45]

In spite of the constraints of communicating by writing, a warm friendship developed between the two men. Hanuman Baba explained to the foreign Master the meaning of certain exercises of Shabda yoga that had been prescribed by Babaji. He also translated texts from the Vedas and Upanishads for him and taught him the special properties of certain plants that grew in the garden.

*
* *

The period that followed this retreat in Babaji's ashram was very different. Master Omraam visited the length and breadth of the country: the big cities, shrines and places of pilgrimage, sacred caves, palaces, and temples. He spent long hours in some of the major libraries and even treated himself to some lessons in Sanskrit.

Throughout his travels on the roads of India he lived as an oriental, partaking of frugal meals which he prepared for himself. In hotels, the personnel respected his wishes and smilingly provided him with what he needed, for they immediately recognized him as a Brahmashari, one who is consecrated in celibacy to the service of God.

As the days passed, he met Indians from all walks of life: members of the different religious castes, businessmen, members of the judiciary, and captains of industry. To all of them he showed the photograph of Peter Deunov he always carried and was moved each

---

45. August 2nd, 1969 (*Harmony*, p. 82).

time to see them take it with respect and touch it to their forehead before returning it. Usually they invited him to a meal, told him of their problems and asked his advice, and to thank him for the honour of his presence, they often took him on a tour of their town or region.

In the temples he visited he could not fail to notice the many sculptures of popular religious symbols, chief among them the lingam, a symbol of procreation, which consists of a concave horizontal form surmounted by a vertical column. In the courtyard of a temple one day, he saw a group of women laying flowers at the foot of one such sculpture. Curious to learn what they knew about the symbolism and having noticed that many women in the towns knew English, he decided to talk to them. Approaching, he asked them what the sculpture represented. One of the women replied that it symbolized the two principles, masculine and feminine.

'Why are they united,' he asked, 'rather than being shown separately?'

In the silence that followed his question, he explained:

'The Rishis have joined the two principles in this symbol, but in human beings they are still separate. In the temples they are united, but not in yourselves. You are either a woman, and in that case you continually seek the other principle, man; or you are a man, continually in search of the other principle, woman. The two principles are separated. If they were not, you would not always be looking for the one that is missing. You are not whole and complete in your own person, this is why you look for a partner to make you whole. Great sages, the Rishis and Saddhus, possess the two principles within themselves: they are both man and woman. This is why they do not need to marry. They possess the qualities of both principles: the love of the feminine principle, and the strength of the masculine principle. They are the perfect lingam.'

By this time he was surrounded by a large group of people who had gathered to listen. In India, there is nothing unusual in such a scene: people recognize a Master who is dispensing knowledge and wisdom; they draw near and stay to listen. Omraam Mikhaël went on to talk about the chakras.

'There is something more,' he said. 'You must develop the Ajna chakra, which will give you the ability to see everything, but as you develop this feminine, horizontal chakra, you must also awaken the masculine chakra, Sahasrara, which is vertical. Only then will you be a living lingam.'

Although he sometimes talked publicly in this way, he was more often content to observe and listen. He spent long periods in isolated villages, observing how the people lived and learning about their interests and their problems. In spite of the wretched conditions, he remained with the poorest of the poor for a long time and adapted to their way of life.

Travelling the roads, he sometimes met saddhus who, renouncing all glory, dressed and behaved like ignorant beggars in order to carry on their spiritual work in peace. His practised eye was not deceived by their appearance, however, and he sometimes stopped to talk to them. They were always willing to converse with him, and some even addressed him as Mahatma, the title reserved for spiritual leaders, ascetics, and sages. He denied that he had a right to the title, but when they insisted, he smiled and said no more.

After the traditional gesture of farewell, he watched them fading into the distance on the dusty road, and reflected on the exceptional conditions in this country for the development of the spiritual life: it was always warm, and in many regions the abundance of fruit in the forests made it possible to live without money. All this made life easier for the saddhus and allowed them to concentrate on developing their spiritual faculties.

From his first days in India, he had noticed that the people still had faith in the power of a blessing. In the streets, buses, and hotels, even in the homes of the rich, people sometimes knelt before him and asked him to bless them and accept them as disciples. At first, this surprised and embarrassed him, but after a time he willingly blessed those who asked.

*
* *

Omraam Mikhaël visited many ashrams, from the humblest to the most renowned. Arriving in the first of these, he was surprised to learn that Babaji had spread word of his presence in India. In all the principal ashrams they knew who he was and were expecting him. At Calcutta he met Ananda Moyi Ma, of whom he said: 'She is a woman who has achieved something very great. There can be no doubt that the spirit is upon her.'

He spent several days at the Ramakrishna Centre. He also visited Shivananda in his immense ashram at Rishikesh, equipped with a hospital, a pharmacy, and a printing press. As soon as Shivananda saw him he exclaimed in delight, jumped up and placed a welcoming garland of flowers around his neck. At the end of the day, after a long conversation, he invited him to join him in a walk along the shores of the Ganga.

At Tiruvanamalai he was able at last to enjoy a few days of tranquillity and silence in the ashram of Ramana Maharshi who had died nine years earlier. The atmosphere here was particularly cordial, luminous, and peaceful. The whole ashram was permeated by a truly spiritual ambience. The Maharshi's disciples received him with the deference due to a great spiritual Master and showed him every mark of confidence. He was conducted to the room that had been Ramana Maharshi's and invited to stay as long as he wished. Speaking later of his experience in that room, he said that he had been 'in communion with the soul of Ramana Maharshi in the light.' He had always had a special affection for this mystic who had refused to be considered a personage of importance, and who had always possessed a lively humour and great common sense.

His visits to ashrams in the four corners of the country taught Omraam Mikhaël a great deal about India. In a civilization in which psychic powers have been highly developed over the course of centuries, there inevitably exists a wide variety of charismatic leaders, from simple fakirs to true spiritual Masters. Several of the saddhus he met were well known and had thousands of disciples, but he also encountered many who had assumed the role of guru, medium, or clairvoyant without real knowledge, and who exploited the credulity of their disciples. On the faces of those who lived in such ashrams he failed to find the signs of spirituality he looked for.

One day he met a saddhu for whom he developed a particular affection. He was a hundred and fifty years old and remained almost constantly motionless in a state of samadhi. The disciples in his ashram saw their guru as a transmitter, a kind of icon, behind whose unresponsive physical exterior was an entity with whom they communicated.

At one point, Omraam Mikhaël interrupted his journey to meet the saddhu Nityananda Maharaj, reputed to be a great sage and an infallible clairvoyant. Arriving in his ashram near Bombay, he found himself before a simple, unassuming man, dressed in nothing more than a dhoti, who greeted him silently and invited him with a courteous gesture to sit opposite him. Without a word, Nityananda gazed at his visitor for a long time, then closed his eyes. The time passed. Sitting face to face, neither of them stirred, and for the disciples present it was obvious that their spiritual guide was in a trance. When Nityananda finally opened his eyes, he seemed to return from a great distance. In perfect English, he said:

'His heart is pure. Peace is in his soul. All powers have been given to him.'

He added that his visitor had lived in India in the distant past, and mentioned an important personage whose name is still known today. Others before him – among them Peter Deunov – had spoken to Omraam Mikhaël Aïvanhov of the role he had played in India in the past. In fact, only a few days before, a saddhu gifted with clairvoyance had told him:

'This is not the first time you have been here. You have already been a Hindu. You have lived here in the past, and you will return.'

Before leaving India, Omraam Mikhaël again visited Ananda Moyi Ma and several of the greater clairvoyants of the time, all of whom spontaneously repeated Nityananda's revelation. Finally, returning to Nainital to see Hanuman Baba, he told him the name that Nityananda had revealed. Hanuman Baba, still silent, took out an ancient book about the great spiritual Masters of India, and showed him a picture of one of them, seated in the lotus posture. Over his head was the figure of the seven-headed cobra, symbolizing the possession of all spiritual and psychic powers.

21

Back In France

On February 9th, 1960, after a year's absence, Omraam Mikhaël Aïvanhov returned to Paris. The happy crowd waiting to greet him at Orly airport were impatient to see him again, for his dynamic presence and his spiritual talks had been greatly missed. But when he appeared at the gates they were taken by surprise. A new power seemed to emanate from this white-bearded patriarchal figure whom they barely recognized. So strongly did he resemble Peter Deunov, that some of those who had known the Bulgarian Master wept openly.

Omraam Mikhaël Aïvanhov was sixty years old. In reality he had been teaching, enlightening, and guiding his disciples with the wisdom of a true spiritual Master for many years, but that day at Orly he seemed both the same and yet transformed. His whole being expressed the stability that had always characterized him, while at the same time radiating a new aura of authority.

The next day and for the following several days, in spite of the fatigue of his long journey, he gave several talks at Izgrev before a hall filled to capacity and received countless visitors. But he did not delay long in Paris and soon left for the Bonfin. Toward the end of his stay in India he had heard of the disaster that had struck Fréjus two months earlier when the rupture of the Malpasset Dam on the Reyran had released flood waters that had devastated the town and left hundreds dead. The Bonfin, a few kilometres away, had been spared.

The spectacle of destruction that met his eyes was overwhelming. For miles around everything was in ruins, and the whole region was impregnated with the terror and suffering of the victims. Powerful,

In the dining room at Izgrev in 1958 and 1960

negative vibrations assailed him on all sides, and he could sense the souls of the dead still clinging to the ruins of their homes. For days, he did everything in his power to communicate with them mentally and help them to free themselves from the horror of the sudden, violent death which kept them tied to where they had lived. By communicating with their spirit, he tried to help them to move toward the light.

After two weeks of this intense spiritual work, he returned to Izgrev, and on March 6th, he spoke about his new name:

'The name Omraam combines the two processes of *solve* and *coagula*. "Om" is the sound that disintegrates all that is negative. It corresponds to the *solve* of initiatic science, which returns things to their source by transforming them into light. The vibrations of "Raam" have the power to condense and coagulate divine realities and make them tangible. This is *coagula.*'

A change of name is not unusual in the initiatic tradition. On condition that it is well chosen – normally by a person of great wisdom – a new name can awaken new forces in the soul. For this reason, the quality of its vibrations is of first importance. Omraam Mikhaël Aïvanhov, who was familiar with the symbolism and power of numbers, calculated the numerological value of his new name, and changed the spelling of his surname from Ivanoff to Aïvanhov. He said that he had been inspired by the Indian pronunciation of his name, but in reality, as he explained later, this change brought the total numerological value of his name to 72, a number that is considered very important in the cabbalistic tradition, being the sum of the nine choirs of angels, each of which comprises eight hierarchies.[46]

At the spring equinox shortly after his return to France, he spent a few days in the mountains. After living as an oriental for months in India, he was finding it difficult to adapt to the rhythm of life in Paris and had even lost all desire to speak. For many years, he had dreamed of communicating wordlessly with his brothers and sisters, and throughout his life, he was to have a sense of regret that this was not possible:

> Not everything that I say to you during these meditations can be put into words. One day you will sense and receive within yourselves what I give you in these moments of silence. In fact, some of you are already capable of this. I could lead you to extraordinary regions, but you are not aware of this, and are not synchronized with my vibrations.[47]

It is true that his disciples were not yet capable of following his lead in this, but neither was he called to live the life of a contemplative. It was impossible for him to be silent. For a long time now, his days had been dedicated to action and a large part of his nights to communion with God. From on high he received the strength that enabled him to live in both worlds.

No sooner had he returned from the mountains than he resumed his task as teacher. The members of the brotherhood were overjoyed. At last their spiritual Master was with them again. To begin with they had been a little uneasy, afraid that the warm, simple relationship of the past might have changed. They could not fail to notice something new and indefinable in him that they had never sensed before. The months he had spent with the yogis and saddhus of India, the privileged relation he had enjoyed with the great Babaji, and the new name that had been given to him in mysterious circumstances – all this was somewhat intimidating.

---

46. Pythagoras taught that the universe was based on numbers. Numerology stems from the notion that each number has both a symbolic significance and a particular vibration, and that each letter of the alphabet corresponds to a number.

47. Unpublished talk, September 1st, 1971.

It was not long, however, before they realized that his attitude had not changed. He was as accessible, cordial, and informal as ever, and no more inclined to allow himself to be put on a pedestal than before. He told them, in fact, to stop singing his praises and start working without focusing attention on him: 'Try rather to understand my ideas and put them into practice,' he used to say. Over the years he repeated that he never told them anything without having experienced and verified it beforehand, and they too, he said, should verify everything for themselves. His constant theme was the light dispensed by the sun to all creatures on earth. He urged his disciples to immerse themselves mentally in light as in an ocean, and to radiate out to the world all the colours it contains.

Omraam Mikhaël Aïvanhov's place is unquestionably at the heart of the Mikhaëlic era foretold by Rudolf Steiner. He belongs to the spiritual family of that great luminous spirit, Mikhaël, archangel of Light, whose mission it is to illuminate and liberate human beings. Far from using his ascendancy to influence or coerce his disciples, he always pointed out the different possibilities open to them. If he saw that some were leaning toward another genuinely spiritual group, he did not try to hold them back. 'We are all members of the same family,' he told them. One could follow him as one follows a mountain guide, without renouncing a particle of one's freedom.

His attitude toward children was equally respectful of their natural development. In his view, it was not the role of the brotherhood to educate them: at some point, they would have to make their own decisions about their orientation. At the same time, however, he invited parents to bring their young children to the Bonfin during the holidays so that they might benefit from the climate of beauty and brotherhood: 'This,' he said, 'is the true pedagogy of the future: this attitude, this silence, and the example of their parents.'

His philosophy of education also attributed great importance to the role of music, and he often advised parents to surround their children with it. In the summer, when the younger ones gave their little open-air concerts, he was always moved by their fresh voices and the trust in their eyes. And when they gave him their drawings, he exclaimed at the beauty of the broadly smiling suns or the multicoloured trees. By encouraging them to do even better, he sought to stimulate in them a taste for perfection. Small children ran spontaneously to him, and even babies seemed to want to talk to him.

Always attentive to the events of his times, he often talked to young people about how to transform themselves before attempting to transform society. He had not forgotten the turbulent energies and impassioned searching of his own youth. As Peter Deunov had once told him, he was the demolisher *par excellence* of stale, outworn ideas. At the same time he knew just how important it was to steer the energies of the young toward life and away from violence and death. One day, referring to the protest movements among the young – such as that of the hippies in the United States, whose chosen symbol expressed an ideal of peace and love – he said that they had been confusedly seeking universal brotherhood and were a manifestation of the age of Aquarius.

In spite of his sympathy for the aspirations of the young, however, he did not attempt to make everything easy for them. Rather, he taught them how to channel their energies and aspirations and give them concrete expression. Aware of their profound dissatisfaction, he urged them to recognize that they would find true strength only in themselves, in their ability to master themselves and to behave with nobility and magnanimity. Explaining the immutable laws of cause and effect, he encouraged them to adapt themselves to the demands of society in order to become capable of transforming it from within.

Cosmic moral laws, the source of all human morality, constituted one of the keystones of his teaching. The first of these is the 'law of recordings', by virtue of which everything that occurs in the world is recorded in nature's memory. Second is the 'law of agriculture', which determines the results of human endeavour, for we reap only what we have sown. According to the 'law of echo', which mirrors our every word or thought, whether we say 'I love you,' or 'I hate you,' those are the words that come back to us. And these laws are effective on the higher planes as well: the negative thoughts that we let slip attract noxious elements which end by poisoning us. Just as every event is recorded in the universal memory of nature, so are our actions imprinted in our own individual human memory and remain alive to torture us or to bring us joy. Hence the importance for human beings to behave in such a way as to create new recordings within themselves, to create new, more positive imprints.

*
* *

In the summer of 1960, there was a large gathering at the Bonfin for the convention. When the Master left his chalet at dawn and saw the long lines of shadowy figures walking up to the Rock, he could not help but be moved. 'Dear Lord,' he thought, 'how beautiful they are, all these brothers and sisters coming to pay homage to your splendour!' One morning, after his talk on the Rock, he confessed that he had been unable to restrain his tears as they sang. Beautiful music often brought him to a state bordering on ecstasy, plucking at the secret chords of his being that linked him to the world of perfection. After his long absence in India, it was a joy to hear the songs of the fraternity again and join his voice to those of his disciples, to measure once again the power of this music to stir the most sensitive fibres of the human heart by linking it to sublime entities.

In India he had noticed that many ascetics did not sing and even considered music a distraction from things of greater importance. That conception of the spiritual life was utterly foreign to him: in his view, music was an essential part of life. He was convinced that harmonious music would soon play a predominant role in the life of people throughout the world. It was classical music that he loved; above all, the sacred music that corresponded with higher realms and facilitated meditation. But his appreciation was not one-sided: when he chose music to accompany certain physical activities, for instance, it was not to the classics that he turned, but rather to Tyrolean yodelling songs or other works equally gay and dynamic.

Even those with little sensitivity to music soon grew to love it here in this spiritual family, where it had such importance and marked the rhythm of the day's activities. When the Master explained that music was the respiration of the soul, or that a beautiful song had a beneficial effect on the singer, even the indifferent responded. The music that resounded in the halls of Izgrev and the Bonfin was of a truly magical beauty. Every day after meals, they listened to the sacred works of one of the composers he loved and whom he referred to as the 'great musical giants': Beethoven, Haydn, Mozart, Handel, and Bach.

Hearing him speak of the deeper meaning of some of these works, one could not help but discover their spiritual beauty. He used to say, for instance, that Beethoven's *Missa Solemnis* could help one to work for greater detachment; that Haydn's *Stabat Mater* was conducive to a continual and tranquil elevation of the spirit; that the Trio for flute and harp from Berlioz's *Enfance du Christ* attracted beings from the invisible world who, unseen and unknown, came to dance. All this was so natural to him that one day he asked the musicians to play the Trio three times running, so that those invisible entities might continue to dance for the glory of God.

To sing with him often became a mystical experience for his disciples, and when they succeeded in silencing the clamorous voice of their own preoccupations and uniting their thoughts with his, he was free for the spiritual work that was the framework of his life. Gathered around the fire one evening in August, 1960, the campers were so stimulated by his words, that they sang one of the most beautiful four-part songs in their repertory with exceptional sensitivity. The Master did not sing with them. The next day he told them that the power of that song had affected him in an extraordinary way, that he had been close to fainting as his soul had taken flight. After leaving them he had thought about the power of their love and, gazing at the stars, had taken a few deep breaths to help him to assimilate what had just happened. 'I know what I do for you,' he said, 'but I want to thank you for what you do for me.'

The year following his return from India saw the beginning of a fraternal centre in Switzerland. On his first visit to the country, his disciples invited him to visit a site they had found at Les Monts-de-Corsier. A long walk through forests and up and down rocky slopes brought them to a broad clearing with a magnificent view. Below stretched the deep blues and greens of the Lake of Geneva, and beyond it the jagged spires of the Dents du Midi pierced the sky. On clear days the great dome of Mont Blanc gleamed in the distance.

Once the Swiss fraternity had bought the land, he returned to visit it again. It was winter, and nature, robed all in white, seemed to have been fashioned that very day by the hand of the Creator. The Master walked for a long time in the snow. Later, when the group asked him to give the future centre a name, he called it Videlinata, meaning 'divine light' in Bulgarian. As always when he dedicated a centre for the brotherhood, he exhorted them to use it with great respect, to be conscious of what it represented and of the work to be done there.

*
* *

At this period, Master Omraam Mikhaël asked those who followed his teaching to intensify their efforts, their attention, and their spiritual work. He spoke of the exigencies of certain Hindu and Tibetan Masters of the past and described the initiatic ordeals to which they subjected their disciples in order to link them ever more closely to the divine source. For his own disciples he had great ambitions, and although he always showed them great love, he could also be severe, even inflexible. The demands he made on himself, however, were a hundred times greater. Wishing to be capable not only of instructing them but of giving them an entirely new vision of life, he constantly sought to perfect himself and increase his own knowledge. He was never satisfied that what he gave them adequately answered their needs.

The references he made at this time to the exigencies of oriental Masters were important. In his view, true universal brotherhood could only come about through a blending of aspects developed respectively by East and West. The spiritual philosophy, clairvoyance, knowledge, and psychic powers of the former allied to the scientific discoveries and material and social progress of the latter were capable of transforming the world.

In spite of the passion of many Westerners for Eastern mysticism, however, he did not hesitate to insist that Eastern methods needed to be adapted, for they corresponded to neither the mentality nor the climate nor the way of life of Westerners. In this he agreed with teachers such as Ramakrishna and Vivekananda, neither of whom had encouraged their disciples to practise rigorous physical techniques; on the contrary, they had declared that traditional techniques whose goal was to develop great mental concentration were no longer appropriate. They too had emphasized the value of spiritual work, of meditation and contemplation as the most effective means of achieving liberation.

Without attaching undue importance to external forms, Omraam Mikhaël Aïvanhov extracted the vital sap from ancient texts, from the maxims of Hermes Trismegistus, from the teachings of Jesus and the Buddha, giving them their true cosmic dimension. By placing himself beyond all religions, cults, and philosophies, he could speak of a solar religion that was capable of preserving the flame of life within changing forms. In his view, only principles are eternal; it is a great mistake to try to perpetuate forms and structures.

At the same time, although he did not approve of the excessively rigid forms established by many religions, he readily acknowledged that pictures or statues could be useful, often serving as a necessary support for prayer. He himself made use of symbols in his spiritual work – the sun, the Tree of Life of the Cabbalah, the rose, the prism, the seven colours of the spectrum – but he always warned his disciples that such symbols must be no more than tools to help them rise toward the divine world. In his initiatic school at Izgrev and at the Bonfin he advocated a spiritual work that mobilized mind, heart, and will. Time and again he talked about the role of these three basic components of every human being. They had an important place in his philosophy, but also in his life:

> I have known the mystical way: the heart, feelings, sensations, love. I have known the spiritual way: study and knowledge. I have also followed the way of concrete realization through work and the exercise of the will. I have tried these three ways one after the other, and in each I have achieved results. And yet I do not want to follow one or the other: I want all three.[48]

---

48. Unpublished talk, August 3rd, 1955.

If he was to continue to reveal to his followers the truths that would enable them to advance, he needed tranquillity and silence. But he saw that an understanding of true silence, the silence that is not merely a conventional attitude but a state of mind, was not accessible to all. Although his disciples were always receptive, he often felt that he was a voice crying in the wilderness. He told them frankly that their lack of resolve and perseverance saddened him. But his regrets were for them, for those who were not yet aware of the value of 'a silence penetrated by thoughts of such an exalted nature, that it is endowed with all the elements needed to form their subtle bodies, even the body of glory.' He told them:

Once you have tasted the gifts this silence brings, you will understand it. Silence is not simply a question of not fidgeting, not moving things about; it is a question of putting a stop to all discontent, to all the vague emotions that drift through one. The first degree of silence is physical. It is necessary to attain that silence before one can go higher and pacify one's astral feelings. The second degree of silence, then, is the pacification of feelings; the third is the pacification of thought. When this silence is achieved, the spirit is free to travel and visit regions it has never seen. In this total peace the spirit can soar aloft and bring back with it joy, health, fortitude, and love. It can bring wisdom to our minds, so that our intelligence enables us to understand everything.[49]

More than once he resolved to demand more of his brothers and sisters. At times he expressed his displeasure in no uncertain terms when they made too much noise at meals. But each year at the close of the summer convention, gathered with them round the fire in honour of the Archangel Mikhaël, it was the magic of love that triumphed. The ambience created by their spiritual aspirations and desire for perfection was so irresistible that the Master was caught up in the current and all his resolutions of severity were swept away. His love overcame all else. Over the years, however, he sometimes interrupted his program of talks and left the convention for a few days in order to give the participants a period of personal reflection. At the same time,

---

49. Unpublished talk, August 6th, 1960.

it was an opportunity for him to renew his own energy and inspiration. On these occasions, he usually went to the mountains. At other times he stayed at the Bonfin and took part in all the activities, depriving the participants only of the spoken word, so that they might learn 'to desire nothing more than the presence of God.'

This presence of God was the object of his own tireless quest. Those close to him knew that when alone he often voluntarily left his physical body or was caught up in ecstasy. They also knew that he slept little, and like all high initiates whose consciousness is always alert and vigilant, was able to carry on his spiritual work while his physical body was resting. He sometimes said that what he could do in the daytime was less than a millionth part of what he could accomplish 'on the other side' at night. It was then that he could speak to the souls of his disciples most effectively.

*
* *

Master Omraam divided his time between Izgrev, Videlinata, and the Bonfin, the three centres at which his followers gathered for conventions at Easter, in the summer, and at Christmas. In addition to his daily talks – only rarely did he miss a day or two – he gave many private interviews and, with great respect for the needs of each individual, took pains to answer his voluminous correspondence personally. He was overburdened with work.

In order to renew his inspiration and consolidate his close bond with the spiritual world, he needed to retire from time to time in solitude. In the mid-sixties, he began to make occasional visits to the Pyrenees to meditate and rest. Finding ideal conditions for his spiritual work, he often spent time there between the brotherhood conventions, alone or with a few disciples. The place, which he called Castelrama, was in a beautiful setting. The view of the mountains was superb, the air pure and invigorating, the silence broken only by the song of birds and the deep voice of the wind.

In his small cottage he consecrated one room for meditation, and encouraged his disciples to do the same at home, adding that the smaller the room the easier it was to concentrate. There were days when he spent many hours in this oratory; at other times he climbed the hill behind the cottage for long meditations, rejoicing in the sunlight and peace of the early morning. Nourished by the natural elements around him, by the currents of energy flowing from the sun, he told his companions that he felt no need to eat. Since his youth he had been accustomed to eat sparsely twice a day, but at Castelrama he usually had only one meal a day. And as his soul had never ceased to vibrate in response to the call of the mountains, he often went off for long, solitary hikes to the high peaks of the Pyrenees.

Omraam Mikhaël recognized the importance of the realities of life in the world, and always tried to remain in touch with the circumstances of his contemporaries in order to understand their problems. Castelrama became a 'transmitting station' from which his spiritual work went out to humanity. But although these periods of retreat were extremely beneficial, he never wished to remain alone for very long. This paradox was a constant in his life: his need to be in permanent communion with the highest planes of being was always tempered by his rare openness and accessibility to his contemporaries and to the brotherhood in particular. He was never so happy as when surrounded by his spiritual family. Before long, there was a continual coming and going of disciples he invited to stay – ten or more at a time – and Castelrama rapidly became a miniature brotherhood centre.

Many surprises awaited his guests: in the Master they discovered a host of unequalled thoughtfulness who personally arranged a vase of flowers in their rooms. He was the *pater familias*, relaxed and warm-hearted, who often invited them to share a meal and at times even prepared a Bulgarian dish for them. He made sure that they all had the opportunity to express themselves, made plans for the future with them, and won their hearts with his informal cordiality. Every so often, local people whose acquaintance he wanted to make – the local gendarme or the mountain-rescue teams – were invited to a meal, and he had the art of putting them all at their ease. The people of the region became truly fond of him and were always happy to know that he was there.

22

I Speak With My Own Voice

It was six years since Omraam Mikhaël Aïvanhov had returned from India, six years since his disciples first gave him the respectful title of Master. In spite of this, he continued to refer to himself as 'a living book' on whose pages Peter Deunov had written for twenty years before sending him to France. Although he loved to talk about the great Masters, he never referred to himself as one. He always said that Peter Deunov had chosen him, his most insignificant disciple, only because he cherished a high ideal and worked in secret to perfect himself.

In spite of his unassuming attitude, he was obliged once again to contend with difficulties caused by calumnies, conflicts, and misunderstandings that resurfaced in his homeland. There were still those in Bulgaria who continued to bear him a grudge, who even reproached him for his physical resemblance to Peter Deunov. To be sure, there were also many Bulgarians who had visited him at the Bonfin and who spoke of his work with enthusiasm, but they were not taken seriously in their home country, any more than others had been twenty years earlier.

In the French brotherhood also, some who had known Peter Deunov continued to reproach Omraam Mikhaël Aïvanhov for the new insights he brought to the teaching. For his part, after a year in India where spiritual guides were accorded unconditional respect, he found himself faced once again with western reticence, with the ever-present tendency to analyse and criticize. One day in July, during the 1966 convention at the Bonfin, deciding that it was time to correct the situation, he declared:

'I speak with my own voice. Peter Deunov spoke with his. If he did not talk about these questions, it was not because he did not know them. Perhaps the time was not ripe to talk about them. Many things need to be revealed before people understand.'

A few days later he reverted to the same question and begged them to pay less attention to persons and more to the light of the sun, to that which is stable and divine. In August, alluding to his illumination at the age of fifteen, he spoke in tones more solemn still:

'It is now fifty years since I was overwhelmed by the light. My work is just beginning and it will become visible to the whole world. I have been waiting for orders from above, and it is only this year that heaven has sent me a sign of the work expected of me. For the first time I have been instructed to reveal many things to you. A different era is upon us, with a different language and different means. My work is different from that of Peter Deunov. Completely different. But there is no contradiction between us. We are following the same path, advancing in the same direction, always toward the light, toward God.'

This declaration was enough to put new vigour into most of his disciples and create a climate of clarity which enabled them to adhere to his teaching without reserve. As for himself, although criticism never prevented him from doing what he had to do, it was always an occasion to purify his motivations and work on humility.

That summer he gave several talks about purity. In fact, he had frequently spoken on this subject before, returning to it over and over again. Drawing on examples from everyday life, he spoke first of the necessity in all realms of life of sorting the pure from the impure, to avoid poisoning oneself. Then he insisted on the importance of choosing one's pleasures, on every plane, with great care. His explanation of what he called 'the divine algebra' was particularly striking: when the intellect is freed from all impurities it attracts light and understanding; when the heart is purified it becomes capable of happiness; when the will is freed from apathy, it becomes stronger, and when the physical body is freed from the wastes that encumber it, it regains health. It is as logical as an equation.

With the skill of a painter, he described the beauty of the river of life, the 'path of wisdom' that flows from the highest realms of the invisible world, pregnant with celestial energies. He explained mental exercises that one could use to slake one's thirst at this river and recapture the purity that dwells at the summit of all that exists. He explained to couples how to live their love for each other without sinking to levels that sterilize the spiritual life. Of paramount importance in his view is to recognize the potency of sexual energy and use it for one's spiritual development.

> The sexual organs are a synopsis of creation as a whole. The force that lies hidden in human beings is a sacred, divine force by means of which they can attain all their desires. Let me give you an example: if you live on the fifth floor, the water you need has to be pumped up to you, and this necessitates a certain amount of pressure. If you do away with that pressure, the water will not reach all the floors. But men do their best to lower the pressure within themselves and reduce it to zero. They cannot endure it. And yet, this force should be allowed to rise through all the floors and reach the brain. It is the pressure that causes it to rise so that you can use it. But most people continually rid themselves of it, and consequently can never make use of it on the higher planes.[50]

It was in this sense that he liked to talk about the beauty of the work achieved by the high initiates, who instead of squandering these energies had learned to use them to create a dazzling light in the brain, a divine state of soul. He himself had chosen celibacy and continence in order to dedicate his life to helping humanity, but he had never feared this force which, following Hermes Trismegistus, he called 'the strength of all strengths.' Neither his spirituality nor his behaviour was ever inspired by a repudiation of the sexual force; on the contrary, in his view, the sexual energies with which cosmic intelligence has endowed human beings contain the seeds of evolution and transcendence.

His attitude toward women was always one of respect and spiritual love. What he looked for was the beauty that is so abundant in nature. The sight of a woman singing moved him deeply because she was a reminder of the divine Mother, but it was above all the

---

50. Unpublished talk, August 26th, 1958.

emanations of inner beauty he sought in the visible countenance. When he spoke about his attitude toward women, he did so in order to help other men. He declared without ambiguity that nothing was more beautiful than the sexual organs of men and women when considered as organs destined to accomplish the designs of God.

His teaching about love and sexuality is balanced and vivifying, but it is a teaching for the future. He himself acknowledged that very few human beings today are ready to work at self-dominance – even and perhaps especially, within the state of marriage – for the sake of achieving something great on the spiritual plane. Yet, considering the potency slumbering in the etheric centres of the chakras, such spiritual work could reach gigantic proportions.

There is a close relationship in his philosophy between sanctity and sexuality. Human beings can attain perfection only when they achieve control of these special energies and direct them to the higher spheres. And they can succeed in this endeavour only by adhering to the high ideal of seeking to resemble the heavenly Father and the divine Mother, only by opening their hearts spiritually to all creatures on earth:

> Love is an exchange, and exchanges exist on other planes beside the physical, they can take place between two people at a distance, through a look, a thought, a word, without ever embracing or touching. [...] When I speak of love I mean love that is life, light and beauty, an exchange with divine creatures. That is the love I think about night and day, and this love brings me blessings.[51]

And yet to renounce something without putting anything in its place had no meaning for him. As he often said, he himself had renounced nothing: he had simply transposed his choice of pleasures from the physical to the spiritual plane, thus gaining a profound joy that was nourished by mystical experiences. The beauty of children, of nature at sunrise, of the stars, the oceans, the mountains – all these things spoke to him of the perfection of God.

---

51. February 8th, 1971 (*The Mysteries of Yesod*, p. 175f).

23

The Yoga of the Sun

Omraam Mikhaël Aïvanhov's dominating passion was to set fire to hearts and minds. His personal path was the path of light, and all his teaching was imbued with this element so essential to life. His aspiration, he sometimes said, was to be a Prometheus: to steal fire from heaven and give it to human beings.

A series of talks given during the summer of 1967 constituted a synthesis of his teaching about the sun. For many years he had spoken of the yoga that he called 'Surya yoga' – Surya being Sanskrit for sun. This yoga of the sun, he explained, was known to the ancient Greeks, Egyptians, Persians, Aztecs, Mayas, and Tibetans, and it was the one he favoured above all others, for it included and summed up all other forms of yoga. He used to say that he taught many different kinds of yoga, among them the yoga of nutrition, but that he had rediscovered the richest, most ancient, and most vital of all: Surya yoga.

He loved to talk about the Spirit of the sun. In this respect his philosophy coincided with the age-old philosophies of the Vedas and Puranas, which teach that the true sun is not the star that is visible in the sky, but the supreme Intelligence that reigns at the summit of the firmament, above the realms of physical creation. He revealed that behind the physical sun existed a subtler, immaterial sun, a sun that is hidden to all but the most highly developed consciousness. Through love, it is possible for human souls to communicate on the level of the super-conscious with all creatures in the light of that sun. 'In our planetary system,' he added, 'the sun is the representative of God, the supreme sun of the universe.'

That year, aware that his ideas were not always easy to grasp, he spelled them out in great detail. In one particularly long talk he explained that by leading people to the light, the yoga of the sun could lead them to God, the unique source of all light. When we contemplate the sun in the morning, at the moment when it is most beneficial, we can rise mentally to the subtlest planes and there obtain elements that are lacking in our organism. 'It is really very simple,' he used to say, 'it is not even necessary to know which elements will restore your health; that is not important.' It is the soul and spirit that are capable of finding what a human being needs.

He realized, of course, that he was not always properly understood, that while he always refused to institute new forms which would become inflexible, most people tended to devise structures and adopt set habits. All spiritual Masters must certainly have experienced similar difficulties: they speak of eternal truths, but they see their disciples crystallizing these truths into rigid forms that mask and stifle the life within them.

In Omraam Mikhaël Aïvanhov's philosophy, the sun was not set up as an idol as in certain ancient solar religions; his 'solar religion' is simply a way of finding God, the true light that shines within each human being. The sun is no more than a doorway opening on to the deity, the best example we have of selfless love, because it gives without ceasing and asks for nothing in return. It is a dwelling place, an authentic temple for the spirit of truth, the spirit of purity and selfless altruism. And yet, as he declared, the man-made temples or churches on earth are not useless:

> [...] there is nothing wrong in having churches and temples; on the contrary, they are excellent and necessary. I have never suggested that they should be destroyed. Even a house can be a temple. But when men are ready to grasp the truth, they will stop going to man-made temples. They will worship in the great temple built by the hand of God himself, the universe. And then they will understand that man himself is a temple of God, and that he must progressively cleanse, purify, and sanctify himself so as to be a perfect sanctuary.[52]

---

52. September 4th, 1967 (*The Splendour of Tiphareth*, p. 202).

In the pure light of the Mediterranean mornings he talked of that which was closest to his heart: light. For him, light was the 'water' that flowed from the sun, the true source of life in which are contained the seven colours. Since the age of fourteen when he had discovered the beauty and symbolism of a prism, he had always used one in working with the seven rays. For him, the seven rays represented seven Spirits imbued with love, wisdom, and understanding with which he seems to have had a vital bond. He always carried a stick on which was mounted the large crystal he used as an instrument for this work. Knowing the influence of the colours of the spectrum, he often repeated that one could achieve great results by surrounding oneself with them, wearing them, and working to incorporate them in one's aura.

'I often turn the crystal of my stick to the sun and look at the seven colours. I pause for a moment to contemplate them, then I give thanks to heaven and go on with my work.'

*
* *

Omraam Mikhaël Aïvanhov was capable of communicating with the mysterious intelligences of the universe, but he had a particularly close relationship with one Being who, he said, was a spiritual sun for our planet, who illuminates the world and protects life on the subtler planes. This was Melchizedek, of whom he had already spoken in his first talks in 1938 and whom he called 'the Master of Masters.' His great love for Melchizedek was apparent in his frequent references to him, and his disciples had come to realize that he lived in uninterrupted communion with him.

The existence of Melchizedek is recognized both in the Judeo-Christian tradition and in certain oriental traditions. In Genesis he appears as the high priest of God who goes out to meet Abraham with bread and wine, the sacred symbols of the two principles. St Paul says of him that he had 'neither beginning of days nor end of life.' And in Revelations St John the Evangelist describes him as a 'son of man', clothed in a long robe girded about with a golden belt, with hair as white as snow and a face shining like the sun in full force.

> As the representative of God he is the divine flame on earth, and all initiates turn to him to light their candles. Make haste to unite with God, with fire, for it will be your salvation. Melchizedek has dominion over the angelic hierarchies; nothing can withstand him. He manifests where and as he wishes, and all Masters are his disciples. St John saw him, he was with him. It was Melchizedek who revealed the destiny of the world to him and inspired the images of the Apocalypse.[53]

In 1969, Master Omraam Mikhaël decided to visit Patmos, the island where St John had lived in exile. He had a special affection for this Apostle, but it was perhaps especially his love of Melchizedek that led him to visit the birthplace of the Apocalypse or Revelation, at the heart of which shines this great being depicted as an old man with eyes of light.

After spending a few days with the members of the brotherhood in Athens, he boarded a boat bound for Patmos, accompanied by a small group of disciples. The island of Patmos is closer to Turkey than to Greece, and the journey, which lasted thirteen hours in heavy seas, was a real hardship for the passengers. At four o'clock in the morning, the Master, refreshed and full of energy, was knocking on their cabin doors, bringing coffee and rolls for all. Soon they disembarked near a village whose inhabitants were still asleep, and a stalwart porter took charge of their baggage. Every line of his face expressed his admiration for the one he called 'the man of God', and although he understood no French, he followed closely on his heels,

---

53. Unpublished talk, September 2nd, 1960.

anxious to hear the sound of his voice. Every few minutes he asked, 'What is the man of God saying?'

Once rested and restored, they climbed into the hills to the monastery of Khora. The priest who acted as guide in the museum was at first voluble in his explanations of its sacred treasures, pointedly ignoring the occasional comments of the white-haired visitor about the secret symbolism of a cross or an icon. Gradually, however, his attitude changed and he became silent until Omraam Mikhaël asked him to tell them about the life of St John. This he did, speaking with greater moderation, after which his face became radiant and he exclaimed:

'I don't know what is happening to me. There is such an extraordinary climate of sympathy between us. I have never felt this with anyone before.'

And he began to weep with joy.

In the afternoon Master Omraam Mikhaël visited the grotto where St John had lived and in which he had written Revelations. Following him, his companions – who were themselves in a state of mind rarely experienced in this life – saw him descending the thirty steps that led through a garden full of flowers to the grotto: he seemed to be flying. The grotto made a deep impression on him – with the stone bed on which St John slept, the shelf carved out of the rock at which he dictated his Gospel to his disciple, and finally the rock that had been split in three by a bolt of lightning as the Apocalypse was revealed. Toward the end of the visit, asking his companions to leave him, he remained alone in the grotto for a long time.

He stayed on Patmos several days. At the time there were few tourists on the island, and he found the atmosphere very pure and blessed, still redolent of the presence of St John. He loved being there and was captivated by the beauty of the country, by the kindness of the people and their sincere, friendly expressions, by the solicitude of the monks who called on him constantly. On his return to France, he commented that the inhabitants of Patmos had the sensitivity of mediums and were capable of prophecy, as though they were still permeated with the ambience of the Apocalypse. For his part, he made a great impression on the villagers, who watched him wherever he went and showed him the deepest respect.

One day, while out for a walk in the country with his companions, a peasant woman approached, stopped in front of him, and asked shyly:

'Are you a monk?'

Without waiting for an answer, she made the sign of the cross and kissed his hand, murmuring:

'I wish you good health. Be happy with your monk's crown.'

She stood before him as though before an icon, while he, for his part, gazed at her with an expression of astonishment and delight. When she left them, he remained lost in thought for a moment. He explained later that before setting out on this walk he had meditated in his room and had asked something of the invisible world:

> When her words were translated for me, I realized that they were the answer to the questions I had been asking. Heaven had spoken to me through that old woman. You cannot imagine how happy that made me![54]

Leaving Patmos he returned to the Greek mainland where he visited Mount Athos with two of his companions. Here, the numerous monasteries, often situated in almost inaccessible spots, shelter some 3,000 monks and are known for the ancient manuscripts in their care. When a monastery they wanted to visit could not be reached by land, the three visitors were obliged to hire a small motor boat. And to their surprise, at each monastery the scene was the same: without knowing who he was, the monks manifested the utmost respect for Master Omraam Mikhaël and gave him the room reserved for the Orthodox bishop. In each place he asked the same question:

'Do you know of the existence of Melchizedek?'

Several years before, while in India, he had asked some of the great saddhus if they knew of a being who dwelt in the Himalayas and who had neither beginning nor end, neither father nor mother. There too they had known of his existence, but their name for him was Markande.

---

54. June 1st, 1969 (*The Book of Revelations: a Commentary*, p. 14).

24

The Universality of a Mission

Since 1960, the universal dimension of Omraam Mikhaël Aïvanhov's spiritual work had become increasingly apparent. His published talks were disseminated in several countries, and in the years following his return from India, he was invited to speak in a number of European towns and cities.

The purpose of his travels was always to extend his spiritual work to every part of the world. He was often invited to address groups of professionals, scientists, or political leaders, but in many cases, knowing in advance that he would be wasting his time, he refused. His ideas about how humanity could be transformed by means of spiritual galvanoplasty, for example, were too advanced for the world in which he was living. When he did address a particular group, however, his manner was exactly the same as when he spoke to his disciples; it was with the same fire, the same ardour, that he explained the principal themes of initiatic science.

On one occasion, at a meeting of scientists at the French nuclear research centre at Saclay, he listened with interest to their scholarly dissertations and discussions and when his turn came to speak he led their minds imperceptibly closer to the spiritual dimension, intending in this way to stimulate in them a level of reflection beyond that of pure science. His ideas about light, for instance, differed dramatically from the scientific notions of the other speakers, but they had the merit of leading the participants to personal discoveries on a subtler plane.

On another occasion, in a discussion with a group of police inspectors in Paris, he talked to them about light in a way that,

almost certainly, they had never heard before:

'Do you think you can fight crime by increasing the number of policemen and gendarmes or by improving your methods of surveillance and investigation? Well, you are mistaken. External methods are ineffectual in this area. The only effective means is light.'

To the five inspectors listening to him, this seemed a strange solution.

'Light?' one of them asked. 'How?'

With his usual colourful images, he talked about criminals and how they prepared their thefts, kidnappings, or assassinations, in the conviction that no one knew about their plans. Then he added:

'But suppose people possessed an inner lamp that enabled them to see in advance and from far away the mischief that threatened them: they would take precautions, and the evildoer's plans would come to nothing. Thus the only way to eliminate crime is by means of light. This is why human beings must be taught to cultivate their inner light: it will take a very long time, but it is the only sure way.'

The inner light he spoke of was the light of a genuine spirituality capable of transforming every human being. Light, the living spirit that bears within itself love, wisdom, and truth. Although well aware that most people are not sufficiently developed spiritually to perceive the subtle reality of light, he still insisted on the necessity of concentrating on it as often as possible, of drawing it into oneself so as to refine one's perceptions and generate new vibrations in the cells.

His first concern was to set people in motion. In fact, to this end, he often deliberately shocked or disappointed them. But although he was sometimes severe, his sense of humour and his great kindness were never absent.

The aspirations and inclinations of those he met did not escape him. He recognized their scale of values and often called it into question without fear of disconcerting them. On occasion, when he was the guest of people who expected to hear him talk about sublime subjects, he limited himself to a few apparently random remarks about their preoccupations: about money which was always on their minds, or about their sex life with which they were obsessed. This was sometimes the only way to reach them. As for his hosts, they often understood only later why he had talked about things which had seemed so trivial at the time. After the first instinctive reaction had faded, they realized that he had stimulated something, that he had opened the flood gates and the 'water of life' was flowing.

No human being was insignificant in his eyes; he looked for the divine spark in everyone he met. In hotels he treated the employees with such exquisite courtesy that their expression became animated, their eyes lit up, and they turned to watch him as he passed. In conversation with flight attendants, guides at an exhibition, or taxi drivers he had the gift of creating the ambience he wanted. If he saw that they were tense or shy, he told them a funny story to make them laugh and open the way for dialogue.

As always, his personal needs were modest, and the hotels he chose to stay in were always the least luxurious. The only condition he looked for was the possibility of seeing the sunrise from his room. When his travelling companions complained about the rudimentary accommodations they had to put up with, he insisted on the importance of a simple way of life.

When travelling by car or train, he worked to perfect his knowledge of English, listening to recorded texts on cassettes to improve his accent. 'A new activity triggers a renewal of life in the whole organism,' he commented. Wherever he went, his sole purpose was to become always more useful to humanity. One of those who often accompanied him confided:

> He was like a father, a marvellous educator. Travelling with him was a veritable apprenticeship, for it is impossible to be close to someone of that calibre without constantly calling oneself into question and striving to transform oneself. But his spontaneous expressions of approval for one's efforts were very comforting.

*
*   *

Quite often while travelling, he left his companions for several days at a time, and whenever possible he meditated in the midst of nature, the true temple of God. On the other hand, he also liked to pray in the religious sanctuaries of the world – in temples, mosques, and basilicas – for he considered that they were all sacred.

In the spring of 1970 he was in Japan and stayed for a week in a Zen temple deep in the mountains not far from Tokyo. The twelve monks in residence welcomed him as one of their own and set aside a small temple decorated with numerous Buddhas, in which he was free to pray, read, and sleep without being disturbed by the noise of the monastery. From the first day, they invited him to take part in their religious rites which were attended by many people from the neighbouring town.

Very early in the morning, the participants gathered for a ceremony followed by a two-hour meditation. They sat round the four sides of a room, facing the wall, in the ZaZen posture, which includes precise rules for the position of the head and hands. A monk moved quietly about in the centre of the room, a long 'warning stick' in his hand, watching the backs of those meditating. When he saw someone becoming drowsy, he tapped him sharply on the shoulder.

Master Omraam Mikhaël knew that the blow was intended to touch a particular nerve, not only to prevent somnolence and remedy a slack posture, but also to induce greater clarity in the brain and rally flagging energies. Naturally, he wished to experience it for himself. But when he asked the monk to give him the traditional tap during the meditation next day, the latter was very embarrassed and refused politely, protesting that he did not need it. In the face of the foreign Master's insistence, however, he finally acquiesced, and the following morning, coming up behind him during the meditation, he bowed with great respect before tapping him on the shoulder. In his turn, Omraam Mikhaël bowed his head to signal his thanks. He found the experience instructive, for the blow did indeed trigger in him an interesting reaction of lucidity in the mind. Wishing to continue the experience, he asked the monk to repeat the gesture every morning. The latter reluctantly did as asked.

Relating this incident after his return to France, he made it clear that although the aim of ZaZen is to arrest thought and create an inner void, the void must never be a goal in itself. It can even be dangerous if it does not serve to attract fullness. To create the void without danger one must have already worked to purify one's inner self and must begin one's meditation in a state of calm and emotional peace:

> [...] then, after a few moments, you must be active and dynamic and focus your thoughts and feelings on whatever subject you have chosen, projecting and intensifying them until you feel yourself expanding, filled with a sense of awe and wonder. Only then is it safe to pause and try to empty yourself, to stop thinking and allow yourself only to feel. At this point you will be in no danger.[55]

Each time he returned from his travels to Izgrev or the Bonfin, he was so happy to be with his spiritual family once again that he spent the day giving thanks. He often said that we should give thanks a thousand times a day; that the magic of gratitude was extraordinary, more beneficial than all the medicines in the world. For him, the single word 'Thanks' was a potent mantra, an 'antidote capable of counterbalancing every kind of poison.'

*
* *

The following year he had the joy of seeing his mother again in the village of his childhood in Macedonia, which was now part of

---

55. August 14th, 1971 (*'Know Thyself' – Jnana Yoga II*, p. 105f).

Yugoslavia. It was not the first time he had been back there: in May 1964 he had visited his village and happily renewed many sixty-year old memories. At that time some members of the family still lived there, among them the cousin whose weaving he had ruined at the age of four. On his return to France, he had commented humorously on that visit:

'They were still alive and very old, and I gave them something to make up for the distress I had caused them. One must never neglect anything. Sooner or later we have to pay our debts.'

This second visit to the land of his birth was for the purpose of meeting his mother, who made the long journey from Varna to Serbtzi with one of her sons. She was now ninety-five years old and had not seen her eldest son since 1937, for it had always been impossible for him to visit Communist Bulgaria without losing his right to return to France. When the time came to part after this short stay in Macedonia, they both knew that they were seeing each other for the last time. Back in Varna, Dolia told one of her granddaughters:

'I was afraid I would cry when I saw him with his hair quite white, but I managed to hold back my tears. I was very moved, but I wanted the ambience to be beautiful. Above all I did not want to upset him.'

On August 5th, 1973, two years after seeing her son again, her long life drew to a peaceful close.

25

True Power is the Fruit of Love

For Omraam Mikhaël Aïvanhov, everything in nature was transparent, everything was luminous and alive. His bonds with the powers of the invisible world were strong, and in this sense the 'marvellous' that accompanies all great spiritual beings was ever present in his life. From the beginning, he had always been conscious of the state of mind of his disciples and of the inner changes manifested in their eyes. When he saw their light growing fainter, he assured them with great kindness: 'If you think I have no idea of your difficulties, you are mistaken.' He was well aware of their problems, for he himself had not had a sheltered life, but he also told them: 'It is you who have to free yourselves, otherwise you will never evolve.'

Often after a talk, some of his followers thanked him for having spoken about their personal problems and given them the specific advice they needed. In fact, this happened so often that he acquired the reputation of being able to tune in to all the questions and problems of a sizeable gathering. In addition, many people told him of inexplicable events such as a cure or an apparition that had occurred when they had called on him. Some had escaped unharmed from an accident after saying his name, while others had seen him before them in his physical body, although in reality he had been elsewhere.

He listened to them but steadfastly refused to be considered a miracle-worker. 'My mission is not to heal,' he had said in the past, 'but to enlighten.' In order to preserve the integrity of that mission, he almost always denied that he possessed any special powers, even those that had been natural to him since his youth. His relationship with his disciples had to be free of the aura of fascination that inevitably surrounds clairvoyance, mediumnity, or the power of healing. Without fail he turned their attention to the light, to the angels, to God. Shortly after his return from India he had begun to talk about the 'OMA firm', explaining that he had become a collective entity, that the credit belonged to those who worked with him and whom he himself did not know. Any thanks should be addressed to this collective being: 'Don't blame me,' he used to say. 'It was Omraam who did it.'

One could sense that he had immense respect for all the invisible beings who supported him and whom he sometimes referred to as angels, at other times as devas or simply as entities. While confident that he could always call on their assistance, he never forgot that he was addressing free beings who must not be burdened with self-centred requests. From time to time he asked the Angel of Air to disperse the clouds so that everyone could contemplate the sun, but he recognized that the Angel had the right to refuse.

This consciousness of his responsibility toward those who helped him in his work gave him a sense of being no more than a single link in the chain of beings working for the good of humanity. His attitude toward nature was one of respect and humility; he did not attempt to go against her laws or change the natural order of things. This approach had allowed him to forge the mysterious bond with animals, trees, and even inanimate objects that had sometimes enabled him to talk to a car that had broken down so that, to the surprise of all present, it inexplicably started up again and functioned just long enough to reach his destination. 'This does not mean that metals are intelligent or that plants have a soul,' he explained; 'but there is a cosmic intelligence which suffuses all created things and works through them.'

The truth is that he attached little importance to powers of this kind and never encouraged others to try to acquire them. He insisted, rather, on the importance of working in one's own way rather than relying on conventional methods: in seeking self-transformation, only our own efforts can be relied on. It was in this sense that he reacted during a pilgrimage to Israel, where he went in part to meet Cabbalists, but primarily to seek traces of the spirit of Jesus. On the shores of Lake Tiberius several people told him the legend of the miraculous powers of this lake: it was enough to bathe in it to be purified. This sort of thing meant nothing to him. He was indifferent to fables which many people considered highly important, and was always careful to restore things to their true proportions. On his return to France, he spoke of this with a touch of humour, saying that it was not by immersing oneself in water that one could be purified, but by working consciously, inwardly as well as outwardly. One of those who had been with him in Israel recounted:

> It was after the Six-day War, and we had received permission to visit Jerusalem, which was occupied by Israel. The Master also wanted to visit the synagogue marking the place were Jethro lived, and he spent a long time meditating there. On another occasion we visited the grotto where Shimon Ben Yohai, one of the authors of the Sepher Ha Zohar, had lived. It was the day after a big feast-day. Thousands of people had been there on pilgrimage to the grotto, which is on a wooded hill, and the ground around the sacred shrine was strewn with litter. Seized with a holy fury, the Master appealed to the Angel of Air to clear it all away. Immediately, torrential rain began to fall and continued for several hours. All the rubbish was swept away. It was such an unusual event that all the newspapers mentioned it the next day. But when the Master was angry, it was never for long. He always regained his normal good humour with staggering speed.

In Omraam Mikhaël Aïvanhov's view, genuine psychic powers could be obtained, sustained, and enhanced only through love. He had always rejected powers that were used to dazzle people in order to dominate them, and wishing to avoid any possible coercion of his disciples, he tried not to manifest his full psychic strength. Those who were often with him or who lived near his cottage, however, could not fail to notice the mastery he exerted over himself and, consequently, over the elements. The fact is that he knew how to influence nature by using the infinite possibilities with which cosmic intelligence has endowed creation.

An instance of this occurred toward the end of one summer in the seventies. Forest fires, which are frequent in the south of France, were raging in the region, and the Bonfin was in danger from the flames being blown in that direction. Night was falling. Master Omraam

Mikhaël, accompanied by others, climbed up to the Rock of Prayer to call on the Angels of Air and Water. 'Leave me alone to pray,' he told them, and ten minutes later, out of a sky that had been cloudless only a moment earlier, rain poured down and put out the fires. More than once over the years, this phenomenon was repeated, and when he spoke of it, it was always to say that he had asked the Angels of Air and Water to put out the fire, adding that one had to conquer a great many things in oneself before obtaining power over the elements.

The meaning is clear: all that exists in nature also exists within each human being. Each of the four elements can be an agent of purification, but it is possible to control the external elements only if one has purified and learned to control the 'elements within.' An effect obtained in this way is not properly speaking a miracle; it is rather the result of an individual's personal mastery, comparable to the control exercised by a lion tamer over wild animals, or by a snake-charmer who neutralizes the venom from a snake bite by force of will.

Springs, waterfalls, rivers, lakes, and oceans represented for him forces that can be used for the greater glory of God. When he was on a ship or in a plane, he contacted the intelligent beings that inhabit the elements of water or air. 'We should speak to animals, flowers, and spirits, to the naiads and sylphs,' he used to say. 'We should ask them to work for the coming of the kingdom of God.'

On one of his visits to the United States, the house he stayed in was close to the ocean. Every morning he went to the beach for the sunrise and stayed there for hours engaged in his spiritual work. He never explained what that work was, but simply said, 'I am sowing seeds.' Later he said that he had been working spiritually with the powers of water:

Water represents the universal fluid, the blood of the earth, and it has tremendous powers. You must learn to have the right attitude towards it, learn how to talk to it, how to create a bond with it, because it can change certain elements within you by diluting and dissolving them. Water, you see, has power over certain substances that fire is incapable of changing.[56]

---

56. April 10th, 1968 (*The Splendour of Tiphareth*, p. 305).

If he was able to work in this way it was because he was familiar with the links that bind together the different elements of the universe, which is truly a single organism. It was because he lived in complete harmony with that organism that the various elements of which it is composed responded to his appeal. Birds and animals were not afraid to approach him; when he was in the country deer gathered to watch him meditating, squirrels came into his room to be close to him. A travelling companion who was with him when he visited Arizona in 1979 described this in her diary:

> One morning he came to find us, saying: 'Come quickly!' We followed him out to a small open plateau. Looking around him in surprise, he exclaimed, 'They're not here any more!' Then he called out, and immediately a swallow arrived out of nowhere. 'But you're all alone,' he said, 'Go and fetch the others!' The swallow flew away, and within minutes, a multitude of swallows was flying round us. Another day, when countless swallows were circling round him, a golden eagle came and hovered high overhead. It was an impressive sight, and it happened again several times. These great birds seemed to be more and more interested in him. One day while he was talking to us, an enormous eagle alighted very close to him. It stood there motionless by his side for a long time. We were absolutely astounded. But you should have seen the Master's unaffected delight, his ingenuous wonder when things like this happened.

It was as though animals instinctively sensed in him the harmony and love that could restore humankind to a state of grace, that could recreate an earthly paradise.

26

A New Season of Love

As the years passed the Bonfin became more and more beautiful. At every summer convention for twenty-six years Omraam Mikhaël Aïvanhov had been present and had spoken daily to the hundreds of participants. With unfailing regularity he had given thousands of unrehearsed talks for which he sought inspiration only in the realms of the spirit. His method faced him with a constant challenge, but he delighted in the unexpected, and as he said with the utmost frankness, these exercises on the tightrope forced him to advance:

> I can only speak if the subject is presented to me suddenly, as a suggestion from the divine world. Then, in spite of all the defects, in spite of my mistakes in French and all the unscholarly language, it works![57]

In 1980, the convention lasted three months and included participants from the five continents. At dawn, as usual, hundreds congregated on the Rock of Prayer for meditation. The sun was already high in the sky when the Master turned and saluted them. Then, advancing slowly between the participants crowding both sides of the path leading down to the Bonfin, he manifested his great love for each one with a glance, a word, or a brief recommendation, showing a special solicitude for the children who accompanied their parents. Those moments with him on this rocky hill were filled with a special sweetness. The ambience was light-hearted and gay because he wished it so.

---

57. April 20th, 1968 (*La pédagogie initiatique II*, p. 107). Our translation.

'Greet each other consciously, with great love in your eyes and in your hand, and project that love out for the benefit of the whole world.'

Every noon he performed the exercises with the participants and later, as he entered the hall and stood to face his audience, they saw him bathed in an indescribable aura. There were days when he seemed to be inhabited by a mysterious presence: sitting perfectly still, his eyes closed, he talked soberly and succinctly. At other times he expressed himself with tremendous energy, like a prophet who had been sent to shake his contemporaries out of their well-worn rut. Usually, however, he spoke to his spiritual family with the simplicity of a father speaking to his children. His laughter, totally spontaneous and unaffected, expressed a profound joy in life. From time to time in the intervals of silence, he could be seen writing a few words on a scrap of paper. In this he was faithful to a habit acquired in his youth of repeatedly writing or saying, in his mother tongue: *Da băde blagosloveno i sveto imeto vi văv veka Gospodi.* May your name, O Lord be blessed and glorified throughout the ages.

In the last few years he had taken up the different themes of his teaching one by one. One might think that after forty-three years of regular talks he would have exhausted most of his subjects, but he was still able to cast new light on them and treat them with ever new dynamism. Rather than attempting a meticulous academic discourse, he gradually explored his topic, shedding light on it from different angles. His goal was to inflame hearts and create links between those listening to him and the light of the higher worlds.

From his earliest youth he had never abandoned his dreams for a peaceful and harmonious humanity. It was in this sense that he continued to talk about the role of women in the transformation of the human race.

'Speak to him while he is sleeping and impregnate him with all the colours of the rainbow.'

He had long asserted that women possessed a reservoir of extraordinary substances capable of realizing Heaven's designs, but that for the most part they were unaware of it:

> [...] once they decide to dedicate themselves to Heaven, so that all that marvellous substance may be used for a divine purpose, we shall see pockets of light bursting out over the whole face of the earth, and everybody will speak the language of the new culture, the language of the new life, the language of divine love. What are women waiting for?[58]

---

58. September 11th, 1962 (*Love and Sexuality I*, p. 134).

The example of spiritual galvanoplasty, based on woman's power of formation and transformation, continued to be one of the themes he most liked to develop. Within the spiritual family of the brotherhood, couples tried to live in harmony and to follow his recommendations for an ideal way of life during the period of gestation in order to suffuse their children with beauty and peace. This was all done in the utmost simplicity. His brotherhood had never been the preserve of an élite; it was a family of ordinary men and women in which each one was free to learn, to grow, to advance on the path of perfection, to work for the kingdom of God on earth. As he often said:

> The brotherhood is a trial run, an attempt at the social actualization of a spiritual family whose members all support and help each other with love. Each one contributes something beautiful from his or her own soul. A perfume emanates from a brotherhood, as from a flower as it opens, which nourishes the souls and spirits of all its members.[59]

The kingdom of God that he so ardently desired to see established on earth corresponded to a veritable Golden Age which he called 'the new season of love.' To him, this was not so much a physical realization as an inner state that reflected all created beauty; it was the reign of love, joy, and peace that could be materialized on earth thanks to a truly fraternal spirit. His one preoccupation was to prepare the way for this reality, and to gain the collaboration of his disciples in his work. And, as he explained, before the reign of wisdom, justice, and love could be established on earth, those who looked forward to it must establish a synarchy within themselves, a way of life founded on the harmonious alliance of heart, mind, and will.

One morning in January 1981, at the Bonfin, he spoke at length about the meaning and beauty of this ideal form of government of self and of the world. He asserted that the era of synarchy had already begun and that one day the whole world would live together in love and brotherhood. Immediately after this talk – which he gave by exception at seven o'clock in the morning – a brilliant rainbow

---

59. Unpublished talk, November 19th, 1961.

appeared above the Bonfin, as though the heavens were confirming his words.

At this period of his life he was more interested than ever in the correspondences between objects, thoughts, feelings, and actions. Modern technological advances fascinated him and offered him many new analogies with the spiritual life. He often used these analogies to great effect when explaining to his disciples how to exploit their innate powers to achieve self-transformation and exert a beneficial influence on the world.

Already the year before, and not for the first time, he had given a long talk on the laser, its symbolism, and its spiritual applications. He had explained that if a great many people concentrated all at the same time on light, they could produce a powerful beam of light and accomplish a work of peace and love. For him this was one of the most beautiful exercises, and one that he loved to do with his disciples.

*
*   *

In June 1981, Master Omraam Mikhaël saw his homeland again. Forty-four years after leaving Bulgaria, he was invited, as an eminent man of letters, to attend the festivities marking the twelfth centenary of the foundation of the Bulgarian State. He was received with great courtesy at Sofia and took part in several activities.

Izgrev, the brotherhood estate in Sofia at which he had spent so much time in his youth, no longer existed. Only one small plot had been preserved, now in the centre of the town, and it was here that Peter Deunov was buried. His tomb was surrounded by roses and other flowers, planted each year by members of the Bulgarian brotherhood. Omraam Mikhaël visited the tomb briefly, went to a few of the places he had loved best in the region of Rila, and then spent a week in Varna with his family.

These three weeks in his country were inevitably full of contradictory impressions, for although he was glad to see his family and visit the haunts of his youth, the atmosphere he had known in the past could no longer be found.

The following year he returned to India. During his previous visit a saddhu had told him, 'You have lived here in the past, and you will return,' and now, twenty-two years later, that prediction came true. In February 1982, he was welcomed by friends at Delhi. Here he met an aged guru through whom he received important revelations. The guru in question was a learned man who had studied medicine in England and was now recognized by a large number of disciples as an extraordinary clairvoyant. On seeing Omraam Mikhaël Aïvanhov for the first time, he exclaimed:

'Master, you appeared to me in a vision fifteen years ago. I saw you descending from the sun. You revealed certain truths to me. I saw you exactly as you are now. Five years later you spoke to me again, and I am so astonished to see that you are exactly the same. On your forehead I see the symbol that designates a Brahma Rishi, the highest of all symbols.'

After this first meeting, the guru visited him often, and at one point Master Omraam told him of the mysterious statement Nityananda had made in 1959, and the name that the latter said had been his in that far-distant incarnation. Greatly intrigued by this, the old guru searched in some specialized libraries and found texts foretelling the incarnation of a solar Rishi in the era known as *Kali Yuga* – the era in which we are living today. The prophecy foretold that he would be born in the eighth month of gestation, that the initial letter of his first name would be M, and that of his second name A. It also said that during a stay in the 'land of the devas', the name Omraam, after the sixth incarnation of the Hindu Avatar Rama, would be given to him unexpectedly by three sages.

These extraordinary revelations were made in successive stages, for the guru, not content with his initial discoveries, extended his research to other libraries. In the meantime Omraam Mikhaël's hosts invited him to stay in one of their residences in the mountains.

Here, his mornings were spent in solitude. At first, when he joined them for meals his companions hoped to hear him talk about elevated subjects, but in fact he said almost nothing. Taking a few moments to touch some of the beautiful objects on the table gently and with great love, he commented: 'When the experience one is living through is extremely powerful, it is best to talk about small things.' His radiance was intense. Many people came, and kneeling at his feet, asked him to bless them and their homes.

The house was situated in a beautiful spot in the Himalayas at an altitude of more than eight thousand feet. It was spring, the orchards were in flower, and the great forests of conifers and rhododendrons spoke of the power of life. One of his travelling companions remembered those days:

The Master told us every day to express gratitude a thousand times over. He himself never ceased to thank heaven. He told us: 'Listen to the silence… Try to listen to the silence!' He explained that the coming of the kingdom of God was not a question of time but of space. And I must say that when we were watching those magnificent sunrises in the Himalayas, we had the feeling that the kingdom of God was truly close at hand.

*
* *

Back in France the following summer, he spoke of all that he had received in India, saying that if he was at last talking openly about his mission, it was because he had been given the right to do so. At the same time he repeated that he had not yet begun his real work, that all he had done so far had been 'no more than minor preliminaries.' Never, he insisted, had he felt himself to be adequately prepared for his work; he continued night and day to prepare himself. In his eyes, nothing was more important than to work, first and foremost on himself: 'I say that I have not yet begun my real work because I have found that it helps me to advance.' It was also one way of developing humility. As he said, pride is the lichen that follows a human being even to the top of the mountain, and it is important continually to practise ways of defending oneself against it.

Paradoxically, it was perhaps his constant work to achieve humility that enabled him to speak of his mission in terms that left no doubt as to its universality. And, as he mentioned at this period, it was the invisible world that counselled him to devote less time to his talks so that he could be free to focus on certain specific places on the planet, for, as he said, one has to know 'which button to push to open the door.' Also, apart from this particular spiritual work, he was always glad to visit the different brotherhood centres in the world.

That autumn he was in England. After several months in the home of some disciples, he travelled to Egypt with three of them and spent time in a small port lying between the Red Sea and the desert. In the mornings he walked far out into the sand dunes to contemplate the rising sun, returning wrapped in a supernatural aura of silence and space that his disciples were careful not to disturb. He loved the stark simplicity of the desert where the sun was absolute monarch. In his eyes it was a privileged region, frequented by benign spirits which facilitated spiritual work. Some mornings he preferred the sea, and as the tide drew out, uncovering the great rocks along the shore, he waded out and settled down on one of them to meditate, as though on an island: 'All around there was nothing but water. It was truly extraordinary!'

As always, after these excursions, he returned to the Bonfin or Izgrev to join his brothers and sisters who were waiting for him at the different conventions, but he was soon called away again on his pilgrimage through the world. During his absences his spiritual family was always in his mind. He often spoke of it as the 'wife' to whom he was espoused, and worked for it unflaggingly. During these years, although he accepted that he must remain with those who adhered to his teaching, that he must continue to talk to them and awaken them to life, he said more than once: 'If the brotherhood were not there, I would abandon everything and settle in the Himalayas or the Andes.'

In April 1984 he gave several talks in the United States. In Los Angeles, disciples had gathered from many directions to hear him speak, bringing their friends with them. The Master entered the room, greeted his guests, and then sat down and closed his eyes. The minutes passed in silence. Gradually his audience realized that the talk they had looked forward to was not going to materialize, that Master Omraam Mikhaël Aïvanhov did not intend to speak, but would only meditate with them. At last he stood up, his gaze rested on each one in turn, and with a final salute he left the room. Many of those present were deeply disappointed, but for some the experience was a veritable revelation: never had they known moments of such intensity in the presence of a spiritual Master.

Mysteriously, he had chosen to do this – something he had long wished to do – with a group that was unprepared and distinctly heterogeneous. But perhaps he knew that among those present were some who were well able to unite their thoughts to his and collaborate in his work with the light.

On another occasion, having been invited to speak on a television program in Los Angeles, he talked about peace, describing it as neither a thing nor a virtue, but a state of consciousness:

> Everyone clamours for peace, but they do not know what it is. They are at war within themselves: their hearts and minds pull in different directions. As long as people have not achieved peace in themselves, they will never achieve it outwardly. It is not possible unless one is capable of harnessing all one's inner powers in the service of an ideal.[60]

After his stay in the United States he went on to visit Canada. He was eighty-four, and his energy was still astonishing. In June he talked to audiences of a thousand people; in one two-day period he gave seven talks in different places.

In May of the following year, he went one last time to Québec, where he consecrated a rural property newly acquired by the brotherhood. He named it *Blagoslovenie*, which means 'fullness of blessings.' Here, as always, he spent many hours talking to those who asked for a private interview. But he took the time also to commune with nature, to pray for long hours among the trees, calling down heaven's blessings on the centre.

---

60. Recounted by himself on August 11th, 1985.

27

I Am With You Even More Than Before

For some years already, Omraam Mikhaël Aïvanhov had been preparing for his final departure from this earth. On his return to the Bonfin in June 1985, he reduced his activities considerably, giving no more interviews and answering no more letters. During the summer convention, the last to benefit from his physical presence, he spoke only once a week, on Sundays. Although no one imagined that his talk on the evening of September 29th, the feast of the Archangel Mikhaël, would be his last, the atmosphere that day was one of particular intensity.

As always on this special day, he spoke of fire and light. 'Fire is the greatest of all mysteries…' In this last talk, as in his first public talk, he spoke of the major themes that had always enthralled him: fire and water, good and evil, the yoga of nutrition, and the yoga of the sun. Of fire, he said:

'Visible fire is the symbol of an invisible reality. By our love, our soul, and our consciousness, we try to unite with celestial fire. This is why it is important to contemplate fire. We must ask the Angel of Fire, Agni, to inflame us with the celestial fire of divine love, so that we may burn with that love; so that wherever we go, we may create the new life by radiating and emanating that warmth and that love.'

After a few minutes of meditation, he again spoke of brotherhood and unity, of the harmony that is so necessary to every organism, whether it be that of an individual or of the world. His closing words were:

'I am always with you, even if I am not physically present. I am with you even more than before.'

In October he withdrew completely. His participation in that spiritual feast day had been his last encounter with the brotherhood on the visible plane. The day of his departure from the world was drawing near. During the whole of 1986, while he prepared himself in solitude, his spiritual presence in the brotherhood was almost tangible. On the mental plane, he was in touch with each one of his disciples.

In this last year of his life, he sent messages of encouragement to help them gradually to get used to his physical absence. He asked them to channel their love so as to become models and work for the benefit of all humanity. He declared with conviction that a new day was dawning over the world, that the sun of love, wisdom, and truth would soon shine more brightly than ever before. Reiterating that he dearly loved his brothers and sisters, he begged them not to be upset by his absence but to work to transform themselves. And he made it clear that he had to withdraw in order to work on other levels, that henceforth his real work lay elsewhere.

He departed this world on the feast of Christmas, that great cosmic celebration that brings a spiritual renewal to humanity each year. Since the day of his illumination at the age of fifteen, he had worked with all his might to realize the kingdom of God on earth, but he could be truly effective only by abandoning his physical body and regaining total freedom of action in the invisible world.

Death, he had always said, is birth on a higher plane:

Death is a change of place, a voyage, a transformation, one energy transformed into another energy. Death does not exist, there is only life.[61]

On December 25th, 1986, fully conscious of his passage into the beyond, Omraam Mikhaël Aïvanhov left this earth. In accordance with his express wishes, the news was delayed for three days, for he had let it be understood that he had important work to do during this period, and that his body should be left in peace.

On December 31st, a number of his disciples gathered at the Bonfin for a last farewell. The silence was extraordinary, a silence in

---

61. July 26th, 1973 (*The Key to the Problems of Existence*, p. 189).

which each one tried to understand what his departure meant and to accept his physical absence. The room in which he lay was suffused with such a sense of life that it was impossible not to think of his own words about the death of great spiritual Masters: when they leave their physical body, their body of glory continues to be present and radiant, continues to vivify all who come in contact with it.

That same day, throughout the world, thousands of his disciples were united to his spirit in prayer and meditation. In many of the brotherhood centres they gathered to re-read his last messages and give thanks, a thousand thanks, as he had so often recommended.

Omraam Mikhaël Aïvanhov had chosen to leave for the higher world on Christmas day, the day on which Christ, the cosmic Spirit, returns each year to illuminate the universe.

> December 25th marks the day when nature sees the birth of the Christ-principle, the life, light, and warmth that is destined to transform everything. Rejoicing is also going on in heaven that day: the angels are singing and all the saints, the great Masters, and initiates are gathered together to pray, glorify the Almighty, and celebrate the birthday of Christ who is truly born today in the universe.[62]

---

62. December 25th, 1958 (*Au commencement était le Verbe*, p. 95). Our translation.

Chronology

1900, January 31	Birth at Serbtzi, in Macedonia.
1907, Spring	Destruction of his village. Goes to Varna, in Bulgaria.
1908, October 3	Death of his father.
1909	Discovers Book of Proverbs.
1915	Illumination.
1917, Winter	First encounter with Peter Deunov in Varna.
1923	Attends university in Sofia.
1930	Teaches in secondary school near Sofia.
1934 or 1935	Principal of college.
1937, July 22	Arrival in France.
1938, January 29	First public talk, Place de la Sorbonne in Paris.
1944, Christmas	Publication of first volume of talks: *Love, Wisdom, Truth.*
1944, December 27	Death of Master Peter Deunov, aged 80.
1948, January 21	Brother Mikhaël arrested on false charges.
1948, July 17	Sentenced to four years in prison.
1950, March	Released from prison.
1950, March 19	Renews contact with the brotherhood at Izgrev.
1953, July 8	First brotherhood convention at The Bonfin.
1959, February 11	Departure for India.
1959, June 17	First meeting with Babaji in India.
1960, February 9	Returns from India.
1960, September 28	Officially rehabilitated by Court of Appeals, Aix-en-Provence, France.
1961, Spring	Visit to the United Kingdom
1962, May	Visit to Spain.
1964, May	Visit to Italy and Greece. Return via Serbtzi.

1965, Spring	Visit to Sweden, Holland, and Germany.
1965, June	Visit to Spain.
1967, May-June	Visit to United States and Canada.
1968, May-June	Visit to Israel.
1969, May	Visit to Greece and Turkey.
1970, April 25	Visit to Japan with stopover in Sri Lanka and Hong Kong.
1971, May 6	Visit to Morocco, Egypt, Ethiopia, Lebanon, and Greece. Return via Yugoslavia where he meets his mother.
1971, September 18	Participation in the 4th Esoteric Symposium in Berlin.
1973, August 5	Death of Omraam Mikhaël Aïvanhov's mother in Bulgaria.
1974, April	Publication of first volume of O.M.A.'s Complete Works (Collected talks).
1975	Thirteen volumes are on sale in book shops.
1976	Publication of first foreign-language editions of the Complete Works.
1977, May-June	Participation in the *Congrès Interreligieux* in Paris.
1978, December 17	Leaves for North America: United States, Caribbean and Martinique.
1981 Spring	Visit to Canada and the United States.
1981, June 18	Visit to Bulgaria.
1981, October 12	Leaves for the United States; public talks.
1981, December 10	Leaves for Thailand.
1982, February 5	Leaves for India.
1982, November	Visit to England and Scotland.
1983, January	Visit to Egypt.
1983, April 28	Leaves for Scandinavia.
1984, January 18	Leaves for the United States.
1984, May 6	Leaves for Canada; public talks.
1985, January 25	Leaves for the United States, Mexico, and Canada.
1986, December 25	Omraam Mikhaël Aïvanhov departs this world.

Sources

Omraam Mikhaël Aïvanhov's talks and messages, published and unpublished, identified by date.

Publications by disciples of Omraam Mikhaël Aïvanhov and Peter Deunov.

Reminiscences and testimonies from members of Omraam Mikhaël Aïvanhov's family, neighbours, friends, and disciples.

Part One: **Youth**

1. Everything is Foreshadowed in Childhood
Talks: 1938-06-09; 1939-01-...; 1944-05-11; 1945-03-27; 1945-04-03; 1945-11-24; 1946-11-26; 1954-09-11; 1960-...-...; 1962-08-26; 1963-02-03; 1966-04-11; 1966-08-03; 1968-01-14; 1971-07-22; 1973-08-09; 1975-09-29; 1977-07-13; 1979-08-29.

Reminiscences of Mikhaël's mother and family.

2. Varna
Talks: 1938-03-05; 1943-05-05; 1944-04-06; 1944-04-24; 1946-01-19; 1951-01-28; 1951-03-24; 1951-03-28; 1954-04-18; 1958-03-22; 1958-08-24; 1960-12-28; 1961-04-02; 1961-08-28; 1962-11-11; 1964-08-10; 1965-04-15; 1965-12-26; 1967-08-22; 1968-04-10; 1975-03-23; 1977-02-25; 1978-01-03; 1978-03-15; 1978-08-15; 1980-07-29; 1980-09-10; 1983-07-21.

Family reminiscences. Testimony of neighbour.

3. 'Hear, my Child'
Talks: 1951-03-28; 1960-...-...; 1962-08-22; 1966-07-17; 1967-08-22; 1977-09-25; 1979-05-04; 1979-08-29.

Reminiscences of Mikhaël's mother.

4. The Power of Thought

Talks: 1939-01-...; 1945-11-24; 1946-06-04; 1956-01-22; 1956-07-16; 1956-07-24; 1962-03-24; 1965-12-26; 1968-07-15; 1971-05-02; 1971-07-20; 1971-08-04; 1974-09-26; 1975-03-23; 1976-07-27; 1979-08-29; 1980-06-30; 1980-07-29; 1981-02-28; 1981-06-15; 1982-07-26; 1983-04-05; 1983-08-20; 1983-08-27; 1984-08-18; 1985-02-03; 1985-04-05; 1985-05-22.

OMA, *The Book of Divine Magic*, p. 18ff; Reminiscences of Mikhaël's mother; Testimony of a teacher, communicated by her son.

5. The Aspirations of Adolescence

Talks: 1945-05-10; 1956-01-22; 1957-08-07; 1958-04-13; 1961-01-06; 1962-03-24; 1962-11-11; 1963-04-15; 1963-06-22; 1966-03-06; 1966-08-16; 1967-08-17; 1967-08-18; 1969-08-13; 1971-08-11; 1974-08-04; 1976-03-14; 1976-09-24; 1977-10-31; 1978-03-15; 1978-04-17; 1978-07-30; 1980-08-02; 1982-09-26; 1984-08-01; 1985-01-04.

OMA, *Creation: Artistic and spiritual*, p. 52; *Youth: Creators of the Future*, p. 120.

6. Illumination

Talks: 1938-03-12; 1938-11-19; 1941-06-10; 1942-08-08; 1945-04-19; 1946-06-04; 1954-08-21; 1955-08-05; 1956-07-14; 1957-01-06; 1960-05-22; 1961-12-27; 1965-04-14; 1966-07-14; 1966-08-19; 1967-08-22; 1968-04-10; 1968-07-27; 1971-07-20; 1972-08-12; 1975-09-29; 1976-01-02; 1976-02-28; 1976-03-14; 1977-02-13; 1978-09-29; 1980-08-14; 1983-08-27; 1984-08-01; 1985-03-18.

OMA, *Looking into the Invisible*, p. 185. Family reminiscences.

Part Two : **The Disciple**

7. The Beginning of a New Life

Talks: 1938-03-12; 1943-04-27; 1944-04-02; 1945-03-26; 1946-06-04; 1947-03-25; 1951-02-11; 1952-04-02; 1954-08-22; 1954-09-11; 1955-08-13; 1957-01-24; 1957-04-28; 1957-08-23; 1959-01-01; 1960-03-27; 1960-04-18; 1963-02-10; 1963-09-...; 1963-12-25; 1965-07-20; 1965-12-05; 1965-12-26; 1970-01-02; 1974-08-26; 1975-07-19; 1976-07-27; 1977-04-04; 1977-07-07; 1981-01-20; 1981-04-15; 1982-04-22; 1983-08-06; 1984-08-12.

OMA, *The Book of Divine Magic*, p. 106. Reminiscences of Mikhaël's mother.

8. Retreat in Ternovo

Talks: 1938-01-29; 1938-04-09; 1939-03-11; 1939-04-10; 1942-05-25; 1943-04-07; 1944-06-14; 1947-04-21; 1955-02-06; 1944-09-18; 1958-06-21; 1958-08-11; 1961-04-06; 1964-08-23; 1964-08-31; 1964-12-25; 1965-04-15; 1966-07-14; 1966-07-23; 1966-08-13; 1966-12-31; 1967-08-15; 1967-09-04; 1967-12-30; 1968-08-10; 1970-07-27; 1971-07-20; 1973-12-28; 1975-09-27; 1978-03-14; 1980-04-07; 1980-04-10; 1982-08-18; 1983-04-05; 1983-08-20.

Family reminiscences. Testimony of Bulgarian disciple.

9. Back to School

Talks: 1938-03-12; 1939-03-11; 1942-04-25; 1942-06-07; 1943-04-17; 1943-05-05; 1947-05-15; 1953-02-27; 1956-07-14; 1957-12-29; 1960-05-22; 1960-08-14; 1965-07-15; 1965-07-20; 1965-12-26; 1966-07-26; 1966-08-03; 1971-04-14; 1971-07-20; 1971-09-30; 1972-08-12; 1976-07-28; 1976-08-07; 1976-12-30; 1977-10-31; 1978-01-22; 1978-04-09; 1978-08-15; 1980-04-07; 1980-09-10; 1981-06-08; 1981-07-18; 1981-08-16; 1985-01-12; 1985-01-26.

OMA, *What is a Spiritual Master?*, p. 171; *'In Spirit and in Truth'*, p. 144. Commentaires sur les chants de la fraternité (Unpublished text, only in French). Reminiscences of Mikhaël's mother and Bulgarian disciples.

10. The Seven Lakes of Rila

Talks: 1938-02-05; 1938-03-12; 1944-04-16; 1944-05-09; 1944-06-17, 1945-04-09; 1946-04-13; 1946-04-18; 1946-10-26; 1950-07-02; 1952-12-25; 1953-08-03; 1955-02-06; 1955-08-15; 1958-05-04; 1958-08-07; 1958-08-11; 1961-04-06; 1962-04-25; 1962-08-28; 1967-08-15; 1984-09-30; 1985-07-28.

Paneurythmie, by Peter Deunov's disciples. Family reminiscences. Testimony of Bulgarian disciples.

11. The Wondrous Powers of Thought and Word

Talks: 1938-02-26; 1938-03-12; 1938-04-02; 1951-03-24; 1951-03-28; 1958-04-07; 1963-08-01; 1963-12-31; 1966-11-01; 1971-04-07; 1978-01-05; 1978-04-17; 1980-03-12; 1980-03-23; 1980-04-10; 1980-08-02; 1984-09-30; 1985-02-05.

Reminiscences of family and neighbours.

12. A Look is Enough

Talks: 1942-09-12; 1955-09-18; 1956-09-29; 1962-07-24; 1963-12-26; 1964-07-27; 1966-11-01; 1974-04-20; 1978-03-14; 1985-05-12.

Message of January 9th, 1949. Reminiscences of Mikhaël's mother.

13. I Will Give You a Precious Stone

Talks: 1938-03-12; 1946-04-18; 1955-01-16; 1956-09-29; 1957-01-06; 1957-12-09; 1961-01-01; 1964-07-27; 1965-11-21; 1966-12-31; 1976-09-15; 1978-07-30; 1979-09-21; 1981-02-01; 1982-09-20; 1983-07-16; 1985-01-27; 1985-03-01; 1985-05-22.

Message of January 9th, 1949. Reminiscences of family and Bulgarian disciples.

Part Three: **Brother Mikhaël**

14. Paris

Talks: 1939-04-10; 1951-04-04; 1954-08-07; 1978-01-03; 1978-03-14; 1980-03-15; 1984-08-12.

OMA, *Creation: Artistic and Spiritual*, p. 71. Svezda, *Vie et Enseignement....* Jean du Bonfin, *Qui est le Maître Mikhaël?*. Testimony of disciples.

15. The First Public Talks

Talks: 1938-06-09; 1938-11-19; 1939-04-10; 1939-05-20; 1939-06-03; 1941-05-15; 1941-05-16; 1941-05-17; 1942-04-10; 1942-04-12; 1942-06-07; 1943-04-27; 1944-05-25; 1944-06-21; 1945-04-08; 1945-04-09; 1945-04-22; 1945-05-01; 1945-05-23; 1945-05-27; 1947-05-12; 1955-08-16; 1955-08-20; 1956-09-05; 1957-04-28; 1960-09-01; 1963-02-03; 1963-07-13; 1966-07-26; 1967-07-26; 1969-04-02; 1970-07-12; 1972-08-28; 1975-09-20; 1978-08-11; 1979-08-02; 1980-07-18; 1980-09-13; 1982-08-29.

OMA, *Education Begins Before Birth.* Svezda, op. cit. Jean du Bonfin, op. cit. Letter of October 26th, 1938, from Boyan Boëv to Brother Mikhaël. Testimony of disciples.

16. A Fraternal Community

Talks: 1942-04-25; 1942-05-25; 1944-04-19; 1944-04-25; 1944-06-11; 1944-07-02; 1945-03-25; 1945-03-31; 1945-05-17; 1946-03-24; 1946-04-13; 1951-03-30; 1951-04-11; 1960-08-27; 1963-12-31.

Svezda, op. cit. Jean du Bonfin, op. cit. Testimony of disciples.

17. The Conspiracy

Talks: 1944-06-06; 1945-04-09; 1945-04-19; 1945-05-05; 1946-06-02; 1947-04-24; 1947-05-05; 1947-06-26; 1947-09-28; 1947-10-21; 1950-03-19; 1951-02-11; 1951-04-08; 1951-10-06; 1966-08-03; 1971-12-30; 1976-03-14; 1977-08-20; 1977-08-21; 1982-04-22.

Message of January 1st, 1947. Svezda, op. cit. Jean du Bonfin, op. cit. Testimony of disciples.

18. Prison

Talks: 1950-03-19; 1950-06-20; 1950-10-29; 1951-02-11; 1951-03-22; 1951-03-31; 1951-10-06; 1954-09-28; 1956-07-16; 1956-08-05; 1956-08-11; 1966-07-28; 1985-02-15.

Message of January 9th, 1949. Extracts from Records of Court of Appeals of Aix-en-Provence. Jean du Bonfin, op. cit. Testimony of B. Robillard & ex-prisoner. Testimony of disciples.

19. The Bonfin

Talks: 1952-06-18; 1953-08-17; 1955-01-16; 1957-05-11; 1958-06-17; 1958-08-19; 1958-08-24; 1958-08-28; 1958-09-29; 1969-07-09; 1975-12-27; 1985-02-04.

Jean du Bonfin, op. cit. Testimony of disciples.

Part Four: **The Master**

20. The Land of the Devas

Talks: 1960-02-10; 1960-02-12; 1960-03-06; 1960-03-07; 1960-04-03; 1960-04-14; 1961-01-01; 1961-01-02; 1962-09-01; 1962-09-10; 1966-08-09; 1969-04-09; 1974-08-29; 1975-09-27; 1976-09-24; 1978-08-21; 1981-09-23.

Message of July 6th, 1959.

21. Back In France

Talks: 1945-05-06; 1945-05-21; 1946-04-30; 1952-04-01; 1956-07-28; 1958-08-03; 1960-03-06; 1960-04-12; 1960-04-13; 1960-08-10; 1960-08-17; 1960-09-01; 1960-11-20; 1960-12-26; 1961-03-05; 1961-12-30; 1962-07-21; 1962-09-29; 1965-04-18; 1965-07-20; 1965-08-16; 1969-02-02; 1975-09-28; 1975-11-23; 1976-07-08; 1978-03-11; 1979-08-11; 1980-08-11; 1982-04-22.

OMA, *'In Spirit and in Truth'*, p. 41ff. Message of July 6th, 1959. Svezda, op. cit. Testimony of disciples.

22. I Speak With My Own Voice

Talks: 1964-07-27; 1965-11-01; 1966-07-26; 1966-08-25; 1966-08-26; 1967-12-23; 1971-04-07; 1971-09-30; 1976-02-17; 1976-08-18; 1978-04-05.

Testimony of disciples.

23. The Yoga of the Sun

Talks: 1959-01-04; 1959-01-05; 1960-04-12; 1966-07-21; 1967-07-30; 1967-08-15; 1967-08-17; 1969-06-01; 1971-03-20.

OMA, *'In Spirit and in Truth'*, p. 182.

24. The Universality of a Mission

Talks: 1964-07-27; 1968-01-14; 1972-08-11; 1974-08-15; 1981-07-14; 1982-08-28.

OMA, *Light is a Living a Spirit*, p. 50.

25. True Power is the Fruit of Love

Talks: 1957-08-14; 1958-01-02; 1963-08-01; 1968-07-27; 1972-08-11; 1974-01-01; 1974-01-20; 1978-08-15; 1979-07-10; 1979-07-13; 1980-09-28; 1981-09-27; 1982-09-12; 1984-07-25.

Testimony of disciples.

26. A New Season of Love

Talks: 1957-09-15; 1961-05-07; 1965-12-30; 1969-12-11; 1980-03-22; 1980-08-19; 1980-08-20; 1981-01-20; 1982-09-18; 1983-07-21; 1983-08-27; 1985-04-09; 1985-04-11; 1985-08-18.

Testimony of disciples.

27. I Am With You Even More Than Before

New Year Message 1986. Easter Message 1986.

Bibliography
of Books Quoted

By Omraam Mikhaël Aïvanhov

Complete Works Published by Prosveta, Fréjus, France
Volume 1 – *The Second Birth*, 2nd edition, 1988
Volume 2 – *Spiritual Alchemy*, 1986.
Volume 6 – *Harmony*, 2nd edition, 1988.
Volume 7 – *The Mysteries of Yesod*, 1988.
Volume 9 – '*Au commencement était le Verbe*', 1974 (In French).
Volume 10 – *The Splendour of Tiphareth – The Yoga of the Sun*,
   3rd edition, 1994.
Volume 11 – *The Key to the Problems of Existence*, 3rd edition, 1988.
Volume 12 – *Cosmic Moral Law*, 3rd ed. 1989.
Volume 14 – *Love and Sexuality I*, 4th edition, 1997.
Volume 17 – '*Know Thyself*' – *Jnana Yoga I*, 2nd edition, 1992.
Volume 18 – '*Know Thyself*' – *Jnana Yoga II*, 2nd edition, 1994.
Volume 26 – *A New Dawn: Society and Politics in the Light of Initiatic Science*,
   2nd edition, 1999
Volume 28 – *La pédagogie initiatique II*, 1979 (In French).
Volume 29 – *La pédagogie initiatique III*, 1980. (In French).
Volume 32 – *The Fruits of the Tree of Life, The Cabbalistic Tradition*, 1989.

Izvor Collection Published by Prosveta, Fréjus, France
No. 203 – *Education Begins Before Birth*, 2nd edition, 1986.
No. 207 – *What is a Spiritual Master?*, 1983.

No. 212 – *Light is a Living Spirit*, 2nd edition, 1987.

No. 219 – *Man's Subtle Bodies and Centres – the Aura, the Solar Plexus, the Chakras*, 1986.

No. 223 – *Creation: Artistic and Spiritual*, 1987.

No. 226 – *The Book of Divine Magic*, 1989.

No. 228 – *Looking into the Invisible – Intuition, Clairvoyance, Dreams*, 1989.

No. 230 – *The Book of Revelations: a Commentary*, 1991.

No. 233 – *Youth: Creators of the Future*, 1993.

No. 235 – '*In Spirit and in Truth*', 1994.

Published by Éditions Izgrev, Paris, 1946
(Under the name of Michaël Ivanoff)

Les sept lacs de Rila, Preface by Alfred Laumonier. (In French).

By Other Authors

BERTHOLET, E., *La réincarnation*, Pierre Genillard, Lausanne, 1978. (In French).

CORBIN, Henry, 'Le songe visionnaire en spiritualité islamique' in *Visage de lumière*, NRF Gallimard, Paris, 1967. (In French).

JEAN DU BONFIN (*nom de plume* of André Jahan), *Who is the Master Omraam Mikhaël Aïvanhov?*, Prosveta, Fréjus, France, 1995.

SVEZDA, (*nom de plume* of Stella Bellemin) *Vie et enseignement du Maître Omraam Mikhaël Aïvanhov en France*, Prosveta, Fréjus, France, 2nd edition, 1992. (In French).

Le Kybalion, Bibliothèque eudiaque, Paris, 1917. (In French).

L'Enseignement du Maître Deunov, Publication E.T., Courrier du livre, Paris 1990 (In French).

Paneurythmie, by the disciples of Peter Deunov's École ésotérique (In French).